New Comparisons in World Literature

Series Editors
Upamanyu Pablo Mukherjee
Department of English and Comparative Literary Studies
University of Warwick
Coventry, UK

Neil Lazarus
Department of English and Comparative Literary Studies
University of Warwick
Coventry, UK

New Comparisons in World Literature offers a fresh perspective on one of the most exciting current debates in humanities by approaching 'world literature' not in terms of particular kinds of reading but as a particular kind of writing. We take 'world literature' to be that body of writing that registers in various ways, at the levels of form and content, the historical experience of capitalist modernity. We aim to publish works that take up the challenge of understanding how literature registers both the global extension of 'modern' social forms and relations and the peculiar new modes of existence and experience that are engendered as a result. Our particular interest lies in studies that analyse the registration of this decisive historical process in literary consciousness and affect.

Editorial Board
Dr. Nicholas Brown, University of Illinois, USA
Dr. Bo G. Ekelund, University of Stockholm, Sweden
Dr. Dorota Kolodziejczyk, Wroclaw University, Poland
Professor Paulo de Medeiros, University of Warwick, UK
Dr. Robert Spencer, University of Manchester, UK
Professor Imre Szeman, University of Alberta, Canada
Professor Peter Hitchcock, Baruch College, USA
Dr. Ericka Beckman, University of Illinois at Urbana-Champaign, USA
Dr. Sarah Brouillette, Carleton University, Canada
Professor Supriya Chaudhury, Jadavpur University, India
Professor Stephen Shapiro, University of Warwick, UK

More information about this series at
http://www.springer.com/series/15067

Belén Martín-Lucas · Andrea Ruthven
Editors

Narratives of Difference in Globalized Cultures

Reading Transnational Cultural Commodities

Editors
Belén Martín-Lucas
University of Vigo
Vigo, Spain

Andrea Ruthven
University of Barcelona
Barcelona, Spain

New Comparisons in World Literature
ISBN 978-3-319-87240-7   ISBN 978-3-319-62133-3   (eBook)
DOI 10.1007/978-3-319-62133-3

© The Editor(s) (if applicable) and The Author(s) 2017
Softcover re-print of the Hardcover 1st edition 2017
This work is subject to copyright. All rights are solely and exclusively licensed by the Publisher, whether the whole or part of the material is concerned, specifically the rights of translation, reprinting, reuse of illustrations, recitation, broadcasting, reproduction on microfilms or in any other physical way, and transmission or information storage and retrieval, electronic adaptation, computer software, or by similar or dissimilar methodology now known or hereafter developed.
The use of general descriptive names, registered names, trademarks, service marks, etc. in this publication does not imply, even in the absence of a specific statement, that such names are exempt from the relevant protective laws and regulations and therefore free for general use.
The publisher, the authors and the editors are safe to assume that the advice and information in this book are believed to be true and accurate at the date of publication. Neither the publisher nor the authors or the editors give a warranty, express or implied, with respect to the material contained herein or for any errors or omissions that may have been made. The publisher remains neutral with regard to jurisdictional claims in published maps and institutional affiliations.

Cover credit: Alicia Llop/Getty Images Cover Design by Fatima Jamadar

Printed on acid-free paper

This Palgrave Macmillan imprint is published by Springer Nature
The registered company is Springer International Publishing AG
The registered company address is: Gewerbestrasse 11, 6330 Cham, Switzerland

Acknowledgements

This collection gathers essays written within the framework of two consecutive research projects funded by the national programme 'Excellence in Research' of the Spanish Ministry of the Economy and Competitiveness: 'Globalized Cultural Markets: the Production, Circulation and Reception of Difference' (2010–2013; Ref. FFI2010-17282) and 'Bodies in Transit: Making Difference in Globalized Cultures' (2015–2017; Ref. FFI2013-47789-C2-2-P). We are indebted to the community of research project members who, along with the contributors, engaged in fruitful discussion and gave helpful feedback along the way. The intellectual and emotional support the participants so generously supplied throughout the thinking, writing and editing processes is an integral part of this book, and we are very grateful for their collaboration. We would also like to thank the series editors for so warmly encouraging and welcoming this book project, and also the anonymous reader who offered such pertinent suggestions and positive feedback.

We wish to thank the artists who have kindly granted us their permission to reproduce their materials in this book.

Contents

Introduction: Interrogating the Production, Circulation and
Reception of 'Difference' in Globalized Cultures   1
Belén Martín-Lucas and Andrea Ruthven

Part I   Reading Methodologies

Subversive Translation and Lexical Empathy: Pedagogies
of *Cortesia* and Transnational Multilingual Poetics   13
Merlinda Bobis

The Production and Productivity of Humanitarian Fiction:
Postcolonial Shame and Neocolonial Crises   37
David Callahan

Still Devouring Frida Kahlo: Psychobiography versus
Postcolonial and Disability Readings   57
Zoë Brigley Thompson

The World Republic of Readers   81
James Procter

Part II Counternarratives of the Metropolis

Success and the City: Working in the World's Capital in
Monica Ali's *Brick Lane* — 97
Darragh Patrick Hall

Borderless (Alien) Nations: Disposable Bodies and
Biopolitical Effacement in Min Sook Lee's Docu-Poem — 117
Libe García Zarranz

Public Art in the Production of a Global City:
Jamie Hilder's Clashing Versions of Vancouver — 133
John Havelda

A Nation Goes Adrift: Subaltern Inter-Identity in
José Saramago's *The Stone Raft* — 157
Maria Sofia Pimentel Biscaia

Part III Disruptive Genders

'Something Terrible Happened': Spectacles of Gendered
Violence and Nadine Gordimer's *The House Gun* — 185
Sorcha Gunne

Alternative Modernities and Othered Masculinities in
Mira Nair's *The Namesake* — 203
E. Guillermo Iglesias Díaz

(Un)Veiling Women's Bodies: Transnational Feminisms in
Emer Martin's *Baby Zero* — 223
Aida Rosende-Pérez

Index — 245

Editors and Contributors

About the Editors

Belén Martín-Lucas is Associate Professor in the fields of Postcolonial, Diasporic and Gender Studies at the University of Vigo, Spain. She has published extensively on transnational literature from feminist perspectives and has co-edited nine scholarly collections and journal special issues on globalization and nationalism. In 2010 she co-founded the electronic journal *Canada and Beyond: A Journal of Canadian Literary and Cultural Studies*.

Andrea Ruthven lectures in the English and Modern Languages and Literatures Department at the University of Barcelona, Spain, where she earned an international Ph.D. in Cultural Studies in 2015, and in the English Department at Mediterrani University College, University of Girona, Spain. Her research focuses on contemporary women's writing and feminist theory and gender studies. Publications include the essays 'Pride, Prejudice and Post-Feminist Zombies' in *The Year's Work At The Zombie Research Center* (2014), and 'The Woman Warrior: Rejecting Utopia' in *Experiencing Gender: International Approaches* (2015). She is a member of the editorial team for the journals *Canada and Beyond: A Journal of Canadian Literary and Cultural Studies* and *Abriu: Textuality Studies on Brazil, Galicia and Portugal*.

Contributors

Maria Sofia Pimentel Biscaia holds a doctoral degree in Literature (2005). She has conducted interdisciplinary research in the fields of visual, gender and postcolonial studies, including on South Asian, African, British and Luso-American authors. She has published extensively in domestic and international journals and is the author of *Postcolonial and Feminist Grotesque: Texts of Contemporary Excess* (Peter Lang AG, 2011). She also co-edited the collection of essays *Intercultural Crossings: Conflict, Memory, Identity* (Peter Lang AG, 2012). A co-founder of the Rushdie International Society and its Newsletter Editor, she is currently Visiting Professor in the English Department at the University of Vigo.

Merlinda Bobis is an award-winning writer, performer and scholar who taught Creative Writing at the University of Wollongong for 21 years and is currently Honorary Senior Lecturer at the Australian National University in Sydney. She has published four novels, a collection of short stories, five poetry books and a monograph on creative research. She has performed her dramatic works in the Philippines, Australia, Spain, the USA, Canada and Singapore. Her awards include The Christina Stead Prize for Fiction, Prix Italia for Radio Fiction, The Steele Rudd Award for the Best Published Collection of Australian Short Stories, The Australian Writers' Guild Award, The Philippine National Book Award, The Philippine Carlos Palanca Memorial Award for Literature and The Philippine Balagtas Award for her poetry and prose in three languages. Her latest novel is *Locust Girl. A Lovesong*. She has facilitated creative-critical community workshops on the preservation and sustainability of rivers and watersheds and their communities in the Philippines and Canada. Creative-critical production, transnational story production, rethinking water, climate change, typhoons, and the ethics and politics of care are the focus of her current scholarly projects.

David Callahan is Associate Professor at the University of Aveiro, Portugal. His book *Rainforest Narratives: The Work of Janette Turner Hospital* (2009) was a co-winner of Australia's McRae Russell Award for the best book of literary scholarship on an Australian subject. He has also edited *Australia: Who Cares?* (2007) and *Contemporary Issues in Australian Literature* (2002), and is the editor of the journal of the European Association for Studies on Australia. His articles on postcolonial issues have appeared in journals such as *Interventions, Postcolonial Studies, Critique, Literature & History* and *English Studies in Africa* along with book chapters on postcolonial subjects such as the writing of Abdulrazak Gurnah, Bharati Mukherjee, Jane Urquhart, and latterly, the processing of East Timor in the West.

E. Guillermo Iglesias Díaz teaches at the International University of La Rioja, Spain. His research focuses on transmodernities, masculinity studies and film. He is the author of *Cine, espacio urbano e identidades (trans)nacionales: The Commitments & Trainspotting* (Arcibel, 2013) and Deputy Editor of *Indialogs, Spanish Journal of India Studies*.

Sorcha Gunne is a Lecturer in English at NUI Galway Ireland. Her research interests cover: gender studies and feminism, contemporary world literature, globalization and world systems, literary and cultural theory, postcolonial writing, popular fiction, and South African and Irish writing. She has published a number of book chapters and journal articles on feminism, gender and world literature, including a special issue of *Atlantic Studies: Global Currents* edited with Neil Lazarus (2017). She is the author of *Space, Place, and Gendered Violence in South African Literature* (Palgrave Macmillan 2015) and editor of *Feminism, Literature and Rape Narratives* (Routledge 2010) with Zoë Brigley Thompson. She is a founding member of the World Literature Network.

Darragh Patrick Hall graduated from the University of Warwick in 2013 with an MA in English Literature where he achieved Distinction and first place. He also holds a BA in English and Philosophy from University College Dublin with First Class Honours in both subjects. He is currently an independent scholar working within the financial sector; his academic research interests include globalization, neoliberal economics, migration studies and world literature when theorized as literature of the capitalist world system.

John Havelda is a British language-based artist and poet who teaches Canadian Studies and Translation at the University of Coimbra, Portugal. He holds a Ph.D. in Creative Writing from Roehampton University. His publications include the artist's book *mor* (1997), *Unparalled Candour* (2005), *Echo and Narcissus* and *Combine* (both 2007) and *Hard Luck, Stories* (2017).

Aida Rosende-Pérez is a Lecturer in English at the University of the Balearic Islands. She holds an International Ph.D. in English from the University of Vigo (2015), and her doctoral dissertation was awarded the Doctoral Award. Her research focuses on the analysis of the conceptualization and cultural representation of the body as a repository of (gender, sexual, racial, class) difference, and its circulation and consumption in contemporary globalized societies. She has specialized in postcolonial and diasporic literature and cultural production, focusing particularly on the work of contemporary Irish women writers and artists. Her most recent research explores the critical theories of transnational feminism, posthumanism and affect studies, as well as the field of Medical Humanities. The results of her research activities have been published in specialized academic journals, and in diverse national and international volumes.

James Procter is Reader in Modern English and Postcolonial Literature at Newcastle University, UK. His research focuses on British and black British literature, including migrant and diasporic writing from the Caribbean, Africa and South Asia. He is the author with Bethan Benwell of *Reading Across Worlds: Transnational Book Groups and the Reception of Difference* (Palgrave Macmillan, 2015). He is co-editor with Jackie Kay and Gemma Robinson of *Out of Bounds: British Black & Asian Poets* (Bloodaxe Books, 2012) and with Bethan Benwell and Gemma Robinson of *Postcolonial Audiences: Readers, Viewers and Reception* (Routledge, 2012).

Zoë Brigley Thompson is Visiting Assistant Professor at Ohio State University and a Research Fellow in English and Creative Writing at the University of Northampton. She holds a Ph.D. in English and Comparative Literature from the University of Warwick. She is an academic and award-winning creative writer. In her academic research, she approaches representations of sexuality and violence in literature, film and culture. For her creative writing, she has won an Eric Gregory Award for the best British poets under 30, the English Association's Poetry Fellows' Award and a Welsh Academy Bursary. She was long-listed for the Dylan Thomas Prize for the best international writers under 35, and she was a finalist for the Autumn House Books Poetry Prize.

Libe García Zarranz is a Supervisor at Magdalene College, University of Cambridge, UK and a Research Affiliate for the Canadian Literature

Centre at the University of Alberta, Canada. She is also a Scholar in the Pierre Elliott Trudeau Foundation and a Board Member of CWILA (Canadian Women in the Literary Arts). She has held postdoctoral positions at the University of Innsbruck, Austria and University of Manitoba, Canada. She has published and co-edited special issues on contemporary feminist, queer and transnational writing in Canada; affect and feminist literary and cultural production; and Raymond Carver. Her monograph *TransCanadian Feminist Fictions. New Cross-Border Ethics* was published by McGill-Queen's University Press in 2017.

List of Figures

Public Art in the Production of a Global City: Jamie Hilder's Clashing Versions of Vancouver

Fig. 1	Ron Terada, *The Words Don't Fit the Picture* (2010), 1280 LED light nodes	135
Fig. 2	Myfanwy McLeod, *The Birds* (2010), EPS foam with polyurethane hard coat and bronze, 5 × 1. 52 × 5 m	136
Fig. 3	Ken Lum, *Monument for East Vancouver* (2010), LED lights, 18.2 m	137
Fig. 4	Lorna Brown and Clint Burnham (curators), *Digital Natives* (2011b), electronic billboard	138
Fig. 5	Jamie Hilder, *AESTHETICS* (2002a), acrylic on canvas, 3.35 × 1.2 m	139
Fig. 6	Jamie Hilder, *GIVE AN F.....* (1999a), acrylic on canvas, 5.5 × 1.8 m	140
Fig. 7	Jamie Hilder, *TO DIE, THAT'S EASY...* (2002b), acrylic on canvas, 6.7 × 1.2 m	141
Fig. 8	Jamie Hilder, *FREEDOM THROUGH WORK* (2002c), acrylic on canvas, 6.7 × 1.2 m	142
Fig. 9	Jamie Hilder, *TEAR WIND LEAD READ LIVE BASS* (1999c), acrylic on canvas, 6.7 × 1.2 m	143
Fig. 10	Jamie Hilder *DOVE BOW WOUND CLOSE SOW CONTENT* (1999a), acrylic on canvas, 6.7 × 1.2 m	144
Fig. 11	Jamie Hilder, *Banlieusard* book jacket (detail) (Vancouver, Artspeak, 2005; print.)	145

Fig. 12	Jamie Hilder, 'Take in our spectacularized aboriginalities' *Special Advertising Section, Public Art Dialogue* (2011)	150
Fig. 13	Jamie Hilder 'See our hospitality come out in force' *Special Advertising Section, Public Art Dialogue* (2011)	151
Fig. 14	Jamie Hilder, 'Look out' *Special Advertising Section* (2011)	152
Fig. 15	Jamie Hilder, 'A city designed with you in mind' *Special Advertising Section* (2011)	153

Introduction: Interrogating the Production, Circulation and Reception of 'Difference' in Globalized Cultures

Belén Martín-Lucas and Andrea Ruthven

The eleven chapters in this volume interrogate the ways in which 'difference'—undoubtedly a prominent element within the global flows of people and products—is narrated, whether in terms of gender, sexuality, race, language or geographical location. Moreover, they seek to offer counter-readings that disrupt hegemonic representations of cultural identity in the context of globalization. The marketing of transnational cultural commodities capitalizes on 'difference' and its appeal for consumers in our postmodern globalized world. At what price? What ethical and political conundrums does the artist/writer confront when 'going global'? Which narratives are most often circulated in such global flows? How are transnational cultural texts received in diverse contexts? How is their 'difference' appreciated by readers/viewers/consumers?

B. Martín-Lucas (✉)
University of Vigo, Vigo, Spain
e-mail: bmartin@uvigo.es

A. Ruthven
University of Barcelona, Barcelona, Spain
e-mail: andrearuthven@ub.edu

© The Author(s) 2017
B. Martín-Lucas and A. Ruthven (eds.), *Narratives of Difference in Globalized Cultures*, New Comparisons in World Literature, DOI 10.1007/978-3-319-62133-3_1

From the creative act itself to the marketing of cultural products, and to their reception in diverse contexts, flows of cultural and capital value invest in transnational imaginaries and capitalize on their 'difference'. At the intersection of Globalization, Diaspora, Postcolonial and Feminist Studies, these essays engage critically with world literature by examining a wide showcase of representative examples taken from diverse cultural fields, including humanitarian fiction, multilingual poetry, painting, text-image art, performance or film.

This volume asserts that the neocolonial voyeuristic fascination for the exotic Other and the obsession with 'authenticity' in this postmodern age of simulacra can be considered central factors behind the apparently 'sudden' irruption at the end of the twentieth century of an important number of authors and artists in diverse media who have been variously described as ethnic, diasporic, migrant or postcolonial, and rapidly incorporated into a renewed world literature canon. Their works have been widely distributed—both in the original and in translation—in a well designed marketing operation that volumes like those by Graham Huggan (2001), Sarah Brouillette (2007), Claire Squires (2007) and Om Prakash Dwivedi and Lisa Lau (2014) have analyzed extensively. Our approach takes into account the crucial role played by cultural products as a preferred form of public diplomacy in the context of economic globalization. Literature and film, together with music and visual arts, are understood here as fundamental modes for soft diplomacy, which increasingly intervene in the process of nation branding. This presupposition, while not explicitly addressed in every chapter, is an underlying component of our joint critical analysis.

Each of the authors included aims to read against accepted notions of difference, against what is expected of the 'Other', the 'periphery' or the 'marginalized', and sets up terms of interrogation that attempt to situate their readings within a critique of neoliberal 'difference' that reveals the dynamics involved in its production. Rather than conceiving of difference as a value conferred on the periphery by the centre, the following chapters consider how it may be written into the texts. As such, the bodies—textual, visual, poetic, etc.—discussed are analyzed with an eye to who or what is producing, circulating and consuming these bodies, and how the meaning of difference is engendered through this trajectory. At the same time, they are examined from a vantage point that is critical of the idea of difference as a commodity, and questions how or why certain 'differences' are more prominent within the circulation of texts than others, and how, or even whether, it is possible to read 'differently'.

Given the myriad ways in which difference is produced, circulated and received, each of the essays in this volume approaches the topic by studying a single thematic aspect (such as the production of a global metropolis, the global circulation of rape narratives, or the reception of 'ethnic' literature and art across the world), and contextualizes the discussion through the analysis of one representative case study to exemplify the argument and situate it within a specific national/local context. The case studies are drawn from a wide variety of cultural forms, including diasporic and/or postcolonial fiction (film and literature), humanitarian fiction (also in film and literature), transnational multilingual poetry, and visual arts (painting, text image and performance interventions). These diverse materials are examined through textual analysis methodologies characteristic of Literary and Cultural Studies that combine critical tools from Feminist, Postcolonial, Diaspora and Globalization Studies.

The collection gathers together the work of two consecutive research projects: 'Globalized Cultural Markets: the Production, Circulation and Reception of Difference' (2010–2013) and 'Bodies in Transit: Making Difference in Globalized Cultures' (2015–2017). Each project generated conversations within a truly interdisciplinary transnational team in order to address essential worldwide questions of circulation and exploitation of 'difference' as a commodity in globalized cultural markets. Emphasis was placed on the pernicious effects of such commodification on the material bodies of those marked as Other/different (and ultimately disposable), with an eye to reframing the discursive construction of this difference. As a group and individually, we have questioned the hypervisibility/invisibility of racial, sexual and gender markers of difference in transnational cultural products from Europe and other multicultural societies (Australia, Canada, South Africa, the USA) from the intersection of Postcolonial, Gender, Queer and Citizenship Studies, in order to provide a diagnosis of the influence of market forces, both material and ideological, on contemporary culture.

The book is divided into three Parts—'Reading Methodologies', 'Counter-narratives of the Metropolis' and 'Disruptive Genders'—each of which explores the way in which narratives of difference can be read and interrogated within and across national borders, in this increasingly globalized context.

Part I, 'Reading Methodologies', groups together four chapters sharing the common objective of dislodging hegemonic readings and practices in favour of subversive, disruptive and counter-discursive methodologies that resist the commodification of 'difference' within globalized cultural contexts. Ranging in focus from cultural and linguistic difference to readings of the postcolonial Other in documentary and text, to re-readings and narratives of Frida Kahlo's visual art, and finally to the resistant potentialities of reading against the imperial metropolis, this section opens up a variety of questions around the ways in which global capitalist narratives of difference are contested, both in their readings and in their writings.

Merlinda Bobis's 'Subversive Translation and Lexical Empathy: Pedagogies of *Cortesia* and Transnational Multilingual Poetics' pays attention to the tactful yet subversive meeting of languages in a single text. The essay looks at three pertinent case studies—poems by Merlinda Bobis (1998) (Philippines-Australia) and Sujata Bhatt (1988) (India-USA-Germany), and a play by Guillermo Verdecchia (1997) (Argentina-Canada)—where *cortesia* or 'lexical empathy' (Steiner, 1989) is mobilized in the process of writing, reading and teaching in order not to neutralize, commodify and consume linguistic and cultural 'difference'. When facing linguistic and cultural difference in a predominantly monolingual hegemonic context, as is the case of the Australian university classroom, subversive strategies are most needed to not mute artistic expression in other languages. 'Monolingual' here does not stand for the person speaking only one language, but for the monolithic sensibility that hears and cares for only one tongue.

David Callahan's 'The Production and Productivity of Humanitarian Fiction: Postcolonial Shame and Neocolonial Crises' explores the possibility opened up by Timothy Bewes's concept of 'shame' (2011), a gap between the writing of postcolonial critique and the inability to transcend and master the history of colonialism. This chapter speculates that Bewes's 'shame' could potentially also be applied to texts dealing with humanitarian crises, using as representative examples Zimbabwean Mashingaidze Gomo's verse novel *A Fine Madness* (2010) and the Australian-Canadian television movie *Answered by Fire* (2006), set in East Timor.

Zoë Brigley Thompson's chapter shifts the focus from the relationship between the artist and the urban environment to the way in which the artist herself, in this case Frida Kahlo, is converted into an object for global consumption. In 'Still Devouring Frida Kahlo: Psychobiography versus Postcolonial and Disability Readings', Brigley Thompson assesses

Kahlo's specific status as a postcolonial woman artist in Mexico, and offers an engaged critique from postcolonial perspectives of the commodification of Kahlo as a globalized cultural product and the role twenty-first-century critics continue to play in fostering Orientalist interpretations of Kahlo's art as something personal and not subversively political.

In 'The World Republic of Readers', James Procter attends to how readers outside London take up a variety of positions in relation to the literary capital. Contrary to certain accounts of the deterritorialized audience associated with globalization studies, evidence drawn from the audiences studied here suggests that reading remains a more stubbornly situated and carefully 'staked out' activity than available research has tended to acknowledge. For the reading group members participating in the discussions, 'London' emerges as an opportunity to position themselves near or far from the texts, put books in place, or use them to better understand their own places in the world.

If the preceding Part sought counter-readings of hegemonic discourses surrounding difference, in Part II, 'Counter-narratives of the Metropolis', the authors' concerns focus on the construction of the nation via the metropolis as a site which celebrates the diversity of its Others while simultaneously relegating them to the periphery. In a further selection of texts, documentary, and visual art, these chapters consider how narratives of difference are used to shore up neoliberal claims of unproblematic transnationality while reinforcing racist, sexist, xenophobic and classist categories of belonging.

Darragh Patrick Hall's chapter 'Success and the City: Working in the World's Capital in Monica Ali's *Brick Lane*' focuses on the construction of symbolic violence as manifested in the representation of gender and the migrant class in Monica Ali's novel (2003). The chapter traces the implicit logics coalescing the possibility of remaining within the world's quintessential global city and participation in the capitalist functions that it embodies, arguing that the novel's political thrusts endorse neoliberal logics via its migrant narratives. Through a concurrent analysis of these narratives and the spatial economy of the city, this chapter asserts the need to situate migrant narratives within broader contexts of global capitalism, international migration and the capitalist metropolis.

Libe García Zarranz, in 'Borderless (Alien)Nations: Disposable Bodies and Biopolitical Effacement in Min Sook Lee's Docu-Poem', looks at the shifting expressions of biopolitical life, using as a case study the 2006 collaborative project *Borderless: A Docu-Poem About the Lives of*

Undocumented Workers (2006). García Zarranz discusses how liberal and neoliberal rationalities, as Foucauldian critics aptly argue, privilege some individuals as autonomous self-regulating agents, while subordinating and disciplining others as invisible or dangerous.

The notion of which identities are privileged and visible, and which are subjected to processes of invisibilization is also taken up by John Havelda in his chapter 'Public Art in the Production of a Global City: Jamie Hilder's Clashing Versions of Vancouver', which focuses on Hilder's artistic interventions in the urban space. These situationist mappings reconfigure the city as a text to be written and interpreted, performed and contested; rather than presenting urban structures, they chart urban life and energy flows, or even the lack of energy flows, in a deliberate attempt to subvert the glamour of the *dérive*. Hilder's text-image art and his performances disrupt the spectacle of the global city and expose how visitors to Vancouver are being interpellated as customers or consumers of the designer city.

'A Nation Goes Adrift: Subaltern Inter-Identity in José Saramago's *The Stone Raft*' by Maria Sofia Pimentel Biscaia considers how identity is constructed from within the nation and projected outward. Using José Saramago's (1986) emblematic novel as a case study, the chapter analyzes contesting discourses on Portuguese national identity which address, respectively, two distinct markets: the identity produced by official entities to satisfy the local market of imperial sympathy, and the external market, represented by Britain, Europe and the world at large, which taken together seek to construct a subalternized Portuguese identity. The result is a hybrid, nomadic identity, simultaneously a flaw and the cornerstone of Portugal's postcolonial identity; an ambivalent European consciousness stubbornly driven to territories of its imperial past.

Within popular neoliberal discourses, gender emerges as a fruitful site for the production and exploitation of 'difference' as a cultural commodity. The chapters in Part III, 'Disruptive Genders', consider how hegemonic gender/ed identity participates in both physical and symbolic violence, and offer readings critical of the processes that reproduce systemic representations of gendered bodies: in South African literature, South Asian diasporic film and post 9/11 veil narratives. Through the situated readings of the implications of the production of normative gender identities, globalized and globalizing forces of representation are disrupted.

The question of symbolic and physical violence is explicitly addressed by Sorcha Gunne in the chapter '"Something Terrible Happened":

Spectacles of Gendered Violence and Nadine Gordimer's *The House Gun*'. Looking at the interconnectedness of gender, sexuality, race and class with violence in post-apartheid South Africa, the chapter situates South African contemporary culture within an interconnected world system. Comparing diverse narratives of gendered violence in the media—which include the spectacularized reporting on the gang rape and murder of women in India and South Africa in international media—parallelisms are established between the notorious Steenkamp/Pistorius case and Nadine Gordimer's novel (1998). The chapter discusses non-normative sexualities and the construction of masculinity both in Gordimer's novel and in Pistorius's trial to expose the persistent global circulation of the 'blame the victim' myth.

Gender, of course, is not just a corporeal marker of women's bodies, but also, as E. Guillermo Iglesias Díaz argues in 'Alternative Modernities and Othered Masculinities in Mira Nair's *The Namesake*', works on men's bodies, especially racialized male bodies, in specific and concrete ways. Paying attention to the complex game of hierarchies in geopolitical and economic terms under the reductive signifier 'South Asian', this chapter specifically analyzes the historical (post)colonial clichés around Bengali masculinities, their relevance within radical Hindu nationalism, and their subversion from feminist perspectives in Mira Nair's highly successful film adaptation of Jhumpa Lahiri's novel (2006). This chapter further discusses the tension between competing modes of normative masculinity in contemporary Indian diasporic flows.

In '(Un)Veiling Women's Bodies: Transnational Feminisms in Emer Martin's *Baby Zero*', Aida Rosende-Pérez analyzes Martin's 2007 novel and explores how transnational feminist politics are an appropriate tool to resist and dismantle the dichotomies derived from a 'civilizational clash' reading of the world which turns women and their bodies into its battleground. The chapter focuses first on the ambiguities and complexities that remain hidden behind the iconic status of the burqa, visibilizing the resistant agency of non-Western women who are victimized under local, but also global, patriarchies. It goes on to highlight the imperative contextualization of these multiple oppressions within a wider historical framework of geopolitical power relations. Finally, the chapter moves on to the examination of those other veils that are modelled on the bodies and subjectivities of women in the context of a capitalist society that equates the commodification of women's bodies and sexualities with concepts of 'liberation', 'freedom' and even 'democracy'.

While each of the chapters highlights a specific media and case study, the reader will perceive an ongoing dialogue around the concept of difference running through the book. Reflecting upon the production of difference we find a recurrent concern over the forces that may influence the writer/artist to exploit 'difference' in the creative act—the ethical and moral dilemmas they face when producing a narrative that could help endorse the imperialist drive of neoliberal globalization or, on the contrary, resist and contest it. There is a common exploration of the concepts of nationhood, citizenship and affective solidarity which does not lose sight of the exclusionary practices produced by current neocolonial discourses. In relation to this, all of the authors consider how bodies have become repositories of difference, looking at the ways the 'divergent' body is branded as a cultural commodity itself. The violence of the circulation of racial and gender clichés and stereotypes is staunchly contested in the analyses, which also pay attention to the glocal situatedness in which the act of consumption takes place—the diversity of locations and glocal cultural contexts where such cultural products are read, viewed or experienced.

No matter what the cultural medium analyzed, the essays coincide in offering strategies for resilience and agency versus the necropolitics (Mbembe 2003) of the contemporary scenario: the lexical empathy of multilingual poetry in monolingual Australia; intervention in the urban space through performative protest; denouncing the exploitation of the disposable bodies of the multitude (Hardt and Negri 2004) in neoliberal labour regimes; or unveiling gendered violence in many of its infinite forms. In its balance between criticism and envisioning tools for change, the volume aims to highlight the potential of world literature and its dialogue and interaction with other modes of cultural and artistic expression to mobilize truly diverse affective relationships based on respect and mutual recognition of difference.

Works Cited

Ali, Monica. 2003. *Brick Lane*. London: Doubleday.
Answered by Fire. 2006. Directed by Jessica Hobbs. Australia-Canada: Beyond Simpson le Mesurier, Muse Entertainment Enterprises, Terra Rossa Pictures, Powercorp.
Bewes, Timothy. 2011. *The Event of Postcolonial Shame*. Princeton: Princeton University Press.

Bhatt, Sujata. 1988. *Brunizem*. Manchester: Carcanet.
Bobis, Merlinda. 1998. *Summer Was a Fast Train Without Terminals*. North Melbourne: Spinifex.
Borderless. 2006. *A Docu-Poem About the Lives of Undocumented Workers*. Directed by Min Sook Lee. Toronto: Kairos.
Brouillette, Sarah. 2007. *Postcolonial Writers in the Global Literary Marketplace*. Basingstoke: Palgrave Macmillan.
Dwivedi, Om Prakash, and Lisa Lau (eds.). 2014. *Indian Writing in English and the Global Literary Market*. Basingstoke: Palgrave Macmillan.
Gomo, Mashingaidze. 2010. *A Fine Madness*. Banbury: Ayebia Clarke.
Gordimer, Nadine. 1998. *The House Gun*. London: Bloomsbury.
Hardt, Michael, and Antonio Negri. 2004. *Multitude. War and Democracy in the Age of Empire*. New York: Penguin.
Huggan, Graham. 2001. *The Postcolonial Exotic. Marketing the Margins*. London: Routledge.
Martin, Emer. 2007. *Baby Zero*. Dingle and London: Brandon Books.
Mbembe, Achille. 2003. 'Necropolitics,' trans. Libby Meintjes. *Public Culture* 15 (1): 11–40.
The Namesake. 2006. Directed by Mira Nair. Mirabai Films, Fox Searchlight Productions.
Saramago, José. 1986/1994. *The Stone Raft*, trans. Giovanni Pontiero. London: The Harvill Press.
Squire, Claire. 2007. *Marketing Literature. The Making of Contemporary Writing in Britain*. Basingstoke: Palgrave Macmillan.
Steiner, George. 1989. *Real Presences*. Chicago: University of Chicago Press.
Verdecchia, Guillermo. 1997. *Fronteras Americanas*. Vancouver: Talonbooks.

PART I

Reading Methodologies

Subversive Translation and Lexical Empathy: Pedagogies of *Cortesia* and Transnational Multilingual Poetics

Merlinda Bobis

Bikol:
Pagmundô, pagmunhô, pagbakhô, pagdusô, pagsakit: grief
Paghaya, agrangay: grief with sound
Paghaya, pagtangis: grief with tears
Filipino (Tagalog):
Dalamhati, pighati, lumbay, sakit, hapis
Spanish adapted to Bikol:
Dolor, lamento
English:
Grief, sorrow, anguish

Here is grief in my first tongue, Bikol, the language of the Bikol region in Luzon, one of the three largest islands among 7101 in the Philippines. But in Filipino, originally Tagalog—one of the regional languages elected as the national language in 1937—I would find other words. If I travel around the archipelago with its more than a

M. Bobis (✉)
Australian National University, Canberra, Australia
e-mail: merlinda.bobis@anu.edu.au

hundred languages, I would find more. Given that we were colonized by Spain for more than 350 years and that the Bikol region was thoroughly Hispanized, the Bikolano knows 'dolor/lamento'. With 40 years of American colonization and, as a consequence, English becoming the medium of instruction at schools and universities, 'grief'/'sorrow'/'anguish' can be added to the list. So in the Philippines, we grieve multilingually. Locally, we are translingual. We navigate across different tongues. Back in my first home in the Bikol region, grief is inherently multiple words, multiple sounds, multiple weights in the chest. Multiple stones.

Gapôbatostone

Gapô	Bato	Stone
dusong kasinkinis kan gapo	sakit na singkinis ng bato	grief as smooth as stone
dusong minagatok na sanribong tataramon na nawaran nin nguso	sakit na sumasambulat na sanlaksang salitang walang bibig	grief that shatters into a thousand words without mouth

gapôbatostonegapôbatostonegapôbatostonegapôbatostonegapôbatostone
gapôbatostonegapôbatostonegapôbatostonegapôbatostonegapôbatostone
gapôbatostonegapôbatostonegapôbatostonegapôbatostonegapôbatostone
gapôbatostonegapôbatostonegapôbatostonegapôbatostonegapôbatostone
gapôbatostonegapôbatostonegapôbatostonegapôbatostonegapôbatostone
gapôbatostonegapôbatostonegapôbatostonegapôbatostonegapôbatostone

Gapôbatostone. Gapô is 'stone' in Bikol. Bato in Filipino. Then stone.

The multilingual migrant writer cannot be self-contained stone. Writing about grief in the Philippines primarily in English in Australia can be problematic. Is grief in English 'less true' than grief in Filipino or in my mother tongue, Bikol? But this is a question that may be asked even by those who live in the Philippines. Filipino poet Marjorie Evasco, who wrote in English first and is now also writing in her mother tongue, Cebuano, explains in an interview (Akella 2014, online): 'The national language of the country called Filipino is a legislated and developing language, which is Tagalog-based and is taught in all the schools of the country, and of course reinforced by Manila-based mass media'. The language debate (English versus multiple mother tongues) is ongoing. Regional mother tongues have been decolonizing from English and Filipino, placing themselves at the forefront of literary production, thus changing the old colonial flavour of the literary canon. And when English is used, it is the Filipino's *own* English.

My stone poem (Bobis 2007, 29–31) is in three languages, in three self-contained poems. But when grief shatters, so does the stone now uncontainable, no longer smooth, no longer owned by a specific mouth, in fact mouthless:

gapôbatostonegapôbatostonegapôbatostonegapôbatostonegapôbatostone

Say this incantation. Feel the hard 'g' in the throat for *gapô*, the tiny explosion of 'bh' in lips touching for *bato*, the subtle hiss in stone. And the multiple o's: the glottal ô (*gapô*), the soft o (*bato*), the rounded o (stone). How do they meet in the mouth, in the ear? How do these diverse languages and cultures reverberate in the sensibility, if they do at all? Regularly hearing multiple languages, how do we read these multiple stones in multicultural locations? How do we listen? Do we listen? To what, to whom? And when we read silently, do our eyes include or blur over the 'other squiggles' on paper? Do we extract meaning from the poem only within our own established sounds and meanings? Do we extract the distinct stone—the recognizable grief that is collected, contained and smooth like a hegemonic artefact in the mono-mouth, in the mono-ear? Or do we, because of our multiculturalism, allow ourselves to shatter into a thousand words without mouth? How terrifying to be radically disoriented. To be without mouth. A terrible loss that can come with a terrible grief.

In this chapter I will attempt to avert this grief through subversive strategies for translating linguistic and cultural difference, in order to facilitate my proposed lexical empathy that builds on George Steiner's 'lexical cortesia' (Steiner 1989, 157). According to Steiner: 'Where freedoms meet, where the integral liberty of donation or withholding of the work of art encounters our own liberty of reception or refusal, *cortesia*, what I have called tact of heart, is of the essence' (Steiner 1989, 55). So I will examine the tactful yet subversive meeting of different languages in a single text, in the process of writing, reading and teaching. Translation is a journey from one language to the other, thus from one text to another. But what if the different languages co-habit in one text? How can translation begin as a decolonial urge that facilitates an empathetic collaboration among differences, so they can resolve each other into meaning? To answer these questions, I will reference Steiner and Jahan Ramazani as I chart the negotiation of alterity at the 'micro-level' and the 'macro-level' (Ramazani 2009, 53) of chosen texts by myself (Philippines–Australia), poet Sujata Bhatt (India–USA–Germany) and playwright Guillermo Verdecchia (Argentina–Canada). I will approach these texts as writer, reader, teacher and scholar producing, circulating and receiving language and culture.

These doing-thinking practices will lead this chapter through a 'grassroots theorizing', which I conceptualized early on (Bobis 2013a, 145) and later defined thus: 'theorizing as story-making from the ground up, moving from the specific lived story that creates knowledge and modes of knowledge production, which become a counter-hegemonic discourse to the usual theorizing direction from above: globalized epistemology applied to a specific local experience' (Bobis and Martin-Lucas 2016, 17). This methodology aligns with Linda Tuhiwai Smith's, described by Susan Hawthorne as a '"local" theoretical positioning' that enables the researcher to draw on her own very 'specific historical, political and social context' to develop an embedded critical theory (Hawthorne 2002). It is only in this way, Tuhiwai Smith argues, that the 'oppressed, marginalized and silenced groups' (Tuhiwai Smith 1999, 186) will gain something from research and from the knowledge created[1] (Hawthorne 2002, 13–14). This stance evokes Walter Mignolo's *decoloniality* that 'delinks' from epistemes historically grounded in the European academy, and instead embeds scholarship in the cultural specificity of marginalized corporeal experience (Mignolo in Bobis 2013b).

These concepts ground this chapter in what I term 'the lived and livable framework' (Bobis 2013b), collaborating with scholarship's expected theoretical framework. It is after all grief in the lived body that began this journey:

---

[1] Hawthorne is quoting from Tuhiwai Smith (1999).

grief that shatters
into a thousand words
without mouth

To shatter grief. In order to find multiple words. But they are without mouth. How to navigate this paradox: with multiple words yet without mouth? Inconceivable. So I will begin with the simpler question: how to be without mouth? How to be silenced? Australians have been rendered dumb when travelling in a non-English-speaking country, unless they are travelling in the original home from where they migrated and they still speak its language. But one does not have to leave Australia to be without mouth. This is what a migrant Australian may experience when buying bread at Woolworth's—even when she is speaking in English—because her 'bread' has an accent that does not sit comfortably with the ear at the checkout. But do Australians born to English not have any accent? In non-English-speaking countries, do they not also fumble over saying a basic need, and swallow back the word for fear of being embarrassed or rejected? Thus a silencing—which is what migrant writers in Australia grieve over when the monolingual publisher/critic/reader decides that their English, thus their literature, is not up to scratch. By monolingual, I do not mean someone speaking only one tongue; I mean someone who hears-and-cares for only one tongue. I mean the monolithic sensibility.

Peta Stephenson contextualizes contemporary Australia as 'a nation formed by invasion and colonisation', and: 'In order for Aborigines and future migrant groups to be "accepted" as members of a single Australian community, they had to stop being culturally distinctive and learn to adopt the assumed monolithic and homogenous Australian culture' (1997 online). Counter-arguments in the new millennium declare that multicultural Australia has come a long way from this historical heritage and that cultural plurality is thriving. But Mary Besemeres and Anna Wierzbicka write that 'the hundreds of Aboriginal languages, largely hidden from the view of the dominant English-speaking culture' and, with migration, the 'community languages, some with very large number of speakers' have not resulted in a 'concomitant change in public consciousness of what it means to live with different languages', and 'the country remains locked in an Anglocentric view of the world' (Besemeres and Wierzbicka 2007, xvi). As I have observed elsewhere:

> There is the initial knee-jerk reaction from the sound of difference. The anxiety of Otherness registers quickly and bodily. But if you are born to and have always lived with other voices in your neighbourhood, do you not grow a plural consciousness? Or do you become more vigilant about your cultural identity and thus block out the 'outside sounds'? The anxiety of Otherness does not only plague the ear of an Anglocentric collective, but more so the newly introduced voice of the migrant. Sounding Australian to be understood is a cause of anxiety at the supermarket, at work, in the daily negotiations to survive. Sounding Australian to be accepted is an even deeper anxiety tied with settling in, with being psychologically *at home*. This anxiety can be acute in literary production, where conjuring the right voice is paramount – dissonances are highlighted as the migrant writer attempts to 'settle' the Other voice of the old home in the new country. (Bobis 2010, 4)

In the 1990s, Sneja Gunew, the frontier scholar on Australian multicultural literature, observed: 'the charge of incompetence is a familiar one in reviews of works by so-called ethnic writers' (Gunew 1994, 95). More than a decade later, Mark Davis writes: 'As Gunew says, it is through accusations of incompetence that critics strive to protect themselves from the voice of the Other, which might destabilise the coherence which underpins their own language and subject positions' (Davis 2007, 16). I remember submitting a poem to a journal in the 1990s and receiving a lengthy rejection letter explaining how to use the English language. More than a decade later, some critics still 'quarrel' with the style of my novels; style is the use of the English language, in this case. But the quarrel is no longer about grammar and correct usage, but about how my sentences are constructed in a particular configuration and tone, thus creating a perceived disfavoured dense, mannered or sentimental style. So who and what prescribe these benchmarks of taste? Do critics exercise self-reflexivity about their own otherness in their critique of that 'other style'? Is there any awareness that their own taste and sensibility are as other/as foreign to the Philippine landscape, language and experience that I am translating to English in these novels? Unfortunately, served in a national paper, the Australian critic's own foreign hearing of the foreign is institutionalized. In this respect, it is worth recalling Michelle Cahill's view that:

> Binary fixations of alterity are invariably drawn by arbiters to mark a distinction between what does and does not belong to the benchmark. Yet,

as critics such as Ruth Frankenberg note, the specular currency of Whiteness operates to validate its perspectives through complex processes that are illusory and indiscernible. How many tedious and derivative books by white Australian writers are spared from disparagement and reductive doublespeak? The advantage of White authority in literary production is so blinding and disguised that to unmask it is a fraught process. (Cahill 2014, 209)

Sometimes the issue is a double-bind of gender and culture. Cahill introduces the women poets in the collection *Contemporary Asian Australian Poetry*, pointing out that many of them 'have remained in the footnotes and peripheries of national canons, including those dedicated exclusively to women's poetry' (Cahill 2013, 28). In a recent essay in *Cordite Poetry Review*, she also argues:

More significantly the emergent discourses in a national poetics are economically invested, driven by the neo-colonizing impulse. Every time a review in our mainstream publications – *The Australian, The Sydney Morning Herald, The Age* – fails to engage impartially or seriously with the work of those poets marginalized within the national category (presumably because of their differences of race or language or their struggles to lever cultural access), effectively what happens is that Australian Poetry reinforces itself as a monolith, legitimising its own authority while diminishing a possible range of differences. (Cahill 2016, online)

Worse than being reviewed in such a manner is not being reviewed at all. In his book *Bias: Offensively Chinese/Australian*, poet Ouyang Yu observes:

Anything that does not conform to that 'ethno-politics of an Anglo type' will be rendered obsolete by this WMS (weapon of mass silence) in which no books by Asians will be made reviewable in magazines, viewable on TV or publishable by white publishers and no decent prizes will be made winnable by Asians, so in the end they vacate the scene by themselves. (Ouyang Yu 2007, 168)

Note the resonances of 'lament' among writers and scholars from the 1990s to the present. This is not to say that Anglo-centricism is promoted by all Australian critics/publishers. Some go out on a limb to support writers outside the white mainstream, and in fact make it a rule to engage and disseminate Australia's plural voices; however, they, too, are often in the margins of the literary industry, as I will discuss in greater detail further on. While I admire Ouyang's blast of anger, in this chapter I argue in defence of a discipline of courtesy, a tact of heart in the meeting between different sensibilities and languages, as Steiner proposes. He writes:

> Lexical *cortesia*, the first step in philology, is that which makes us dwellers in the great dictionaries, both general and specialized ... it enables us to *hear* the unfolding of historical continuity and of change inside words themselves and within the bodies of text in which these words are organic ... it takes an ear for temporal tuning. (Steiner 1989, 157)

An ear for temporal tuning will certainly not privilege a singular mouth and will refuse to atrophy in a monolithic sensibility—what a disaster would it be, to be rendered deaf to the multiple, varied reverberations of the universe? Steiner grounds translation in lexical *cortesia*:

> If the poem is speaking out of our own tongue, we seek to ascertain the historical, social, if need be local or dialectal, status of the poet's particular idiom. If the text is in a foreign language – and there is no more concentrated instance of 'otherness' and of its freedom of being than that of our encounters with languages not our own – we do our labored best either to master that other speech or to accept the humbling trust of translation. (Steiner 1989, 156)

How do we accept the humbling trust of a translation? And when we read a poem in its English translation, which is *the poem*? Where is the poem in its original language and do we explore how this sits in the mouth and ear? Unfortunately it is so easy to read the English translation as an English poem (and it has to work in *my* English)—thus the original language and culture disappear. In this case, we may have trusted the translation, but there is hardly any courtesy in the engagement. I would like to move beyond Steiner's lexical *cortesia*. I propose a lexical empathy, but subversively strategized. One can approach this concept as the necessary 'operational empathy' among languages, in order to make meaning together—though I argue that languages make meaning in the body that produces/receives it. In its simplest terms, empathy evokes a bodily process: putting oneself in the shoes of another. So for lexical empathy to work, the reader has to put her/his own mouth-and-ear into the mouth-and-ear of the poem, of the poet, of that language, of that culture.

I propose, then, to unsettle the monolingual reader into empathy, in a translingual poem where Filipino co-habits with English in one text. So the reader must physically meet the untranslated other—must ingest this 'foreign-ness' into their mouth-and-ear—to be thus confounded, disoriented, made awkward, rendered momentarily mouthless. This silencing of the reader, so they can listen, is the poet's aestheticized politics: the creative process begins with the political will to subvert an English-only reading. And the politics is realized in an aesthetic artefact: a poem. According to Liz Lundberg, 'The structures of language are social structures in which meanings and intentions are already in place, always fighting for power and dominance with rhetorical figures and more violent weapons. Poetry and art works are not isolated autonomous aesthetic objects. The language of poetry has the capacity to question, expose and attack the language of power' (Lundberg 2014, 172). In the following translingual poem, I aim to disrupt the structures of the language of power, English, and the silencing violence that it wields in the house of the patriarch (see Giffard-Foret 2013).

Siesta

Take me not
in mid-winter,
only to thaw the frost
of your old bones,
imagining how stallions rear
in the outback,
hooves raised to this August light,

kakaibang liwanag,
kasimputla't kasinglamig
ng hubad na peras.*

But take me
on a humid afternoon
made for siesta,
when my knees almost ache
from daydreaming of mangoes,
tree-ripe
and just right,

at higit sa lahat
mas matamis, makatas
kaysa sa unang halik ng mansanas.**

> *alien light,
> pale and cold
> as a naked pear
>
> plucked from my tongue you have wrapped
> in a plastic bag with the $3 mango
> from woolworths
>
> while i conjured an orchard
> from back home – mangoes gold and not for sale, and
>
> **above all,
> sweeter, more succulent
> than the first kiss of the apple.

This poem (Bobis 1998, 8) was my response to the domestic subjugation and violence experienced by Filipinas married to Australians at the time when the Filipina mail-order bride issue was rife. This is not to say that there were no happy stories of cross-cultural unions—which continue to thrive until now. Moreover, I also continue to question the term 'Filipina mail-order bride' and how it stereotyped and stigmatized Filipinas (see Piper and Roces 2003; Espinosa 2015). Who coined the 'mail-order bride' label, in the first place? Why not, 'Filipinas who were "pen-pals" with Australian men, then married them'? But then, this could make invisible the 'mail-order-bride' attitude and actions of certain Australian men to Filipinas whose accounts told to me reveal that this stigma was their lived life in the new home: their Australian husbands married them to have a housekeeper, a carer, a sex slave (see Elson 1997; Cunneen and Stubbs 2000; Saroca 2006). So I asked, how does one re-instate in this Australian household the disappeared voice, tongue, food, sexual agency and first home? Then, as a poet, I wondered, how do I re-instate my own mouth and render the poetry patriarch (or matriarch) mouthless in the house of Australian national literature—so his only choice is to listen, even for a moment?

And 'Siesta' was born. A siesta is a moment: in Spain and in the Philippines, it is an afternoon nap after lunch. The poetic persona claims her siesta as a moment of agency—an ambivalent threshold, a liminal space where everything is unfixed and fluid. Even language is de-territorialized: English in the first stanza is disrupted yet completed in image by the Filipino in the following stanza. Jahan Ramazani writes about 'the logic of *stanza* as geographic room, [where] the white space in between functions like a doorway between cultural worlds' (Ramazani 2009, 54). In 'Siesta', this doorway is subversive as English opens into Filipino, which opens back into English that returns to Filipino—as the Filipina delineates the parameters of sex. Take me on my own terms: at siesta when I'm 'at home' with my own food, in my own season, in my own language. Also, the poet says: hey critic, you want poetic pleasure? Have it, but on my terms. And I am not translating that soon. Because I want you to put your reader's mouth-and-ear into the poet's mouth-and-ear. Such an erotic moment. Is empathy erotic then? Perhaps. After all, eros is love.

In 'Ethics and Cognitive Science', Alvin Goldman proposes empathy as simply 'the ability to put oneself into the mental shoes of another person to understand her emotions and feelings' (Goldman 1993, 337–360). An interesting framework that departs from the perception of empathy as primarily a feeling. Mental cognition precedes emotional cognition or affect. Frans de Waal's definition of empathy is the reverse, denoting process: 'The capacity to (a) be affected by and share the emotional state of another, (b) assess the reasons for the other's state, and (c) identify with the other, adopting his or her perspective' (de Waal 2012, online). First affect, then critical knowing of the state of the other, then identifying with and adopting the other's perspective.

Both definitions are relevant to my argument about lexical empathy that may be subversively inspired in this translingual siesta: there must be a mental and emotional cognition of the other. More importantly, it is imperative that the reader adopt the other's perspective. The patriarch, to whom the poem is addressed, is forced to read and act in the Filipina's terms, taken out of his comfort zone and linguistically disoriented and made vulnerable. But the poet also has to have empathy for this disoriented reader: she cannot leave him in the dark. Not only for his sake, but also for the sake of the poem: so it is understood. The footnote is written to translate, as much as to argue and further the subversive stance. Note how

> *alien light,
> pale and cold
> as a naked pear

is the translation of the poem's first stanza in Filipino. It is also the translation of the August winter light by the Filipina to herself: your winter light is the colour of a naked pear, pale and cold. Moreover, this footnote is more than a translation. It is a completely new poem, a secret revealed about the silencing: to expose how you wrapped my tongue in a plastic bag with the mango from Woolworth's, my tongue a commodity that you could buy cheaply—unlike back home, where mangoes are 'gold and not for sale'. Where we have a whole orchard of them, where both fruit and tongue are precious—and

> **above all,
> sweeter, more succulent
> than the first kiss of the apple.

is the translation of the poem's final stanza in Filipino and, more importantly, the assertion that my fruit and my tongue are 'sweeter, more succulent' than the fruit that you offer me: 'the first kiss of the apple' evoking the sex in your own terms or the language/poem in your own terms that have displaced my mangoes, my language, my season, my pleasure—that have wrapped them up cheaply, muffled them in a plastic bag. So the new footnote poem subversively serves three functions—to translate, to critique, to re-instate voice—to decolonize from the subjugating triple-bind of gender, race and culture. Even the translation must function on my *own* terms.

You might think: but what a confrontational way to foster lexical empathy. We have this notion of empathy as a fuzzy, warm feeling of being nice to the other. No, empathy is not comfortable or self-congratulatory. Empathy is kinship for another's loss and suffering, which inevitably destabilizes us, and like love, empathy renders us vulnerable. Empathy is a critical and ethical re-positioning of who we are and how we relate to those unlike us. Those who do not speak and sound like us—so we attempt, as Steiner proposes, to 'master that other speech' in the hope that we can, as De Waal argues, 'adopt the other's perspective'. To master, as in to learn—not to master, as in to subjugate—that other speech is a tall order. So I simply propose to resolve the poetic experience among poet–text–reader into some meaningful aesthetic completion. But meaningful aesthetic completion is still a tall order. Even if at line/local level, multiple languages empathize with each other to complete the poem, at cultural/global level, navigating difference is always fraught with ambivalences, fractures, slippages and uncertainties. The journey is often threatened by 'The Undertow', (Bhatt 1988, 89–90), as Gujarati poet Sujata Bhatt writes:

> There are at least three
> languages between us.
> And the common space, the common dream-sound
> is far out at sea.
> There's a certain spot, dark
> far out where the waves sleep
> there's a certain spot
> we always focus on,
> and the three languages are there
> swimming like seals fat with fish and sun
> they smile, the three languages
> understand each other so well. (Bhatt 1988, 89)

The 'three languages between us'—Gujarati, English, German—'understand each other so well'. But unfortunately we do not: 'the waves keep us back,/the undertow threatens' (Bhatt 1988, 89). What is this undertow that scares us? Perhaps the possibility of failure to understand, to connect—or the possibility of losing power? Is the undertow, in fact, the refusal to understand, underpinned by a language chauvinism that holds fast to our fear of those unknown others, lest they pull us down and we drown? Even so, Bhatt's poem is lexical empathy at its best: it is joyful lexical play, in which 'we take one word at a time' like 'dog' (Bhatt 1988, 89):

> કૂતરો (kootro) in Gujarati, *Köter* in Low German
> *Hund* in High German, like hound in English.
>
> Dog   કૂતરો   (kootro)   *Köter*   *Hund*
>
> hound   dog   Köter   કૂતરો   (kootro)
>
> કૂતરો   કૂતરો   કૂતરો
> (kootro   kootro   kootro)

And there is always the undertow. But chased by the threatening waves, the kootro, köter, hund, dog subvert the chase lexically—the threat is disarmed as the waves join the gambol and 'flood the streets', bringing in seals 'through the bookstores', with 'the common sounds' (Bhatt 1988, 90) that overcome us, 'filling our shoes [and 'our love']

                ક   ખ   ગ
                 શ   ક્ષ   સ
            kö   kh   ga
                 sh   ksh   ß

with salt' (Bhatt 1988, 90). The private love story of the three languages overcomes the public spaces. We cannot stop languages from doing what they do: blend and compete as sounds, play, chase each other—perhaps chase away even our fear of the undertow. Unless we are in love with the undertow itself. So there is no hope for us. We are already drowning in our monolithic apprehension of the world. Or, we could keep ourselves safe, never daring to dip into the water for fear of failure to understand, to connect, to become vulnerable. So forever, high and dry on the shore: 'We stand watching, jealous/of the three languages' (Bhatt 1988, 89). But Bhatt enjoins us to engage: to listen and listen again to the dogs, the seals, the sounds, and to allow our shoes to be filled by them, by the indispensable pleasure of 'salt'. That shared other ingredient, which binds different flavours and rounds the palate. At this point, Jahan Ramazani's 'traveling poetry' is crucial. He writes:

> Whereas travel writing, the Odyssean tale, or, for that matter, the travel poem (as opposed to the traveling poem) involve 'the territorial passage from one zone to another'[2] – that is, a macro-level transition, a mimetically plotted border crossing from home to foreign land – the travel in what I am calling traveling poetry often occurs at the micro-level. (Ramazani 2009, 53)

Bhatt's poem (like 'Siesta') is a traveling poem, a transnational poem at micro/local/line level, and at macro/cultural/global level echoing the poet's own border crossing from her first home in India to the United States and then to Germany, where she now lives. And she teaches us how to travel out from the safe shore, as she teaches us how to read: how to master those other speeches, as Steiner advises—'one

---

[2] Brian Musgrove 1999.

word at a time' if only in small 'common sounds', byte-sized morsels for a start. She instructs us: try them, repeat after me: *ko kh ga sh ksh B*. Find them in your mouth. After all, your mouth and ear know these sounds.

But how do I assure my class of Australian students, who speak and write only in English, that they know or can know these sounds? And for those who know another language from their migrant background enough to use it, which is a rarity, how can they be inspired to confidently bring these other sounds to the class? I will now swap my writer's-and-reader's hat for the teacher's hat, and ask: How can I enable my creative writing students to experience lexical subversion, *cortesia*, empathy, joy? In the swimming culture that is Australia, how can I (who literally cannot quite swim) teach my students to overcome their fear of the undertow?

In 2010, with Belén Martín-Lucas and her University of Vigo students (Literary Studies), I and my University of Wollongong students (Creative Writing) began a border-crossing experiment: the Transnational Story Hub (see website). Our students had to 'swim' two oceans (Pacific and Atlantic) towards each other by co-writing an online story, a process that spanned a whole semester. The teaching experiment developed into a four-year story-making project with Galician and Wollongong participants mostly from the original transnational experiment. I do not have room to discuss this project in this chapter, but suffice it to say that it brought to the fore the problematics of storying self and other across different cultures, languages and disciplines, especially if one group is monolingual (Wollongong: English) and the other multilingual (Vigo: Galician, Castilian, English). I saw the undertow at work through both groups' engagement of difference, and as a co-facilitator of the project, I realized that the lived and perceived power dynamics is the strongest undertow that can pull us down. The practicalities of process can threaten to overcome even those with the best intentions. These realities are discussed, examined and critiqued in the project's book outcome, *The Transnational Story Hub: Between Self and Other* (2016), a collection of essays and creative works produced by the project participants.

While the above project was ongoing, I designed a new creative-writing subject: Writing Across Borders. I was led to this recourse after more than a decade of teaching Australian and mostly monolingual students as a Filipino-Australian lecturer bringing a different sensibility (and texts from different cultures) into the classroom. Student responses ranged from the indifferent, perplexed, hesitant, timorous, appreciative, joyful, to resentful and sometimes downright hostile. Thus, I had to dream up a subject that attempts to address these responses through creative writing, and critical reading and thinking across borders. Intended as 'a doing-thinking space', the subject examines story production, circulation and reception across varied cultures, languages, literary forms and genres. The subject aims to unsettle the students (who will be the next generation of writers, critics and teachers) from the singular self in order to accommodate multiple others. Or, at least, to recognize that there are other sensibilities unlike theirs, and to listen to them with, hopefully, courtesy and a tact of heart. However, having retired from teaching at the end of 2015, I did not have enough time to fine-tune the subject according to what I hoped it could become: grow beyond the Creative Writing Program and cross disciplines, so it could be delivered by creative-writing lecturers team-teaching with those from literary and language studies, with students from these diverse disciplines reading, thinking and writing together in a shared creative-critical space. I had hoped to develop a mode of delivery that could live up to the subject's aspiration: cross borders.

The first semester of 2013 was an exciting, difficult and revealing teaching-learning pilot for this new subject. There was discovery/re-discovery of the other and the students' (and my) own otherness; the resisting, stereotyping and welcoming of difference; the challenging of the Anglocentric hierarchy of language and sensibility; then the incessant 'ethical niggle' about how we read and write the other, always with multiple creative and critical interrogations, and lessons learned/unlearned. More interesting for me was how the students responded with their bodies: how they put (or not) their mouth-and-ear into the mouth-and-ear of another language and/or culture. Ours was 'a threshold subject', where we were always in a liminal state, at the brink of knowing and unknowing, of learning and unlearning, of being and becoming. My mode of delivery was often tested and de-territorialized: this was difficult and sometimes stressful but necessary for developing further strategies in transnational knowledge production and dissemination in the academy, which Jahan Ramazani pertinently challenges:

> How would modern and contemporary poetry studies in English – an area now largely subdivided along national lines – look if this transnationalism

were taken to be primary rather than incidental? ... How might the field seem different if the nationalities and ethnicities of poets and poems, often reified by nation-based histories, anthologies, and syllabi, were genuinely regarded as hybrid, interstitial, and fluid imaginative constructs...? ... Unless we transnationalize our syllabi and historical narratives of modern poetry, we may miss such abundant ironies of influence. (Ramazani 2009, 24–47)

Ramazani addresses 'the transnational and cross-ethnic ironies' in possible convergences and influences among contemporary British, Irish and American poets read as only of a particular national or cultural affiliation. My students rose to the challenge beyond authors writing in English, as we also studied world literature in translation from other languages, and they discovered a few ironies themselves, even uncanny convergences and insights; moreover, I found myself coming up against my own border crossings as teacher-reader-writer-migrant.

One of the subject's readings was a play about multiple border crossings: the award-winning *Fronteras Americanas* (1997), a one-man play—autobiography, history, cultural theory and critique, intertextual literature, language play, satire and meta-theatre rolled into one—by the Argentinian-Canadian Guillermo Verdecchia, also the protagonist of the play. I asked the students to do a performance reading of excerpts. At the outset, we kept getting the name 'Verdecchia' wrong in our mouths, so after a while we skipped it. I missed my chance. The lesson should have begun with *Verdecchia* as sounds, as byte-sized morsels. Worse, to avert fumbling, I asked if they would rather I read the Spanish parts in between their reading of the English sections. But one student said: 'Please, can I have a go with the Spanish?' That little request was a slap on the teacher's hand. Yes, always let their mouths-and-ears have a go. Let them find the sounds of the other. Perhaps they can find the other's stories too, and find their own stories of relating with the other.

This is the scene read by the student who asked to have a go:

> **Verdecchia:** I went back to Santiago and looked for some sign of the man who had been shot on the first day of my return. I looked for a scrape, a stain, anything, his shoe perhaps had been left behind.
>
> I wondered who he might have been. I remembered the redness of this shirt, the brightness of the sun. It was five o'clock.

> *A las cinco de la tarde.*
> *Eran las cinco en punto de la tarde.*
> *Un niño trajo blanca sábana*
> *A las cinco de la tarde.* (Verdecchia 1997, 66–67)

Verdecchia's return to Santiago leads him to Federico García Lorca's iconic poem 'Llanto por Ignacio Sánchez Mejías' (García Lorca 1960, 101–108), the lament for the dead matador.[3] Verdecchia quotes Lorca's lines as he looks for signs of the murdered man. But there is nothing, no means available to identify the dead. No name. So he turns to the only remnant of the tragedy: 'I asked about his shoe—the one I saw on the road—no one knew anything about a shoe although they knew he wore size forty-two just like me' (Verdecchia 1997, 68). But here *is* identification that is more significant, shocking: *It could have been me.* Empathy: putting himself in the shoes of the dead man. And the student who read the excerpt in the class happened to have the same shoe size! *It could have been me.* The recognition reverberated around the class and we were all silenced. Steiner is right:

> In a wholly fundamental, pragmatic sense, the poem, the statue, the sonata [or this play] are not so much read, viewed or heard as they are *lived*. The encounter with the aesthetic is, together with certain modes of religious and of metaphysical experience, the most 'ingressive', transformative summons available to human experiencing. (Steiner 1989, 143)

Each text is a map of signs, and we either live them or not to reach a destination. In the class, we came to Verdecchia's text for signs of who he is, what his story is, and ultimately, what we reached was *who we are*. Perhaps it was not so much that Verdecchia translated the tragedy in Santiago for us, but that our safe lives in an Australian classroom were 'translated': translocated to the streets of Santiago, into the shoes of the dead. And now we knew: *It could have been me.* Our self-containment was lost. *Gapóbatostone* shattered. Rendered mouthless, we listened to other sounds, other lives, other griefs chasing away the fear of the undertow. We ventured out to that 'certain spot, dark/far out where the waves sleep', where we met the other's language, culture and lived

---

[3] Translation of lines from García Lorca's poem: 'At five in the afternoon. It was exactly five in the afternoon. A boy brought the white sheet at five in the afternoon' (J.L. Gili 1960: 101).

life. We listened, we mouthed them, and maybe in that moment of being-with-the-other, we repaired.

The wish to repair. The wish to not shatter. What I hoped to teach the monolingual Australian critics when I wrote the poem 'Word Gifts for an Australian Critic' in the 1990s:

> Mate those lips,
> then heave a wave in the throat
> and lull the tip of the tongue
> at the roof of the mouth.
> *Mahal. mahal. mahal.*
> 'Love, love, love' – let me,
> in my tongue. (Bobis 1998, 9)

I wish to teach Australian critics how to read, teach them the sounds of my language, how to move lips, tongue, throat and lungs to make these sounds. I wish to teach them how we love back home, how we sing, how we remember, and that how as migrant—like their parents or great-grandparents who also travelled from far away to settle in this new home—I too have grieved over the lost home and languages. I wish them to know what this grief and loss mean, how cutting they are:

> But if suddenly you pucker
> the lips – *lung* –
> as if you were about to break
> into tears or song – watch out,
> the splinter cuts too far too much – *lunggggggg* –
> unless withdrawn – *kot* –
> in time. *Lungkot.*
> Such is our word for 'sadness.' (Bobis 1998, 9–10)

In 1991, I left the Philippines writing in three languages: Bikol, Filipino, English. In my early years in Australia, I wrote a full epic poem in Filipino.[4] Now, to read this epic, sometimes I have to consult a dictionary. It is as if it was not I who wrote this twenty-thousand-word

---

[4] *Kantada ng Babaing Mandirigma Daragang Magayon/Cantata of the Warrior Woman Daragang Magayon* (Manila: Babaylan Press, Institute of Women's Studies, St. Scholastica, 1993, 1997) was the epic poem in two versions, Filipino and English, that I wrote for my Doctorate of Creative Arts at University of Wollongong (1991–1994).

text. Because I have to keep writing-thinking-feeling in English, in order to survive in the Australian literary industry, I have been losing a language. I wish the monolingual Australian critics could imagine the grief over this loss, even if now I can laugh with them:

> your kookaburras roost in my windpipe
> when I say, 'laughter!'
> as if feathering a new word.
> *halakhak-k-k-kookaburra*! (Bobis 1998, 9)

Even my laughter has morphed into new sounds, as I live with this push and pull between two homes inside, as I bring Australian literature 'words freshly/prised from my wishbone' (Bobis 1998, 9):

> how they flow
> east-west-east-west-east
> in one bone wishing
> it won't break. (Bobis 1998, 10)

In 2016, my fourth novel, *Locust Girl. A Lovesong*, was shortlisted for then won the Christina Stead Prize for Fiction. Unlike my earlier novels, this is not about the Philippines, nor was it written to 'translate' the spirit of my first tongues (Bikol, Filipino). I am very happy with the win but was incredulous that I even got shortlisted, and did not believe at all that I would win. I have lost confidence in my writing in recent years. At times before this win, I thought to myself, maybe the critics, judges, literary institutions are right: my work is not good enough. I hope this loss of confidence does not happen to other writers of difference to an extent that it would stop them from writing. That it would silence them. This would be a great loss to literary production in multicultural Australia.

We need to acknowledge the advocates against this possible loss: the small, independent presses and literary journals, the alternative awards, networks and forums, and television and radio programmes that provide a space for different stories and modes of storytelling even in languages other than English. And there are the teachers and scholars who continue to bring these cultural products into the classroom and the public discourse. Notable is the AustLit, 'an authoritative database about Australian literature and storytelling' powered by 'a network of researchers from Australian universities and the National Library of Australia, led by The

University of Queensland' that 'support research into, and the teaching of, Australian literary, narrative, and print cultures and the expansion of knowledge about the place of story in Australian culture in the past and present' (online). These vigilant networks save writers of difference from total invisibility. And sometimes, there are welcome surprises in the mainstream. In the 2016 New South Wales Premier's Literary Awards, the shortlists and winners of major prizes included several writers of difference whose first language is not English. Moreover, the Indigenous Writers Prize was created for the first time, officially celebrating the voices and stories of Australia's first peoples in the mainstream.

In the media release for the awards shortlist, Senior Judge Ross Grayson Bell is quoted: 'Across all categories, this year's nominees reflect a growing diversity of voices that enriches and broadens the Australian literary canon. By bringing new and fresh perspectives to light, our collective horizons are expanded and our understanding of ourselves, and each other, deepened' ('Shortlists' 2016). So is the 'white ground' shifting? Michelle Cahill, one of the judges for the poetry prize, maintains that the literary recognition of writers of difference continues to be an ongoing struggle, an opinion that could also apply more generally to the whole Anglophone realm. In addition, the Australian nation, still grappling with its colonial history, is only just beginning to recognize its indigenous literatures. Not surprisingly, the celebrated 'Australian multiculturalism' still becomes the topic of contestation, and the other and multiple languages, and the literatures that they produce, are still in the periphery of Australian literature in English. And when these other literature producers write in English, translating their experiences from their first home, they find that the mainstream gate is still a very high wall to contend with.

But I take hope: 'our understanding of ourselves, and each other, [may be] deepened' especially in this age of intensifying conflictual local–global identity politics—if a meeting of diverse voices in the spirit of 'lexical *cortesia*' or empathy continues to be fostered in the mainstream imaginary.

WORKS CITED

Austlit. "Homepage." 2016. http://www.austlit.edu.au/about.

Akella, Usha. 2014. An Interview With Filipino Poet Marjorie Evasco. *Cha: An Asian Literary Journal*. http://www.asiancha.com/content/view/1789/205/.

Besemeres, Mary, and Anna Wierzbicka. 2007. *Translating Lives. Living With Two Languages and Cultures.* St. Lucia: University of Queensland Press.
Bhatt, Sujata. 1988. *Brunizem.* Manchester: Carcanet.
Bobis, Merlinda. 1998. *Summer Was a Fast Train Without Terminals.* North Melbourne: Spinifex.
———. 2007. GapoBatoStone. *Over There: Poems from Singapore and Australia,* Singapore: Ethos Books, 29–31. Originally published in Merlinda Bobis, *Paguli, Pag-uwi, Homecoming. Poetry in Three Tongues* (Manila: University of Santo Tomas Publishing House, 2004).
———. 2010. The Asian Conspiracy: Deploying Voice/Deploying Story. *Australian Literary Studies* 25 (3): 1–19.
———. 2013a. Confounding Light: Subversion and Transnational Sympathy. *Social Identities Journal for the Study of Race, Nation and Culture* 19 (2): 145–157.
———. 2013b. Perhaps Towards New Ground: Navigating Spain-Philippines-Australia. Paper presented at Postcolonial Europe Workshop, Australian National University Centre for European Studies, 5 December.
Bobis, Merlinda, and Belén Martín-Lucas (eds.). 2016. *The Transnational Story Hub: Between Self and Other.* Barcelona: Centre d'Estudis Australians, Universitat de Barcelona.
Cahill, Michelle. 2013. The Female Text. In *Contemporary Asian Australian Poetry,* ed. Adam Aitken, Kim Cheng Boey, and Michelle Cahill, 24–29. Glebe, NSW: Puncher & Wattman.
———. 2014. The Colour of the Dream: Unmasking Whiteness. *Southerly* 74 (2): 196–211.
———. 2016. Extimate Subjects and Abject Bodies in Australian Poetry. *Cordite Poetry Review* 54 (16). http://cordite.org.au/essays/extimate-subjects-and-abject-bodies-in-australian-poetry/2/.
Cunneen, Chris, and Julie Stubbs. 2000. Male Violence, Male Fantasy and the Commodification of Women Through the Internet. *International Review of Victimology* 7 (1–3): 173–175.
Davis, Mark. 2007. The Clash of Paradigms: Australian Literary Theory after Liberalism. *Journal of the Association of Australian Studies* 7: 7–31.
De Waal, Frans. 2012. *The Age of Empathy.* http://www.emory.edu/LIVING_LINKS/empathy/faq.html.
Elson, Amy L. 1997. The Mail-Order Bride Industry and Immigration: Combating Immigration Fraud. *Indiana Journal of Global Legal Studies* 5 (1): 367–374.
Espinosa, Shirlita. 2015. When Solidarity Melts Into Air: Philippines-Born Women Migrants in Australia. In *Documenting Gendered Violence: Representations, Collaborations, and Movements,* ed. Lisa M. Cuklanz, 83–106. New York: Bloomsbury.

García Lorca, Federico. 1960. *Lorca Selected Poems*, trans. J.L. Gili. Middlesex: Penguin Books.
Giffard-Foret, Paul. 2013. Linguistic Hybridity and a Multilingual Australia in Merlinda Bobis' Poetry. *Creative Industries Journal* 6 (1): 29–41.
Goldman, Alvin. 1993. Ethics and Cognitive Science. *Ethics* 103 (2): 337–360.
Gunew, Sneja. 1994. *Framing Marginality: Multicultural Literary Studies*. Melbourne: Melbourne University Press.
Hawthorne, Susan. 2002. *Wild Politics. Feminism, Globalisation, Bio/Diversity*. North Melbourne: Spinifex.
Lundberg, Liv. 2014. Border Poetics. *Nordlit* 31: 171–174.
Mignolo, Walter. 2013. Geopolitics of Sensing and Knowing: On (De)coloniality, Border Thinking, and Epistemic Disobedience. *Confero* 1 (1): 129–150.
Musgrove, Brian. 1999. Travel and Unsettlement: Freud on Vacation. In *Travel Writing and Empire: Postcolonial Theory in Transit*, ed. Steve Clark, 31–44. London: Zed Books.
Ouyang, Yu. 2007. *Bias: Offensively Chinese/Australian. A Collection of Essays on China and Australia*. Melbourne: Otherland Publishing.
Piper, Nicola, and Mina Roces. 2003. *Wife or Worker. Asian Women and Migration*. Maryland: Rowman & Littlefield Publishers, Inc.
Ramazani, Jahan. 2009. *A Transnational Poetics*. Chicago and London: University of Chicago Press.
Saroca, Cleonicki. 2006. Filipino Women, Migration, and Violence in Australia: Lived Reality and Media Image. *Kasarinlan: Philippine Journal of Third World Studies* 21 (1): 75–110.
Shortlists Announced for 2016 NSW Premier's Literary Awards. 2016. https://www.austcrimewriters.com/content/shortlists-announced-2016-nsw-premier%E2%80%99s-literary-awards.
Steiner, George. 1989. *Real Presences*. Chicago and London: University of Chicago Press.
Stephenson, Peta. 1997. 'Race', 'Whiteness', and the Australian Context. *Mots Pluriels* 1 (2). http://www.arts.uwa.edu.au/MotsPluriels/MP297ps.html.
Transnational Story Hub: Wollongong (Australia) and Vigo (Galicia). 2016. http://webs.campusdoman.es/tsh/.
Tuhiwai Smith, Linda. 1999. *Decolonizing Methodologies: Research and Indigenous Peoples*. London: Zed Books.
Verdecchia, Guillermo. 1997. *Fronteras Americanas*. Vancouver: Talonbooks.

The Production and Productivity of Humanitarian Fiction: Postcolonial Shame and Neocolonial Crises

David Callahan

SHAME AND HUMANITARIAN FICTION

One of the characteristics of contemporary cultural production is the spread of representations that attempt to portray the efforts, consequences and dilemmas of people involved in humanitarian work (see, for example, Alexander 2013, Maskalyk 2010, Dallaire 2004). Common to most of this work is uncertainty over the relation of representation to the events and emotions that it is trying to depict. This uncertainty is derived from intertwined anxieties over everything from the efficacy to the morality of intervening in other people's suffering, as well as over endeavouring to organize either the suffering or the intervention in words or images. In part, this anxiety arises from the faultline between the denial of the representability of such breakdowns in human civility as genocide or trauma and what Lauren Berlant summarizes as 'the centrality of affect to the mediation of the present of any historical moment' (Berlant

---

D. Callahan (✉)
University of Aveiro, Aveiro, Portugal
e-mail: callahan@ua.pt

2011, 79). That is, the imperative to produce (true for all) realism in the telling of other people's suffering comes up against the desire for the contemporary validation of any account through the (inevitably limited) personal experience. Disaffected examples of various forms of admission or study of the way petty personal experiences and discomforts take over individuals' initial agendas while on humanitarian work are accordingly not uncommon (see Smirl 2015, Autesserre 2014, Minion 2004, and Cain et al. 2004).

This mismatch between the desires of the tellers and their awareness of their failure to do justice to either the trauma of others, or their own exertions on behalf of those others, raises the question of why people tackle something they perceive as not just impossible, but impossible in ways that call their own ethical commitment into question. The most extreme case of this disjunction is that of the Holocaust, the debate around the representability of which lies behind all apologies and admissions as to the inadequacy of the autobiographical or fictional text that has been produced dealing with humanitarian issues. Yet at first sight, this is an odd aetiology for texts dealing with representational deficit in the present. For while there are many works testifying to people's response to the Holocaust (particularly from survivors and the descendants of survivors), there can be, by the nature of the event, relatively few produced by or about people who went to work among and alleviate the sufferers while the Holocaust was actually happening (perhaps explaining the great impact of Thomas Keneally's *Schindler's Ark* and Steven Spielberg's *Schindler's List*). Bernard Taithe even refers to '[t]he holocaust, against which humanitarians had been so helpless as to become almost complicit' (Taithe 2007, 133).

Despite cultural critics' tendency to reference such figures as Theodor Adorno, Claude Lanzmann or Elie Wiesel, all hostile to the notion of transmuting the Holocaust into direct representation on account of the danger of seeming to contain it, there are many other less gatekeeping analysts of the issues. In the blunt words of one, acclaimed historian Yehuda Bauer, 'humans are related in makeup', so that 'actions performed by any one individual could in principle be performed by others as well, so the explicability of such actions is a prerequisite for human relations' (Bauer 2001, 17). Bauer's pragmatic position does not claim that either the Holocaust or anything else that human beings do will be explained in such a way that everyone assents to the explanation, but rather that human beings are analyzing animals who ceaselessly generate explications of whatever they are involved in or of whatever constitutes a challenge to their categories of understanding. This activity cannot be stopped, and nor can any ultimate arbiter of representational success ever exist.

Given this situation, a more productive response to the interpretations that human beings produce of extreme cases is not to simply dismiss them as insulting or fundamentally immoral in principle, but rather to try to perceive why people feel they want to attempt them, what needs they feel they are addressing and what terms of analysis would be best applied to them. This is what Gary Weissman does, for example, in his exemplary close reading of texts produced by Holocaust survivor Elie Wiesel, non-Jewish academic Lawrence Langer, and Jewish filmmakers Steven Spielberg and Claude Lanzmann. In this, both historian Bauer and textual analyst Weissman are operating in line with Hans-Georg Gadamer, for whom it was a *sine qua non* that human beings are judging animals. Whatever we come into contact with we have opinions on, we judge, we assess, we conclude. It is not an option not to. 'The self-preservation of what is alive', in Gadamer's summation, 'takes place through its drawing into itself everything that is outside it' (Gadamer 1979, 223). For Joseph Slaughter, more specifically: 'That something can be said to be unnarratable is itself the product of a "given narrative"—a narrative about unnarratability' (Slaughter 2010, 213). Even to will some sort of distance or make some ethically generated decision not to represent something is to make a judgement on our relation to it and to produce a form of representation after all.

This necessarily brisk sampling of issues that have aroused complex and lengthy debates also takes its place in a certain theoretical and emotional exhaustion surrounding this theme. Time after time participants in humanitarian work conclude that the only position they can occupy involves some form of incompletion, a shrinking of their initial hopes to a pragmatic size that tastes like failure. The same questions go round and round: what am I doing here, if I were not here I would not be trying to help, what makes me think I can help, these people must be helped, any help will be flawed or in some significant sense a failure, any attempt to tell it how it is will never manage to say anything like how it really was, how can I not try to tell what I have seen even though I know I will fail, am I explaining how the situation really is or am I merely explaining myself and thus putting myself unjustifiably at the centre? That these conundrums continue to be examined over and over in contemporary discourses of different types suggests that while there are many sophisticated analyses of the issues which admit both the imperfection and the necessity of representation, despite arguments over how best to carry it out, there remains a disabling residue of remorse in the whole enterprise.

The Event of Shame

In their continual admission of failure, however, could writers involved in depicting humanitarian crises and efforts to alleviate them perhaps be read through Timothy Bewes's recent notion of the event of postcolonial shame? In Bewes's stimulating account, shame can be split into two conceptions: one is the conventional thematic of shame, in which shame is consciously dealt with as a topic, while the other, more telling in his view, is the representational gap that opens up when certain events or historical sites are dealt with. In Bewes's *The Event of Postcolonial Shame* an awareness of having been abjected by colonialism and its aftermath leads to the production of a shame that is 'an event of incommensurability: a profound disorientation of the subject by the confrontation with an object it cannot comprehend, an object that renders incoherent every form available to the subject' (Bewes 2011, 3). In this confrontation, shame becomes 'a materialization of the discrepancy between content and form, of the inadequacy of form with respect to content' (Bewes 2011, 39). This sounds very much like the experience of the writers of texts representing humanitarian work, and indeed in one of the two reviews Bewes's book was accorded in the journal *Interventions*, Tom Langley ended by claiming that although putatively focused on postcolonial writing, Bewes had produced 'nothing less than a groundbreaking new theory of the novel' (Langley 2013, 143). Could it be that what Bewes has imagined as a reading practice for works incorporating postcolonial critique is actually much more widely applicable—applicable indeed in this case to a type of writing of which 'gap' could be said to be its middle name?

Moreover, the type of humanitarian text that receives most publicity is that dealing with places and events whose structuring vectors are generally located within the history of colonialism and its legacies. From Rwanda to East Timor, from Guatemala to Australia, many human rights violations arise from the grating together of peoples brought about by colonial arrangements and the perceptions of values and entitlements and hierarchies that have ensued. Perhaps reading texts attesting to humanitarian efforts in terms of Bewes's shame as necessary form might be useful in ways that dealing with them in terms of a failure of form may not. That is, instead of measuring them against some potential but inevitably always deferred, not to say defeated, match between the text and its object, it might help to explain the necessity and even the power of such texts if they are seen as inhabiting a formal space which they cannot help but inhabit and in which the shame of representation is a necessary part of what they are doing in the first place.

In the context of mostly Western representations of Western interventions in humanitarian-crisis flashpoints, Bewes's most appropriate example may be J. M. Coetzee, the displaced first-world observer and beneficiary of a repressive social system, brutal and traumatic for those at the bottom, but which he had the freedom to develop a good living in, and then to walk away from, emigrating easily to the generally hostile-to-migrants Australia. This situation loosely parallels that of the peacekeeper or aid worker or journalist who stands outside the repressive or violent system they are commenting on or even intervening in, benefiting from support structures and guarantees that disallow fellowship with the suffering and which can, at any time, also be walked away from.

In Bewes's formulation, 'the substance of Coetzee's shame is not primarily ethical or political, at least not in the usual sense of these terms … shame is not a preexisting subject matter of the writing: rather, shame is so intimately bound up with writing that it is impossible to separate them' (Bewes 2011, 137). While Coetzee may always be writing politically and ethically, he is unable to sum up or dispatch shame. He can only inhabit it. Hence his refusal to deal with the situation in South Africa as directly or openly accusingly as some arbitrators on acceptable political fiction would have liked. Bewes draws on Adorno for a comparison: 'For Adorno, one of the signs of the impoverishment of thought after Auschwitz is precisely the ability to transcend it' (Bewes 2011, 138), with 'transcend' here implying among other things the ability to sum up and explain Auschwitz, something Coetzee refused to do in his work with respect to apartheid. Given that writers who have participated in or support humanitarian actions inevitably ascribe a great amount of the blame to the very Western nations or politico-economic system where most of them normally live and from which they benefit, a similarity can be seen with the situation of writers like Coetzee who face the problem of attempting to 'write conscientiously while also acknowledging the complicity of one's writing in the conditions one hopes to bring to an end' (Bewes 2011, 139). The formal failure of the text that attempts to write the experience of humanitarian witness or intervention could thus be seen as the event of shame of writers even being in a position to represent such a thing; indeed, of potentially being construed by readers as people who believe that they or their writing perform the transcendence of the history they are representing.

Whatever the typical disclaimers about not claiming to tell the full story, or not claiming to be in possession of the one true explanation, and whatever the admissions of failure on the ground, both personally and authorially, the freezing of a Western observer's perceptions in a commercially circulating product is inflected with a type of transcendence of the situation, if nothing other than the opportunity to step physically away from it and reflect upon it from elsewhere. As Bewes says, again in reference to Coetzee, '"disclaiming" is itself an authoritative gesture' (Bewes 2011, 142). Using such notions, it quickly begins to sound as if Bewes can indeed be usefully applied to a type of writing his study does not contemplate: the fictionalizing of humanitarian intervention.

Inhabiting Humanitarian Shame

At first sight, the step from postcolonial to humanitarian fictions is not as large a step as some might imagine, as long as the key decision is taken to see the postcolonial not as an ontology but as a reading practice. That is, in the words of Bill Ashcroft, one of the most insistent supporters of this understanding of the postcolonial as decoding strategy: 'Post-colonial theory may be defined as that branch of contemporary theory that investigates, and develops propositions about, the cultural and political impact of European conquest upon colonized societies, and the nature of those societies' responses' (Ashcroft 2012, xv). In this light, most historical, autobiographical and fictional texts dealing with humanitarian issues and crises in most places in the world may be considered postcolonial, given that no-one doubts that colonial history is centrally implicated in most such issues and crises. What is different between writers in these cases and writers considered postcolonial writers by virtue of national identification is that the former are usually not representatives of or writing out of the cultures they are writing about. In order to briefly test Bewes's usefulness in the analysis of this type of material, I will examine two quite different works: Zimbabwean Mashingaidze Gomo's poetic reflection and narrative *A Fine Madness* (2010), dealing with the breakdown of civil society and African military attempts to intervene in the Democratic Republic of the Congo; and an Australian-Canadian production for television dealing with UN electoral supervisors in East Timor in 1999, *Answered by Fire* (2006).

A Fine Madness

Mashingaidze Gomo's *A Fine Madness* eschews both the reflective sequencing of prose and doubt about its narrator's point of view. Told by an unnamed Zimbabwean, Gomo's text, termed a 'novel' on the back cover, is part chronicle, part reflection and part diatribe generated by a soldier accompanying an African peacekeeping force to the Democratic Republic of the Congo in 1998. However, rather than serve only as a witness through the ordered sequences of narrative memoir, Gomo constructs a collage in the form of poetry, in which thoughts about colonial history are mixed with impressions of the place he has been sent to and observations as to why any of it is happening in the first place.

The poetic form can be said to already deny the usual shaped realism of the witness of prose. Prose is of course just as 'artificial' as poetry, and prose can be used just as much as poetry to construct a mixture of registers, styles, and interior and exterior events. Nevertheless, given the conventions in this area, in which to impart too personal a stylization runs the risk of being accused of aestheticizing what is being signified, it is standard sober and self-conscious prose, prose aware of its limitations, which has become the default option. By using self-conscious reflection, however, such prose also recognizes that claims to serve as some form of depiction of 'what really happened' cannot be sustained. Gomo's refusal of any illusions of an unmediated processing of events from start to finish may offer one African's sweeping aside of the hand-wringing despair of other fictionalizations of humanitarian or peacekeeping work, licensing a rejection of self-critique on account of the identity status of the author as African. After all, all of these problems were caused by '[a] cruel relationship in which Europe came and went as /she pleased and by armed coercion, kept Africa in tow' (Gomo 2010, 85; see Quick 2015, for a clear analysis of the situation in the Congo). Over and over again, the text returns to this clear causality in which the civil dysfunction of the present has this one explanation, pungently declaimed.

One problem, however, is that identified by Bewes in the work of Ngugi: 'How can decolonization ... not be as thoroughly steeped in shame as colonialism itself?' (Bewes 2011, 116). Bewes goes on to identify how the novel form itself, by implication when used in decolonized Africa, instantiates the failure of the supposed re-creation of societies based on local cultural values after political independence. The novel is a form derived from European conventions, exemplified as 'the expectations of its characters; the categories with which they orient themselves ethically ... the unified narrative perspective; the linear chronological framing' (Bewes 2011, 123). Given this description of the novel, Gomo has indeed circumvented many of the shaming gaps opened up by such apparently European novelistic strategies. For a start, *A Fine Madness* does not have conventional characters but rather a speaking voice and a tableau of individuals it comments on. These individuals are not characters orienting themselves according to ethical categories but rather seen and described by the narrator in terms of their physicality, locations and fate. Despite the presence of one overarching speaking voice, the narrative strategy is not unified, as it ranges from sweeping generalizations about Europeans and Africans, to admiring observations of women, to portrayals of daily scenes, to speculations about causes, to memories of home in Zimbabwe and musings as to the meanings and realities of another land and other peoples. And if it has a linear chronological framing, it is bent in all directions by this montage of thoughts, observations, theorizations and accusations. At one moment the voice is making a political comment, such as:

> And it struck me that the history of African resistance to European conquest and prejudice should not be left to myth and ephemeral folk tale alone but in a literary form inculcated into the mental make-up of African children as a security vaccine. (Gomo 2010, 27)

At another moment, he is detailing actions in the field:

> And a hut was set alight
> And I thought to myself that it was the emotional
> turbulence of a living universe
> And men cowered into their bunkers and watched for, as
> at Mt Sinai, God had descended the heavens and was walking the troubled land (Gomo 2010, 13)

Very often he is commenting on local women:

> And Mami came out of one of those homes with the air
> of provisional occupation
> A dark-lipped impala
> Dainty
> Clean-limbed and just as shy
> The older sister is the one we saw first
> Tall, dark and all-woman
> And she could have passed for a Zimbabwean
> (Gomo 2010, 80)

However, it may be that it is not the novel's European-derived form that leaves the African writer with the unavoidable legacy of the gap of shame. In the first place, the destabilization of the novel's formal conventions is as old as the novel itself. So vigorous have novelists been in denying and exploding the supposed belief of novels in the truth of what they are representing that it is doubtful whether any other than generic novelists, and not all of those either, entertain any sort of belief in particular conventions as other than illusions in the service of story. Unless Bewes means not the novel as a whole, but rather those novels that are 'organized according to certain conventional features', it is difficult to see how the novel in all of its potential shapes can be implicated in 'the impossibility of instantiating the revolution' (Bewes 2011, 122). In any event, even if Gomo's rejection of almost all of the conventional features of the novel would seem a potential first step in avoiding the shame of the inherited form, *A Fine Madness* remains a text in which the unrealisability of African peace and order emerges at every turn. Another of Bewes's examples—the work of Caryl Phillips—may perhaps serve as a context for Gomo's direct and strident register. Phillips has often been criticized for the flat and undemonstrative nature of his prose, even when he is dealing with historical outrages and injustice. Bewes rescues Phillips's prose from such accusations by holding it up as an example of the inability to write shame out of history. Writing 'well' would suggest a mastery of what cannot be mastered, a history that cannot be unwritten and whose consequences cannot be risen above in the control or the beauty of fine prose, the 'transcendence' Adorno referred to in another guise. Perhaps shame over the legacy of the breakdown of relations between peoples occasioned by colonialism, a breakdown which may lead to the need for humanitarian intervention on the part of outside nations, can be countered by the refusal to produce elevated or subtle writing, by Gomo's direct anger and would-be blunt and plain speaking.

When we read over and over of 'the thoroughly evil interests of imperial Europe' (Gomo 2010, 21), there is no attempt at historical analysis from any point of view save one: the destructive effects on African peoples of European colonialism. Indeed, another of Bewes's examples, Ngugi wa Thiong'o, no apologist for European colonialism, supplies a preface to Gomo's prose poem, in which he casts doubt on this strategy: '[b]y subsuming class divisions in Africa under the struggle between two colour monoliths, he denies himself a perspective that might better explain the emergence of postcolonial dictatorships and their actual relationship to the Western corporate bourgeoisie' (Thiong'o 2010, 2). That colonialism contained contradictions, ambiguities, confusion, and even opposition on the part of sectors of European populations is irrelevant to the poem's speaker's analysis: the results are what we see, and here is the speaker having to help another African people because of 'the European sponsors of destabilization in Africa' (Gomo 2010, 113). All responsibility for the present is stripped from its current actors in a flatness of causality which, for some observers, might be enough to condemn Gomo's work as nothing but a naïve tract. Oliver Nyambi characterizes it as participating in an 'emergent corpus of pro-state literary texts [in Zimbabwe] that are covertly and sometimes audaciously aligned to the state's philosophy and practice of counter-discourse' (Nyambi 2016, 219). This differentiates it from the postcolonial texts which have received the most critical attention, texts which tend to be oppositional to authoritarian regimes and attempts to impose government support roles on writers.

Having regard to Bewes, however, it is not what Gomo refers to that is the central enactment of his work. It is Gomo's form which constitutes the gap of shame occasioned by colonial history and the humanitarian flashpoints in Africa which are traceable to it. The colonial history that structured what can be called a country, a border or a people, that determined who now has jurisdiction over and responsibility for peoples, and therefore who can be accused of having lost control or having perverted control, is certainly a history that cannot be left out of the account. And yet, so apparently all-structuring is colonial history that Gomo may be seen as having been left little space in which to develop a more local response to the situation in the Congo. The contending planes of his book figure the impossibility of fitting together the continuity of the local people, landscapes and customs with a hypothetical time receding into the past in more or less explicable fashion: an imagined past in which local peoples had sometimes been friends and sometimes enemies, but in which at least some of the logic of present events appears to arise out of the relations between them. Instead, here in the Congo as in Zimbabwe, history has undergone invasions, sunderings and forced rearrangements by people who are not neighbours. Further, their business in this part of the world was of such an alienating and intrusive violence that the speaker is unable to develop a representation that grants any agency to the people in the Congo at all. Clear-headed and practical analysis is constantly disordered by an inability to get past the framing conditions of colonial history. Rather than a mere rant, however, Gomo's 'fine madness' could be seen as a fine evocation of the gap of a text that is unable to come to form. Instead of seeing Gomo's attempt to tell of his time in a humanitarian force acting in another country as flawed history, flawed social analysis and skewed memoir, it is possible to see its disjointed shape and emotive registers as an appropriate representation not of 'what happened' but of a relation to a situation which 'should not be' resolved into controlled prose.

Film and *Answered by Fire*

When it comes to controlled representational narrative forms, it is some form of 'realism' that is considered the most controlled. Many years have passed, however, since realism's cover was blown. Revealed as a loose set of conventions just as artificial as any other in Wayne C. Booth's influential *The Rhetoric of Fiction* (1961), and vilified in the heyday of post-structuralism as complicit with social structures which attempt to mask the production and consumption processes on which contemporary societies are based (see Belsey 1980), from one angle realism could be considered as a form whose shame consists of its supposed belief that it transcribes reality better than any other fictional form.

Bewes includes in *The Postcolonial Event of Shame* a concluding chapter in which he deals with a text that he feels offers strategies that enable it to remain aware of the shame of colonial history but nevertheless to deal positively with this inheritance. This text is a film, Louis Malle's three- or seven-part *Phantom India* (1969), of which Bewes says that Malle felt he was telling 'a story that is truer than any that could be told in the former colonial language' (Bewes 2011, 180). While fictional film in many ways possesses specificities or resources that written fiction does not, it also has to deal with the same or related representational bargains to those in written fiction. However, where Bewes has dealt with postcolonial shame through novels, his one example of a partial escape from the aporia of shame as representation is a documentary film, a form associated even more than fictional realism with truth-telling. In this choice Bewes echoes James Dawes's difficulties in his *That the World May Know: Bearing Witness to Atrocity*, in which, after a chapter dealing with writers bearing witness through the mediation of fiction, Dawes has difficulty making a case for why people would use fiction in such cases as opposed to more documentary discourses.

Malle claims that '[w]e're not filming to defend an idea, or demonstrate one' (qtd. in Bewes 2011, 181), evidencing a somewhat naïve belief in the realism of direct representation. Bewes reads the gap between the voiceover and the images as a discrepancy that might be resolved 'in the presence of the camera, which elevates the discrepancy into a formal principle' (Bewes 2011, 182). The voiceover commenting on this discrepancy does not instantiate the formal principle, but rather becomes part of it. Instead, it is the camera that establishes in some way 'a center of consciousness that is outside the human subject' (Bewes 2011, 183). To call this consciousness, however, begs the question as to the way in which this centre is conscious, given that human choices drive everything from the on/off switch to where the camera will be pointed and for how long, not to mention what will be edited out later. Bewes refers to an event in which the people being filmed looked back at the camera but were not embarrassed by it, merely curious, later choosing to ignore it and get on with the more important matter of a marriage. At the same time, those filming were also not uncomfortable because the agency enacted by the Indians meant that Bewes's quote from Fanon did not apply: 'the black man has no ontological resistance in the eyes of the white man' (qtd. in Bewes 2011, 184). Malle and his camera eye/I are looked at by Indians but then assigned just one more place in the visuality of what is already a highly stylized event, ensuring that the Indians are unavailable for the easy consumption of the explanatory documentary and that the 'ontological resistance' of the Other prevails over the gaze of the white man. This refusal is problematized for actors in a fiction film, given that they are generally not representing themselves, and may also be construed in terms of the meanings that might have accrued to them as stars through other, very different films, in addition to the generically situated types of characters they are playing.

Apparently 'the world of immediacy and intimacy that beckons to Malle is that of the cinema, the plane of immanence in which the shameful condition of being stapled to a fixed point of consciousness ... is overcome' (Bewes 2011, 186), for 'what is transcended ... is the logic of *his, their, our*' (Bewes 2011, 187; italics in the original). It is difficult to know what to make of this. Throughout the analysis Bewes has used Malle's comments on the film and the process of making the film and subsequently editing it, a series of Malle's personal relations to the film that would seem not to transcend any personal pronoun. While a film is a text produced by a collective of people much more obviously than a book, a collective which these days is generally drawn from a variety of cultural flows, it is still produced within a financing and a distribution system which would also seem not to transcend notions of origins or belonging. But Bewes ascribes to film itself the possession of a 'plane of immanence' which might 'overcome' the 'shameful condition of being stapled to a fixed point of consciousness'. It is not documentary or travelogue cinema or factual cinema, but cinema in general that apparently has this ability, although it seems apparent that the relative absence of narrative of *Phantom India* is central to Bewes's suggestion that the film evades the logic of 'the West', summarized as 'a structure of domination predicated upon the separation of identity and difference, the principle of self-expression, and a regime of organic description that assumes the independence of the object from its perception' (Bewes 2011, 187). Clearly the cinema as a medium cannot be imagined as inherently outside any of the things named here, whether in the widely critiqued excesses of ethnographic documentary or the structured and generic narratives of fiction. Let us see what this might mean through the very different example of a realist historical film.

Answered by Fire is a 180-minute Australian-Canadian co-production, originated by Canadian writer Barbara Samuels, but funded 70% by Australia and 30% by Canada, and first broadcast in two parts in 2006. It was the first such Australian-Canadian co-production, and according to the Australian Broadcasting Commission's head of drama at the time, Scott Meek, 'If you were looking for a model of what two not-particularly-wealthy public broadcasters can do together, it's here: a story that happened in the real world in which Canadians participated and Australians participated, a story that has meaning in both places' (qtd. in Enker 2006). In one review of the series, however, East Timor is described as nothing more than 'a boutique cause' in Canada (Mascarenhas 2006), explaining why the series was never in fact broadcast on a mainstream channel in Canada. To most intents and purposes, it can be read as an Australian text.

The somewhat naïve but committed *Answered by Fire* would seem to indicate some of the problems of cinema, just as much as writing, when dealing with humanitarian issues. *Answered by Fire* is told from the point of view of the realistic camera position, observing the lives of an Australian policeman and a Canadian policewoman, along with those of the East Timorese and Indonesians they come into contact with on both sides of the division that was to erupt into killing and destruction during and after the referendum on the continuance or not of Indonesian control in East Timor in 1999. While fictionalized, it is also attempting to serve as a type of docudrama, a representation of a history which can serve as a type of record of what was not recorded in this form at the time. The production is unashamedly supportive of the East Timorese desire for independence and critical of the cynical and ruthless Indonesian perpetrators and instigators of murders and intimidation. In its attempt to stay close to the versions of the facts from an anti-Indonesian viewpoint there is not much scope for fictional (re)construction, for fictional manipulation one might say, and yet it is precisely this scope that has proved too much of a temptation and which debilitates the narrative. In the well-known presupposition that Western publics cannot be interested in a story that is entirely populated by non-Western 'Others', the narrative constructs a supposedly humanizing story of the romantic relations between a female Canadian officer and an East Timorese man, her last words being 'I've applied for an extension', and the last image one of her with her arm around him as the Australian leaves. The official duty to promote humanitarian principles is always going to come under pressure in the field from individual entanglements and agendas, not to mention the all-too-frequent sexual predation on the vulnerable whom humanitarian workers are supposed to be protecting, so that the film's investment in a serious and hypothetically long-term relationship on a personal level becomes metonymic of a desired Western commitment and ethical responsibility. In filmic terms, it has the virtue of avoiding the cliché of the lead actor, and male, major Australian star David Wenham, being the one to develop a romantic relationship, while it also posits the younger Canadian as the prospective learner from the East Timorese man instead of as the bringer of Western knowledge or superiority. Significantly also, Canada is not perceived as a threat in East Timor while Australia is correctly perceived as having neocolonial interests in everything from East Timor's resources to its choice of official languages.

Jill Bennett's suspicion in *Empathic Vision: Affect, Trauma, and Contemporary Art* that artworks involving human beings depicted within the conventions of realism make some form of empathetic response inevitable appears confirmed here. Typically, in productions that attempt to mediate the suffering of others to Western audiences through the intervening acts of Western characters, the institution of an 'empathy grounded in ... affinity' moves the drama away from being something 'that entails an encounter with something irreducible and different, often inaccessible' (Bennett 2005, 10). Given that Western audiences are presumed not to be able to relate along the axis of affinity with other peoples, the irreducibility of peoples or collectivities who suffered or who may be still suffering is translated from an impasse of the inaccessible to the comforting empathetic conventions of fictions centred on personal relationships. There is a caveat here though. For Westerners to go to East Timor in 1999 was to place themselves within stories so extraordinary and anguishing that by most accounts they are worth telling. To act as peacekeepers in other countries is to ask serious questions and demonstrate priorities, in this case of Canada and Australia's values and commitment to helping weaker polities (on the case of Canada, see Callahan 2014). The circulation of information which becomes part of the currency in which nations value each other or not, and the experiences in which these questions become vivified, seem legitimate material for the forms of transcription of both memoir and fiction. This is where the praxis of exemplification and comparison between representations comes into play, not to provide any guarantor of absolute rules but to subject an archive to constant assessment and filtering. It may be messy, but only a never-ceasing dynamic engagement with the issues can help us to live in a state of theoretical impasse without becoming impassive.

Despite being unable to remand the choices made by the writers and producers of *Answered by Fire* to any absolute category of the illicit and appropriative, and indeed not wishing to critique too harshly the film's moving and anguished portrayal of the pain and determination of the East Timorese people during the period of the UN-sponsored referendum, the difference between Louis Malle's supposedly 'erased'

I, and that of the side-taking *Answered by Fire* is obvious. The marks of Bewes's 'West' have not been avoided: there is a clear 'separation of identity and difference' between the East Timorese and the outsider UN officials, and this is not just registered narratively (*we* have to save *them*), but would also seem to guarantee the '[non-] independence of the other from its perception' (Bewes 2011, 187). But do these 'failures' typical of realism render the mini-series one more event of appropriate formal shame, given that it does not refuse the appearance of mastery of something whose representation cannot be mastered or explained? Unlike my other example, *Answered by Fire* does not consciously destabilize its form, a conventional form that does not appear to question that there is a story to be told about humanitarian intervention and which has made a sincere attempt to do just that.

Dominick LaCapra calls attention to Annette Wieviorka's naming of the present as the 'era of the witness' (qtd. in LaCapra 2009, 60), but adds that 'the problematic distinction, which should not be taken to binary or dichotomous extremes, is between bearing witness, giving testimony, and offering commentary of one sort or another' (LaCapra 2009, 61). This era of the witness tends to give an absolute priority to the eye that has seen and reported, as opposed to the I that has heard about and commented upon. In this case the representation of the history of East Timor, even including the success that was the outwitting of the Indonesian military in the transport of the ballot boxes and the counting of the votes faster than the latter were expecting, posits the Australians in particular as formerly inhabiting a history that was incommensurable with their visions of themselves, given that Australia had officially supported Indonesian oppression throughout the whole brutal period of the latter's occupation. Now they are shown as doing the right thing, and suffering for it to authenticate it even further. For anyone aware of the history of the relation between Australia and East Timor there is no way the story can be told in which this gap between the unspoken past and the redeeming present does not appear at the centre of the film. In addition, given the mission's failure to save enough people, its failure to tell the story to power (the Australian government, the United States, the United Nations itself) in a manner convincing enough for the violence to stop, and the discontinuity between the mission being represented and the subsequent and safe mission of the production of the film (in Australia) seven years later, are only clumsily resolved through the narrative device of leaving the Canadian behind in East Timor to become part of the rebuilding process.

It may be over-ingenious to claim that the naïve realism of *Answered by Fire* enacts the event of shame because a more sophisticated fragmentation of its narrative points of view would imply that it understood contemporary theories of representation and was attempting to transcend or demonstrate inwardness with respect to the problems through this knowledge. That is, the more 'knowing' the form, as in Malle's *Phantom India*, the more it would imply that what has been represented has been known more authentically. Indeed, Bewes's event of shame has to involve some sort of self-conscious struggle with representational conventions until the conventions break open in some way and deny that they are a neutral window onto reality. That critics often believe that realism is an always already broken form (see Chouliaraki 2013, 36–9) might not, however, be enough to qualify it as an event of shame, given the absence of the self-conscious element. Nevertheless, it is also true that nowadays the use of conventionally realist narrative strategies is much less innocently entered into than formerly. From documentary to historical fiction filmmakers are well aware now that, in the words of Sonia Tascon, film in the context of humanitarian issues 'is a powerful tool. Its power does not lie simply in its utilitarian application, but rather, like all media and communications modes, in its ability to be non-neutral' (Tascon 2012, 865). Given this self-conscious context at the level of the actual filmmaking, then, if not at the level of apparent on-screen attitudes to mimesis, it seems appropriate to interrogate realist narrative modes in relation to other narrative modes.

Conclusion

After synthesizing the history of humanitarian writing and action since the nineteenth century, Bernard Taithe comes to a present in which '[t]he limits that humanitarians fear they have reached and which they have described as compassion fatigue refer ... to the superabundance of emotional politics—to the over-emotionalising of world representations' (Taithe 2007, 136). This recalls my citation of Lauren Berlant at the beginning of this article and, at first sight, it might seem as if I am adding an emotionally charged accusation to the impossible situation of people who try to construct narratives that might help others better understand particular humanitarian crisis points in the contemporary world. To associate these creators with the term 'shame' appears to brand them with public failure in a stigmatizing and scornful manner. However, my intention is rather the opposite. Bewes is not accusing writers but rather holding them up as exemplary figures whose forms embody a gap of shame that is entirely appropriate to colonial history and its aftermath. Perhaps also then, as I suggest, the same gap is appropriate for those constructors of humanitarian-issue fiction whose representations strive so anguishedly to deal with something they do not feel equipped to deal with, but which they do not feel they can leave to the affective resources of memoir and its different types of authority either. This article has discussed very different types of fictional representation, and whether their forms articulate such a gap or not. Within the space available it has not been possible to discuss a wider sample of textual variations, but the general link between humanitarian fiction and the idea of apparently failed or at the least compromised narrative strategies as those actually most appropriate for representing crisis and limit situations seems well worth further consideration.

WORKS CITED

Alexander, Jessica. 2013. *Chasing Chaos: My Decade in and out of Humanitarian Aid*. New York: Broadway Books.

Answered by Fire. 2006. TV film, directed by Jessica Hobbs. Australia-Canada: Beyond Simpson le Mesurier, Muse Entertainment Enterprises, Terra Rossa Pictures, Powercorp.

Ashcroft, Bill. 2012. Introduction: A Convivial Critical Democracy: Post-Colonial Studies in the Twenty-First Century. In *Literature for Our Times: Postcolonial Studies in the Twenty-First Century*. ed. Bill Ashcroft et al. xv-xxxv. Amsterdam and New York: Rodopi.

Autesserre, Séverine. 2014. *Peaceland: Conflict Resolution and the Everyday Politics of International Intervention*. Cambridge: Cambridge University Press.

Bauer, Yehuda. 2001. *Rethinking the Holocaust*. New Haven: Yale University Press.

Belsey, Catherine. 1980. *Critical Practice*. London: Methuen.

Bennett, Jill. 2005. *Empathic Vision: Affect, Trauma, and Contemporary Art*. Stanford: Stanford University Press.

Berlant, Lauren. 2011. *Cruel Optimism*. Durham: University of North Carolina Press.

Bewes, Timothy. 2011. *The Event of Postcolonial Shame*. Princeton: Princeton University Press.
Booth, Wayne C. 1961. *The Rhetoric of Fiction*. Chicago: University of Chicago Press.
Cain, Kenneth, Heidi Postlewait, and Andrew Thomson. 2004. *Emergency Sex and Other Desperate Measures: A True Story from Hell on Earth*. New York: Miramax.
Callahan, David. 2014. Canada's Humanitarian Reach and Maggie Helwig's *Where She Was Standing*. *Journal of Commonwealth Literature* 49 (1): 113–126.
Chouliaraki, Lilie. 2013. *The Ironic Spectator: Solidarity in the Age of Post-Humanitarianism*. Cambridge: Polity Press.
Dallaire, Roméo, with Brent Beardsley. 2004. *Shake Hands with the Devil: The Failure of Humanity in Rwanda*. New York: Carroll and Graf.
Dawes, James. 2007. *That the World May Know: Bearing Witness to Atrocity*. Cambridge, MA: Harvard University Press.
Enker, Debi. 2006. Fire in their hearts. *The Age*, 18 May. (31 May 2016). http://www.theage.com.au/news/tv–radio/fire-in-their-hearts/2006/05/17/1147545333698.html.
Gadamer, Hans-Georg. 1979. *Truth and Method*. 2nd English edition. Translated by William Glen-Doepel. ed. John Cumming and Garrett Barden. London: Sheed & Ward.
Gomo, Mashingaidze. 2010. *A Fine Madness*. Banbury: Ayebia Clarke.
LaCapra, Dominick. 2009. *History and its Limits: Human, Animal, Violence*. Ithaca: Cornell University Press.
Langley, Tom. 2013. The Event of Postcolonial Shame. *Interventions* 15 (1): 141–143.
Mascarenhas, Alan. 2006. Fire Power. *Sydney Morning Herald*, 15 May. (31 May 2016). http://www.smh.com.au/news/tv–radio/fire-power/2006/05/13/1146940773476.html.
Maskalyk, James. 2010. *Six Months in Sudan: A Young Doctor in a War-Torn Village*. Edinburgh: Canongate.
Minion, Lynne. 2004. *Hello Missus: A Girl's Own Guide to Foreign Affairs*. Sydney: HarperCollins.
Nyambi, Oliver. 2016. The Lion Has Learnt to Speak? The Novel *A Fine Madness* and Third Chimurenga Counter-Discourse in Contemporary Zimbabwe. *Journal of Black Studies* 47 (3): 217–234.
Quick, Ian D. 2015. *Follies in Fragile States: How International Stabilisation Failed in the Congo*. London: Double Loop.
Slaughter, Joseph. 2010. Vanishing Points: When Narrative is Not Simply There. *Journal of Human Rights* 9: 207–223.

Smirl, Lisa. 2015. *Spaces of Aid: How Cars, Compounds and Hotels Shape Humanitarianism*. London: Zed Books.

Taithe, Bernard. 2007. Horror, Abjection and Compassion: From Dunant to Compassion Fatigue. *New Formations* 62: 123–136.

Tascon, Sonia. 2012. Considering Human Rights Films, Representation, and Ethics: Whose Face? *Human Rights Quarterly* 34 (3): 864–883.

Thiong'o, Ngugi wa. 2010. "Preface". *A Fine Madness*. Banbury: Ayebia Clarke. 1–3.

Weissman, Gary. 2004. *Fantasies of Witnessing: Postwar Efforts to Experience the Holocaust*. Ithaca: Cornell University Press.

Still Devouring Frida Kahlo: Psychobiography versus Postcolonial and Disability Readings

Zoë Brigley Thompson

When the New York Museum of Modern Art (MoMA) hung Frida Kahlo's self-portrait *Fulang Chang and I* (1937) in 2009, a unique decision was made. The curators resolved to hang the painting alongside a mirror that Kahlo had gifted to her friend Mary Sklar (as an accompaniment to *Fulang Chang and I*). In a blog entry for MoMA's website *Inside/Out*, curator Veronica Roberts explains that: 'As a gesture of gratitude for a different painting Sklar purchased from the Levy show, Kahlo gave her this one, telling Sklar that she had added a mirror so that they could always be together' (2009). For Roberts, Kahlo's gift of the painting and mirror is 'a fundamentally generous gesture – an open invitation to enter the work' as '[w]e are invited to see ourselves (literally) and to enter her world' (Roberts 2009).

The hanging of the painting at MoMa alongside the mirror, however, turns the private gesture between Kahlo and Sklar into an exhibit for public consumption. The mirror reflects a significant motif of Kahlo's

Z. Brigley Thompson (✉)
The Ohio State University, Columbus, USA
e-mail: zoe.brigley@gmail.com

© The Author(s) 2017
B. Martín-Lucas and A. Ruthven (eds.), *Narratives of Difference in Globalized Cultures*, New Comparisons in World Literature,
DOI 10.1007/978-3-319-62133-3_4

art—self-examination—but it also signals Western attitudes to Kahlo and economies of intimacy that reflect an Orientalist fascination with the 'uncivilized', tempestuous life of this Mexican artist.

Studying scholarly and critical articles published on Kahlo mainly from the last fifteen years or so, this analysis extends previous commentaries on the dumbing down of Kahlo and her artistic works, drawing especially on Margaret A. Lindauer's *Devouring Frida*. Lindauer emphasizes the need for critics and commentators to discriminate 'between the "painter" and the "paintings"' and to consider those paintings 'as a product of labor implicated in dynamic political negotiations to liberate women from the construct of "women"' (1999, 151–2). Lindauer's exhaustive study interrogates biographies, critical studies of the artist and media representations, pinpointing the tendency to use 'Kahlo's paintings as a means to diagnose the artist' (1999, 108). In her discussion of critical discourse, Lindauer is troubled when 'the paintings [are being] approached as if they provide direct, unmediated access to the artist's psyche', and she questions the use of a psychobiographical approach—uniting the artist's biography with psychoanalytic models—to analyse Kahlo (1999, 108).

The analysis that follows will critique twenty-first-century critical readings and cultural commentaries surrounding Kahlo and her artworks, focusing on how psychobiographical readings fail to recognize Kahlo's complexity. Such criticism universalizes Kahlo as a subject appropriate for consumption by Western viewers/readers. Kahlo's art in such readings is not political but personal: her roles as the wife of a faithless husband, or as an infertile mother, dominate the interrogation of Kahlo's artistic intentions, denying the more subversive potential in her relationship with Mexican culture and her experience of bodily impairment.

Psychobiographical readings of Kahlo place her firmly in a Western model of family, which often dictates her being framed in terms of loss and pity: a mistreated wife and failed matriarch. The preoccupation with these aspects of her biography occludes the possibilities of her generative and playful artistic practice. The universalizing and simplification of Kahlo's story also ignores both her political status as a postcolonial woman artist and the significance of her disabilities as a result of the polio she suffered as a child and the debilitating bus/trolley crash to which she was victim in 1925. By uncovering the erasure of or incomprehension towards Kahlo's Mexican and disabled identities, this analysis suggests that Western colonial fantasies and gendered assumptions are still very much at work in modern psychobiographical readings of Kahlo.

The Problem with Psychobiography

Psychoanalysis still has a major influence on Western art criticism. Elizabeth Wright suggests that the tendency to psychoanalyze the artist has parallels with nineteenth-century pathographies, which provided 'a study of the artist not for the sake of the work or even the man, but for the purpose of classifying a particular pathology' (2006, 34). Tracing such studies to twentieth-century psychoanalytic critics—Marie Bonaparte writing on Edgar Allen Poe, for example—Wright confirms that such arguments are often gratuitous, because 'the assumption of classical criticism, that the text is the patient and the reader the analyst, no longer holds' (2006, 39, 193). In spite of objections to psychoanalyzing the artist, critical readings of Kahlo after 1999 (when Lindauer's *Devouring Frida* was published) continue the obsessive focus on Kahlo's biography and employ dubious psychoanalytic readings. Such approaches transform the complexity of the artist's processes and political ideas into literal biographical readings. They reduce Kahlo's art to mere expressions of certain biographical events, framing the artist as a romantic sufferer or a victim without any account of the impairments and inequalities that Kahlo lived with as a postcolonial, disabled subject.

In facile psychobiographical readings, Kahlo is a problem to be unravelled or uncovered, and her artworks become clues. David Cohen registers the origins of this approach in twentieth-century art critics who were early luminaries in their use of psychoanalysis. Critics like Herbert Read, Adrian Stokes, Peter Fuller and Richard Wollheim adopted the 'notion of a simple key to the meaning of art (and life)' which could be sought out in the works of a particular artist (Cohen 1993, 165). This interrogative approach is inflected, Luke Thurston suggests, by a partial (or even mis-) interpretation of Jacques Lacan's definition of anamorphosis. Anamorphosis refers to the practice of artists hiding secrets in their works that can only be perceived from a particular viewing point—for example, the anamorph skull in Hans Holbein's *The Ambassadors* (1533). Lacan, however, extended the meaning to refer to 'the interpretative pleasure produced by deciphering, solving riddles or making things legible', an emphasis that fits with the traditions of Freudian readings of art (Thurston 2004, 50). Anamorphosis is more complex, however, because even Lacan recognizes that it is 'no longer the purloining of interpretative self-mastery we identified as Freudian traduction' but 'something beyond analysis, impossible to transpose into a readable image' (Thurston 2004, 50). There is a 'real' beyond the text, but it is not 'some safe realm of praxis' (Thurston 2004, 50).

Thurston points out the irony then, that in 'applied psychoanalysis' (a term despised by Lacan), the certainty of being able to uncover secrets about an artist or artwork has gained 'extraordinary popular currency as a tool of cultural criticism' (Thurston 2004, 51). This approach fails to recognize that Lacan's understanding of anamorphosis also acknowledges 'the untranslatable, the unworkable' (Thurston 2004, 51). Certain twenty-first-century readings of Kahlo's life and work simply ignore the impossibility of intimacy with the artist, but reach towards a certainty that is never authentic.

Much of the critical discourse on Kahlo is preoccupied with the problem of unlocking her supposed mystery, of breaking her open as I have written elsewhere (Brigley Thompson 2010). Martha Zamora in *The Letters of Frida Kahlo*, guarantees that the 'selection of letters and other writings' will 'allow us to unlock the mystery of Frida Kahlo', and Barbara Levine in *Finding Frida Kahlo* promises 'an intact album of Frida Kahlo's world, and how she imagined her place in it' (Zamora 1995, 5; Levine 2009, 21). In a particularly intrusive and insensitive volume, Salomon Grimberg's *Frida Kahlo: Song of Herself* (2006) presents an archive of documents including James Bridger Harris's psychological assessment, and other medical records, inclusions that make overt reference to the idea that Kahlo is a pathology to be unravelled.

In other volumes, manufacturing a sense of authenticity is paramount. *Frida Kahlo: Photographs of Myself and Others* presents photographs of Kahlo and her contemporaries (from the Vicente Wolf Collection) in an album format with inspirational quotations alongside, and in the centre is a facsimile where photographs appear on dogged and wrinkled pages, with even the traditional photograph corners reproduced. This is described as Diego Rivera's 'personal album', and it is included despite the fact that it features Rivera's life with his second wife before his relationship with Kahlo (Kahlo 2010, 60). Some pages are completely empty of photographs with only the corners left behind, as if some hand had removed them moments ago. The emphasis is on authenticity, as if the album had just been passed from Kahlo's hand to the viewer's (despite it belonging to Rivera).

While the collection manufactures authenticity, it is actually carefully edited, and the whole effect is to minimize unpalatable aspects of Kahlo's life and practice. For example, one featured photograph of Kahlo shows her in a wheelchair, her expression uncomfortable, while a visitor leans over her, grinning. The caption quotes the well-known phrase from Kahlo's diary: 'Feet, what do I want them for if I have wings to fly' (cf. Kahlo 2010, 33). As well intentioned as this juxtaposition might be, it does not consider the day-to-day experience of impairment that Kahlo lived, but promotes that image of her as a 'strong woman' who simply decided to not be affected by her physical problems. Carol Thomas (1999) notes that so often in hegemonic narratives on disability, the emphasis is on the tragedy of disability and not the lived realities of everyday impairment. It is also telling that the Vicente Wolf anthology presents few of Kahlo's views on politics or Mexican culture, but most of the quotations featured alongside the photographs offer commentary on how Kahlo overcame her physical difficulties, or they feature Rivera's and Kahlo's views on their troubled relationship.

Many critics rely solely on Kahlo's turbulent experiences with her husband, the Mexican artist Rivera. In 1999, Lindauer criticized Herrera for creating a narrative about Kahlo's art that depended on her status as wife of Diego Rivera, and framed Kahlo's artistic career as dependent on her husband (11). This suspect tendency has continued in critical readings since 1999. Grimberg suggests that Rivera was instrumental in creating Kahlo the artist, at best, giving too much primacy to the husband's influence on his wife. Grimberg's claim that in 1931, 'Diego was carefully tending to the seeds of what [Kahlo] would become and paint' is questionable, and Grimberg resurrects a dubious myth of Pygmalion when he writes that Kahlo was 'clay in [Rivera's] hands, allowing herself to be molded to meet his needs' (Grimberg 2006, 13). Grimberg suggests that Rivera's many affairs created Kahlo's supposedly 'characteristic, hard, self-absorbed look' (Grimberg 2006, 13). Tanya Barson even reduces Kahlo's androgyny—related here to her hirsute features—to a trite 'gesture of retaliation for Diego's affairs' (Barson 2005, 56). In Western discourse, Kahlo is too often framed as an inspirational figure, overcoming her relationship woes through art. While it is positive for a Mexican woman to be foregrounded as a role model, the real inequalities and difficulties faced by Kahlo as a postcolonial artist and subject of physical impairment are very often ignored.

Many of Kahlo's paintings are self-portraits that mimic the size and placing of the mirror alongside *Fulang Chang and I*, so her face acts as a kind of mirror too, a reflection that questions notions of intimacy between the artist and the viewer. Her striking visage with knitted eyebrows and haughty expression has become an icon, rudimentarily reproduced on refrigerator magnets and T-shirts. Too often, however, Kahlo's identity is circulated as 'one of those strong women'. The character of the 'strong woman', as John Branch (2015) suggests, fails to challenge gender stereotypes, because it suggests that all that is needed are 'women who are agents rather than mere instruments or objects', as if it is simple enough to make that choice.

Kahlo's face is regularly interpreted in a psychobiographic mode which ignores the subversive aspects of Kahlo's Mexican and disabled identities. Writing about twentieth-century artists' resistance to simplistic psychobiographical readings, Charles Harrison describes the desire 'to liberate painting from its subservience to the self-enchanted spectator, whose incurable tendency it was to look into paintings in search of congenial likenesses and reflections', rather than speculating on artworks 'on their own terms' (Harrison 1993, 26). On its own terms, Kahlo's painting of her own face is far more complex than has been suggested by self-enchanted psychobiographical readings. While critics highlight Kahlo's statement that she wanted 'to try to be myself as far as possible' in her painting, the reality is far more complicated (Kahlo 2006a, 315).

Psychobiography Versus the Postcolonial

Kahlo's specific status as a postcolonial woman artist is not always addressed, especially in readings that pursue psychobiographic approaches, and psychoanalysis itself has been defined as complicit with discourses of colonialism and empire building. Ranjanna Khanna rightly pursues this idea and concludes that psychoanalysis is, at its heart, 'a product of colonialist and nationalist ideology that commits an epistemic violence upon those who cannot be founding subjects' (2004, 58). Khanna's conclusions are built on Gayatri Spivak's engagement with psychoanalysis and colonialism, Spivak having been troubled by the application of psychoanalysis to colonial, postcolonial, migrant and post-emancipation discourses because 'the shifting dynamics of the ethical moment in psychoanalysis, which is lodged in the shuttling of transference and counter-transference, is emptied out in such theoretical activity' (1999, 107). The quest for a psychoanalytic 'cure' or 'intelligibility', so integral to a psychobiographic approach, might be irrelevant in the postcolonial context, and psychoanalysis certainly seems to be blind to the exigencies of the postcolonial situation. Jacques Derrida (1995) emphasizes that the aspiration of psychoanalysis to provide a universal narrative inevitably denies specificity to the rest of the world, that is, countries beyond the West, and consequently, it mimics imperialist ideology.

Considering psychobiographical commentaries in the specific context of postcolonial Mexico, William Nericcio's discussion of the circulation of 'Mexican-ness' in the United States is very illuminating. Nericcio notes that Western representations of Mexican-ness often replicate familiar Orientalist and colonial imaginaries; Mexicans are 'seductive hallucinations with an unambiguously sexual and decidedly violent inheritance' (Nericcio 2007, 65). Mexican subjects become what Nericcio terms 'Hollywood Mexicans'; the focus remains on Kahlo as a 'strong woman' who overcomes the crippling trolley accident of her youth and her difficult marriage to the faithless painter and muralist Diego Rivera.

While Kahlo's art subverts notions of personal and artistic identity, some critics reveal Western assumptions about postcolonial artists in their readings of her Mexican-ness. Schaefer suggests that Kahlo uses a 'literal or figurative' mask, which 'covers the "shadowy" space behind it, which is composed of an uncharted and unconquered terrain that [Kahlo] suggestively exploits and explodes' (Schaefer 1994, 13). Schaefer's phrasing, of course, recalls Freud's comparison of femininity to a 'dark continent', and, as Khanna notes, that comparison evokes a colonial and patriarchal story endorsed by Freud's language: 'a heroic narrative of discovery and a feminization of the land' (Khanna 2004, 52). Schaefer makes explicit such colonial fantasies when she writes of how Kahlo disrupts 'the tantalizing lure of the "exotic" or Other', inviting the viewer to regard Mexico 'through the spaces of the so-called *Cortina de nopal* (cactus curtain)' (Schaefer 1994, 13).

In trying to unlock the secrets of Kahlo's face, many critics have commented on the stoic, emotionless gaze that Kahlo presents in her self-portraits and expressed anxiety about the lack of feeling in a female subject. Barson writes that Kahlo's face repels the viewer, as 'Kahlo's habitually inscrutable expression' means that 'she paradoxically reveals more feeling [in a mask] than she does unmasked' (Barson 2005, 70). Carlos Monsiváis suggests that 'Frida is the face that is effaced' (Monsiváis 2000, 13). Other critics like Jack Rummel fall back on Kahlo's relationship with Rivera, asserting that Kahlo's refusal to present the visible 'face' of pain is a means of revenging herself on her faithless spouse (Rummel 2000, 104). As I have argued elsewhere, Kahlo's face is a refusal that is not simply biographical; rather it is a means of questioning identity and its expression, a kind of epistemological trauma that refuses to give up the subject to the viewer's gaze (cf. Brigley Thompson 2010). Kahlo's refusal to present the visible 'face' of pain is inextricably linked to her Mexican politics and her presentation of the disabled body, because her face is usually marked as a Mexican body.

Psychobiographic readings, however, tend to view Kahlo's identity in universal rather than specific terms, such that her Mexican identity is subordinate to her experience of a supposed Electra complex (Knafo 1991). Kahlo's marriage is a preoccupation of many psychobiographic readings: the narrative is an obvious one involving the roles of the faithless husband and the wounded wife, a safe story for Western consumption, which highlights the problem of normalization in psychoanalytic discourse. Such readings focus on Kahlo's marriage but not so much on her particular status as a Mexican woman living in a postcolonial society. Susan Billingham points out that in 'certain formulations of psychoanalysis and the therapeutic culture that has grown out of them ... psychoanalytic theories tend towards ahistorical explanations of subject formation according to archetypal categories that foreclose materially- or contextually-specific accounts of agency' (Billingham 2010, 108). Billingham draws on Lois McNay (2000) who argues that the introspective dynamic and confessional operations of psychoanalysis normalize identity and close down the possibility of selfhood being subverted. Billingham concludes that the interrogative method of orthodox psychoanalysis 'privilege[s] the (male) individual in relation to the nuclear family, overlooking the fact that gender identity is formed by extended as well as immediate intersubjective relations—that is, by impersonal symbolic and material structures which are historically and culturally specific' (Billingham 2010, 108).

This oversight is particularly significant in relation to the postcolonial subject since, as Stef Craps points out, in postcolonial society there is 'no such natural agreement between the family and the national culture'; Kahlo's experience cannot simply be read in terms of a universalized family or nation (Craps 2013, 30). Psychobiographic readings, however, foreground Kahlo's status in her roles as wife and mother. For example, Kahlo's adoption of Tehuana dress is often attributed solely to her husband's influence. Burrus describes how 'rather like a woman, taking the veil, [Kahlo] dressed now for [Diego Rivera's] benefit, in the shimmering traditional costume of Tehuantepec' (2008, 37). Similarly, Margaret Hooks suggests that it was solely Rivera's painting of indigenous women in his murals which 'inspired Frida to adopt their clothing as her own' (2007, 14). Beyond the influence of the men in Kahlo's life, however, critics have begun to note the influence of Kahlo's Catholic, Mexican mother, and the women in her family who were dressing in indigenous clothes long before Diego Rivera arrived on the scene (cf. Rivera 2006, 407; Barson 2005, 56–7).

As Lindauer wrote in 1999, apolitical readings of Kahlo's work 'insidiously sequester the artist from the broader social contexts' (5), and Nadia Ugalde Gómez demands that critics 'approach her painting from another perspective' in order to 'emphasize her deep interest in the traditions of the Mexican people' (Lindauer 1999, 17). Despite such normalization or universalization, some commentators still apply Western, psychoanalytic ideas to Kahlo's family life, an operation that recalls Nericcio's comments on 'the sometimes slow, sometimes fast process of secretion, absorption, and evaporation' of Mexican identities, a process which he defines as 'XicanOsmosis' (Nericcio 2007, 196).

Kahlo's genuine investment in exploring 'the identity and culture of the common people' (Gómez 2006, 18) is often sidelined by Western critics who pose Kahlo as heavily influenced by European Surrealism, a movement with inextricable ties to psychoanalysis through Andre Breton's preoccupation with Freud (cf. Burton 2005; Polizzotti 1995, 162–3). Kahlo, however, wrote that Surrealism was not a great influence (cf. Kahlo 1995a, 104, 2006a, 365), and her paintings certainly depart from Surrealism's sexualized, dehumanized female bodies. Kahlo's defiant, confrontational self-portraits could not be more different from the faceless bodies of women in Marcel Duchamp's *Étant donnés* (1946–1966) or René Magritte's *Le Viol* (1934).

The difference lies in Kahlo's adoption of a specific gendered and postcolonial context; the body presented is not simply an eternal woman, but a specific woman anchored in a Mexican context by her dress, props and paraphernalia. Burrus is right to point out that Kahlo's art exceeds the aspiration to 'shock the spectator out of conventional middle-class attitudes'; indeed the stern, stoic figures in Kahlo's self-portraits challenge not just the bourgeois but the Western, Orientalist, eroticizing gaze (Burrus 2008, 70). Freixas and González write that 'Kahlo uses an American primitivism to construct an identity that distinguishes her from the European Surrealist matrix', and they link Kahlo instead to specific traditions of portraiture in Mexico which included inspiration drawn from mortuary portraits, *retablo*s, ex-votos, devotional painting and still lives of the *costumbrista* movement which offer simple portrayals of folk life (2000, 221; cf. Gómez 2006, 22).

Critical responses and commentaries on Kahlo's *Four Inhabitants of Mexico* (1938) reveal some of the drawbacks of employing psychobiographic methods that ignore the specificity of postcolonial contexts. The painting features a Mexican *zocalo* with four imposing figures and a small Mexican girl in Tehuana dress sitting cross-legged contemplating the bizarre group. The four inhabitants are a Judas figure wired to explode, a pre-Columbian female idol, a skeleton and a straw man riding a donkey. All of the figures relate to pre-Columbians or folk traditions in Mexico. The female idol recalls pre-Conquest Aztec or Mayan ideas of fertility and fecundity, while the Judas figure refers to Easter festivities in Mexico where effigies of Jesus Christ's betrayer are burned, and the straw man resembles a Mexican revolutionary fighter. The figures also recall traditions of Mexican toy-making: the creation of straw or corn husk dolls and toy skeletons which are also linked to the Mexican Day of the Dead. As a group, the caricatures represent different aspects of Mexico: pre-Conquest indigenous cultures, Catholicism, the Mexican Revolution and cultures of death and morbidity.

Responding to the painting, Gerry Souter remains 'puzzled by it all', and, in a reference specific to Western literature, describes the painting as having an 'Oz-like whimsy' (Souter 2011, 101). Marjorie Agosín suggests that the painting relates to Kahlo's 'continuous feelings of loneliness and rejection … experienced in childhood' and 'when she felt particularly disabled', without any further explanation or reference to Kahlo's lived experience of disability (Agosín 1998, 130). Burrus focuses mainly on the figure of the child in the painting, describing the work as a means to 'interrogate the adult world' (Burrus 2008, 134). Barbara Broadman relates the painting to Kahlo's interest in Eastern philosophies as parallel to Mexican cultures of death; her conclusion suggests the painting as a 'means of better coping with anxiety and isolation born of her own unique circumstances and a collective *Western* consciousness' (Broadman 2011, 102 my italics). All of these readings wholly or partially eclipse the specific cultural situation of Kahlo's painting and consequently produce reductive readings that signal glib answers to the ambiguity of the scene.

All fail to acknowledge the complex reading of the painting by Lindauer, which begins by noting the work's ambivalence towards 'the optimism of the era in which it was produced' when President Lázaro Cárdenas was introducing widespread reforms that benefitted Mexico's indigenous peoples (Lindauer 1999, 135). Lindauer is right to point out Kahlo's scepticism regarding the possible liberation and enfranchizement of indigenous Mexicans, and she notes that the 'frailness and/or innocence of the characters does not bode well for the country's future generations' (1999, 136). Drawing on folklore, Kahlo manages, in the words of de Caro and Jordan, 'to explore her own connection to a nationalist artistic endeavour, its politics, and its aesthetic, and—within that larger aesthetic—to create and re-create her own self through artistic projections of that self' (2004, 184).

The Mexican painter, Juan Rafael Coronel Rivera, offers another illuminating perspective on *Four Inhabitants of Mexico*, however, highlighting the importance of Mexican culture and heritage in interpreting Kahlo's painting. For Rivera, the painting is not necessarily a negative parody or a set of sarcastic caricatures, but he cites the significance of the skeleton in Mexican mythologies. He explains: 'In Europe, death has an especially traumatic content, born as it is of devastating consequence: the plague and decimation of populations it caused', but '[i]n the Americas, … rites of human sacrifice were essentially festive, and dying as a sacrificial victim was the highest honor to which a human being could aspire' (Rivera 2006, 99). The skeleton has a different significance for European and Mexican critics, because, in Mexican traditions, 'skeletons were images that included the concepts of honor, devotion, transcendence and celebration' (Rivera 2006, 99). This alternative reading of the skeleton challenges conventional readings of *Four Inhabitants of Mexico*; the caricatures are not necessarily negative satirical stereotypes, but wry shorthand for Mexican values of honour and heroism.

Four Inhabitants of Mexico is a deeply complex painting that cannot be explained through psychobiographical approaches that merely emphasize certain tragic or poignant events in Kahlo's life. While every artist is a product of their experiences, to make Kahlo's art simply an outpouring of such events is to infantilize her, to make her into a barbarous, uncivilized Other and an object of fascination for the Western gaze. Fred S. Kleiner stresses that to read Kahlo's paintings as merely related to her personal woes is to 'overlook[s] the powerful political dimension of her art' and the fact that such paintings also represent 'the struggles of her homeland' (Kleiner 2010, 736). Terry Smith even suggests that Kahlo was more politically effective than her husband Diego Rivera, because while Rivera's art 'spoke visibly of Mexico to tourists', Kahlo made 'little effort to disseminate her work on any scale despite its popularizing visual language' (Smith 1993, 276). While Diego Rivera's art was, in Smith's view, ready for Western public consumption, Kahlo sought to subvert that gaze both practically and aesthetically.

Psychobiography Versus Disability

If psychobiographic readings of Kahlo's identity tend to overlook her Mexican-ness, they also fail to examine her disability in much complexity. Kahlo suffered polio as a child, and, in adulthood, her right leg was described as noticeably thinner than her left. In 1926, she was the victim of a traffic accident when the bus she was riding in crashed into a streetcar; she was impaled on a steel handrail and suffered fractures of her spine and pelvis. After her marriage to Rivera, she suffered a number of miscarriages related to her injuries. She was to suffer a degenerative spine condition for many years, and eventually in 1953, her right foot and leg had to be amputated. Kahlo lived with chronic pain for much of her life as documented by Courtney et al. (2017). There is a huge body of psychobiographic work that considers the trauma of Kahlo's disability, but there is less emphasis on what Carol Thomas (1999) describes as impairment, for example the lived experience of disability.

The influence of psychoanalytic theories of trauma is significant in the psychobiographic readings of Kahlo, despite the objections of feminist theorists like Ann Cvetkovich. In *An Archive of Feelings: Trauma, Sexuality, and Lesbian Public Cultures,* Cvetkovich draws attention to the universalizing tendencies in Freud's theories of trauma, noting that trauma can become 'a hall of mirrors in which social problems are reduced to diseases in need of ever refined diagnoses' (Cvetkovich 2003, 45). This focus on the universalized individual is a blind spot of psychobiography, which brings Regina van der Wiel to ask about Kahlo: 'In relation to her broken body, then, why would Kahlo want to paint specifically that which worked so much against her?' (van der Wiel 2009, 143). To such a question, one might ask, what would be the alternative? The only answer is unconscionable, because it would be to hide the disabled body: unconscionable too because the answer replicates a dynamic that forces people with disabilities to disguise themselves from the public gaze. As Mark Jeffreys explains: 'We understood that if our disabilities were framed, our disabilities would frame us, and we wanted to exclude them so we wouldn't vanish behind them' (Jeffreys 2002, 37).

Van der Wiel answers the question of Kahlo's preoccupation with the disabled body by drawing on Freud's classic text on trauma, *Beyond the Pleasure Principle*. Underestimating the urgency of art, van der Wiel compares Kahlo's painting to a child's game: the famous 'fort-da' scene, where Freud's grandson enacts the appearance and disappearance of the child's mother. The comparison is apt, according to van der Wiel, because the game and art both create 'control where there is none', and she denies the escapist or retaliatory potential of art, viewing Kahlo's practice as merely 'ceaselessly re-enacting her founding trauma' (van der Wiel 2009, 153).

What is missed in this reading, however, is an awareness of Kahlo as a person with disabilities living a day-to-day existence where her movements and activities might be interrupted by physical ailments. Thinking about Kahlo's artistic practice in this context changes its significance, because Kahlo's impassive faces and wounded figures are presented to a general view that is often hostile to people with disabilities. Rosemarie Garland-Thomson describes the politics of staring at disabled subjects, noting that pictures of disability have often served as vessels of 'unaccountable, unlicensed, insistent looking' in wonder, in pity or sentimentality, and in an exoticizing manner (Garland-Thomson 2002, 58). The juxtaposition in Kahlo's paintings of the impassive face and wounded body is radical, then, because while sometimes there is a display of the grotesque in exposed body parts or blood, the face itself refuses to become a marker of pity or shame, but meets the stare of the viewer in a challenging and defiant mood. Psychobiographical foregrounding of trauma is inadequate then, while the quest for mastery that van der Wiel described does not merely seek to conquer self, but to conquer that stare that 'registers the perception of difference and gives meaning to impairment by marking it as aberrant' (Garland-Thomson 2002, 56).

People with disabilities are often presented in Western culture as either hypervisible, defined only by their physical impairment, or invisible, conveniently hidden. Zarzycka notes that Kahlo's disability is often ignored entirely, or it becomes only 'a tool for organizing Kahlo's biographical data, turning away from the problem of pain itself' (Zarzycka 2007, 16). When Tamara Rojo choreographed her groundbreaking 2016 ballet about Kahlo's life for the London *She Said* showcase, the response went that because 'Kahlo was disabled' it made her 'an even more unlikely candidate for a ballet heroine' (Mackrell 2016). The desire in this statement is to erase the disabled body, to make it static, quiet and passive, despite Rojo's inspired choreography which, to depict Kahlo at the end of her life, uses 'a cube in which the dance character could be enclosed yet free to move' (Mackrell 2016). Zarzycka offers a more positive reading of Kahlo when she asserts that Kahlo's presentation of the disabled body is not, as so many critics have suggested, about 'disintegration' but '*re*-integration' (Zarzycka 2007, 18). Rojo offers an opening to the viewer to participate through Kahlo's art in the complex and sometimes painful feelings and experiences that can accompany disability.

Kahlo's lived experience of pain should be registered in critical readings, but often the everyday problems faced are reduced to an easy narrative which envisions Kahlo fearlessly overcoming her disability as a stereotypical strong woman. For example, writing in response to the Tate Modern exhibition in London, Harry Eyres describes his favourite painting of Kahlo's as *Portrait of Lucha Maria, A Girl from Tehuacan* (1942), because it presents 'a young girl who is not [Kahlo] but another Frida with the hope perhaps of a less painful life' (Eyres 2005, online). The idea that Kahlo is longing to escape her disabled body and enter that of the able-bodied girl is hugely patronizing, and ignores much of the symbolism that surrounds the girl.

In spite of the psychobiographic trend, debates from contemporary disability studies suggest that Kahlo's display of debilitated bodies is very much a performance. Such staging recalls the display of the patient's body for the doctor, who must then read the signs and symptoms and come to a diagnosis. Petra Kuppers (2003) asserts, however, that the performance of the disabled body is a means to 'remobilize' what the disabled body might mean, and this also demands situating the disability in a Mexican context rather than simply reading it through a Western lens.

Looking in detail at *Portrait of Lucha Maria, A Girl from Tehuacan*, the Mexican context of the painting combines with contemplation of disabled experiences to provide a very different reading. The girl is pictured flanked by the sun and moon, and by the respective temples for each of those heavenly bodies from the ancient site Teotihuacan. Aztec accounts specify Teotihuacan as the place where 'the sun and moon first emerged' and this process was enabled by 'the gods Nanahuatzin and Tecuciztecatl [who] modeled self-sacrifice by throwing themselves into a fire' (Headrick 2007, 96). In such an account, to suffer and feel pain is not weakness, but an act of warriors. Mexican history is conjured again by the shawl that the girl wears, which is not simply comforting in its warmth but in its history, since the *serape*, *rebozo* and *poncho* represent the bringing together of traditions in *mestizo* heritage. Holding a model airplane in her hand that is almost obliterated by clinging vines, the girl is a figure that unifies different spheres, just as in Kahlo's *Self-Portrait on the Borderline between Mexico and the United States* (1932) where the roots of plants become wires underground and connect to the United States' factories.

In such stark contrasts, Robin Adèle Greeley finds in *Portrait of Lucha Maria, A Girl from Tehuacan* a political commentary on the clash in Kahlo's era of 'Mexico's archaic pre-capitalism and U.S. Fordism', with disability not simply being an 'unfortunate accident', but standing in for the 'half-functional physicality' of Mexico (2004, 228–9). Greeley's reading is compelling in its discussion of Kahlo's political motives, which are so often sidelined, but it runs the risk of appropriating the disabled body without much foregrounding of Kahlo's actual views on disability. It is clear, however, that in *Portrait of Lucha Maria, A Girl from Tehuacan* Kahlo embraces what Joanna Latimer describes as 'challenges to the idea of an undivided body-self', highlighting the body's 'instability, hybridity and heterogeneity' (2008, 10). Kahlo's art does not simply represent a longing to be someone else without disability. Instead, she inhabits her disabled body, and presents it in a manner that challenges the viewer's pitying gaze. As Sharon Betcher puts it: 'If the world stares at the disabled, Kahlo's stare dares us to move into regions of life we don't want see' (2007, 186).

Pity is so often the response to Kahlo's disability. Eyres describes Kahlo's art as a 'chronicle' of her 'own gradual martyrdom', a word that is unfortunate in its usage (Eyres 2005, online). Imagery of the martyr—the long-suffering maternalism of the virgin of Guadalupe—is precisely what Kahlo is trying to resist in her work, and the word 'martyr' is a barbed one, since one of its meanings suggests a display of feigned or exaggerated suffering to gain sympathy or admiration. Lindauer notices that the physical pain often figured in Kahlo's art is sometimes read by critics as '"imagined" and "self-inflicted" pain' (Lindauer 1999, 55).

Alongside the mistrust of Kahlo's authenticity in experiencing pain, there is also an imaginary that, in Zarzycka's words, 'transform[s] Kahlo's disability into narcissistic longing' (Zarzycka 2007, 16). Claudia Schaefer, for example, rather dubiously describes Kahlo's state of mind as being burdened by a disabled body, and she describes Kahlo's paintings as 'suffering image[s]' that are 'narcissistic in [their] self-examination and exhibition' (Schaefer 1994, 16). Narcissism is an especially pernicious concept to bring to the disabled artist, since, as Tobin Siebers explains, Freudian psychoanalysis has traditionally viewed the disabled person as so narcissistic that s/he 'inhabits the disabled body like an armored fortress ... [so] its own dear self becomes its most cherished prize' (Siebers 2002, 45). Psychoanalysis views the disabled as self-obsessed, trapped in the disabled body, and therefore resistant to therapy, while still demanding 'special privileges' (Siebers 2002, 45). Siebers emphasizes the repercussions of this prejudice in psychoanalytic theory, which frames the disabled as 'bad patients' and 'bad citizens', an assumption that reveals more about ableist anxieties than it does about the disabled (Siebers 2002, 47).

Doubt over Kahlo's expressions of pain and suspicions about her narcissism are obvious in psychobiographic readings that tackle Kahlo's experience of the infertility that resulted from her disabilities. Commenting on the narration of Kahlo's miscarriages in pre-2000 commentaries, Lindauer notices that: 'Suspicion about Kahlo's "desire" is implied in accounts of the miscarriage in which she is held responsible for the baby's death' and 'cast as a traitor who recklessly put her individual whims before her social responsibility' (Lindauer 1999, 25–6). Kahlo is framed as a bad patient and bad citizen.

Some twenty-first-century critics cast Kahlo as a tragic figure, ready to sacrifice everything to have a baby (a role similar to that in Aida Rosende-Pérez discussion in this volume of problematic sacrificial mothers in the novel *Baby Zero* by Emer Martin). This role is tempered by a narrative of maternal sacrifice and tragedy, however, since after a number of miscarriages, it became clear that Kahlo would be unable to bear a child. Christina Burrus writes rather tritely: 'After her accident, Frida had been advised against trying to carry a child to term. She defied doctors on three occasions, and each time her body had the final say' (Burrus 2008, 38). Kahlo's letter to Dr. Leo Eloesser on 26 May 1932 belies this story, however, since Kahlo explains sensibly that she is quite prepared to have an abortion should a pregnancy threaten her health (Kahlo 1995b).

Such an admission is represented as culpable and dubious in some readings of Kahlo, which lambast her for lacking maternal feeling. Stephanie Mencimer suggests that in *Me and My Doll* (1937), Kahlo 'looks bored and is sitting some distance from the child on the bed—a reflection of, perhaps, her real lack of maternal instincts' (Mencimer

2002). To counter dominant narratives about the primacy of motherhood would be productive, but Mencimer's psychobiographic reading stretches beyond what one can reasonably intuit from the painting, making overblown assumptions about the artist's personality. Mencimer describes the doll in the painting as a 'child', a conflation that simplifies the painting to a mere biographical text. Mencimer's ostensible aim is admirable: to unravel the overblown maternal mythology surrounding Kahlo, but her readings also seem tinged with blame. Later Mencimer explains that: 'When [Kahlo] got pregnant again, she considered another [abortion], but ended up having a miscarriage after intentionally disobeying doctors' orders to stay in bed', adding that Kahlo 'took driving lessons instead'. Mencimer's framing of events poses Kahlo as reckless and self-interested, and it pinpoints this narcissism as the source of her miscarriage. Driving lessons hardly seem to explain a miscarriage, but the ability to drive does represent, especially for women, freedom, independence and mobility. Motherhood as a disabled woman and autonomy seem incompatible in Mencimer's discussion of the miscarriage, recalling Nancy Mairs's (2002) lament for the lack of acceptance or sympathy for the sexual and reproductive challenges facing disabled women.

Frida Kahlo Painting Frida Kahlo

This essay began by discussing Kahlo's self-portrait *Fulang Chang and I* (1937) and the juxtaposition created by hanging the painting alongside a mirror that Kahlo had gifted to her friend Mary Sklar. It ends with an analysis of Nickolas Muray's famous photographic portrait of *Frida Painting the Two Fridas* (1939). Muray's photograph depicts Kahlo in front of one of her most famous self-portraits *The Two Fridas* (1939). Situated alongside her immense twins, the photograph draws attention to Kahlo's art and artifice: how she is an active participant in the making of self, not a mere victim of her biography. Nickolas Muray was very aware of Kahlo's elusiveness when he took the photograph, as her gaze demanded 'the viewer's attention in wonderment, eager to decipher it, but unable to do so' (Grimberg 2006, 32).

As one of Kahlo's largest canvases, *The Two Fridas* is often employed in psychobiographic readings of her art, read as representing Kahlo's pain at her husband's infidelity (cf. Herrera 1963; Chadwick 1985; Lowe in Kahlo 1995c, 245; Kettenman 2003; Grimberg 2006; Misemer 2008). Jennifer Josten notes that the origins of this reading emerge from notes made by MacKinley Helm, an American visitor to Kahlo's studio on an emotionally charged occasion when Kahlo had just received divorce papers from Rivera. Helm's interpretation suggests that one of the women in *The Two Fridas* is the Frida that Diego once loved, while the other is the one he loves no longer (cf. Josten 2006, 27–8). There is no denying that Rivera is significant, since in the painting, the indigenous version of Kahlo holds a photograph of him in an ornate, miniature frame. Josten, however, challenges the supposition that two Fridas are 'dying' and rightly challenges the idea that the painting is merely 'an internalised discourse about physical and psychological suffering' (Josten 2006, 28).

Looking at the painting in detail, two versions of Kahlo are presented, one dressed in European style, and the other in traditional Mexican dress recalling Mexico's *mestizo* heritage. Kahlo was the child of a German father and a Mexican mother, and her paintings often seek to represent different ideas of *mexicandad*, uniting her European and indigenous identities, the *criolla* and the *indigenista* (cf. Lindauer 1999, 146–7; Josten 2006, 28). Juan Rafael Coronel Rivera notes that the face in Kahlo's self-portraits has 'two distinct hemispheres'—Western and indigenous—but they are often connected; for example in *Self-Portrait for Marte R. Gómez* (1946), the two halves are 'united by a swallow, the migratory bird par excellence' (Rivera 2006, 29). In *The Two Fridas*, the European and Mexican versions of Kahlo mirror each other's woundedness, comforting one another by holding hands. Connected by a vein that crosses the space between them, they are linked: one heart exposed and vivid, the other closed. The vein continues under the arm of the European Kahlo and is stopped by surgical scissors, though blood has fallen on her white dress mimicking the red flowers at the skirt's hem. A vein, not a bird, unites the two women, and it is important that these specifically Mexican subjects are framed as suffering, wounded bodies. The specific exposure of the hearts recalls the Catholic traditional icon *el Corazón*—'fiery, wounded hearts' that often stand alone, or in the Milagros, there are hearts that are more anatomically correct as in Kahlo's painting, while, finally, the heart recalls the sacrificial imaginaries of literal human sacrifice in pre-Columbian cultures (de Meng 2010, 123). Kahlo brings together different Mexican traditions in the very wounds that are displayed. Greeley (2004) suggests that Kahlo's portrayal of the wound was part of her very appeal to a Mexican nation that felt itself to be fragmented, to be what Octavio Paz would describe as *chingada*, a state akin to the experience of violation: 'pure passivity, defenseless against the exterior world' (Paz 1985, 77).

Taking care, however, not to make Kahlo's experience stand in for national rhetoric, the exposure of the hearts is significant in relation to Kahlo's lived experience of debilitation. Seldom, however, in readings of *The Two Fridas* is the woundedness of the bodies interpreted in any other way than as an expression of romantic pain. The lack of wholeness or integrity in the bodies presented, however, recalls issues in Disability Studies surrounding 'innocent' versus debilitated bodies, and the challenge that such a performance offers the curious gaze. The exposed hearts and veins unsettle what otherwise might be a mere pastiche of the marriage portrait, *Diego and Frida Rivera* (1931). Admittedly, the hearts removed from their proper place within the body do not directly concur with Kahlo's actual sites of pain: her back, pelvis and legs, but they do suggest a dynamic where a subject is laid bare to the scrutiny of another: Paz's *chingada* again. By using an imagined rather than an actual wound, Kahlo manages to elude the pitying, anxiety-ridden gaze that is cast on disabled bodies by hegemonic standards, while the fact that there are two Kahlos suggests a sense of doubleness and denies that the wounded women are solitary aberrations. Kahlo's self-portraits are so subversive because so often all their parts do not settle into a whole portrait of the individual.

In Kahlo's diary, her own account of doubleness questions the primacy of the relationship with her husband, and suggests far more complex ideas on art and identity. Kahlo recalls an imaginary friend from childhood with whom she would play. This dream-like scenario is from the period of recuperation after Kahlo experienced polio. Kahlo imagines following a girl 'to a dairy store called PINZON' and '[t]hrough the "O" in PINZON' she descends to a magical place *'the entrails of the earth*, where "my imaginary friend" always waited for me' (Kahlo 1995c, 246; italics in the original). This imaginary friend, a mirror of Kahlo and inspiration for *The Two Fridas*, represents the lonely pleasures of creativity. Kahlo asserts that she is '*Alone* with my great happiness' in remembering the girl, and she adds that though 'It has been 34 years since I lived that magical friendship … every time I remember it[,] it comes alive and grows more and more inside my world' (1995c, 247 italics in the original).

Kahlo's account of the creative process counters dominant critical readings that *The Two Fridas* was merely a response to her husband's infidelity, but suggests instead the primacy of imaginative consolation. The account of Kahlo's imaginary friend frames the hand-holding women as an inspiring, comforting presence: 'I do remember her joyfulness—she laughed a lot. Soundlessly. She was agile and danced as if she were weightless. I followed her in every movement and while she danced, I told her my secret problems' (Kahlo 1995c, 246). The imagination, personified in her alter ego, brings joy to Kahlo and playfulness or performance of identity is healing. As in Nickolas Muray's photograph, *Frida Kahlo Painting the Two Fridas*, the artist delights in multiple identities: the painted Mexican and European Kahlos, the Kahlo who poses for photographs in Mexican traditional dress and the 'real' Kahlo who remains unknowable behind such popular images.

Kahlo creates a hall of mirrors, where beyond safe narratives appropriate for Western audiences the viewer is forced to doubt the superficiality of their first impressions and must admit the limitations of their viewpoint. Western universalizing models of gender, community, family and identity are not enough to illuminate the paintings on display. No obvious psychoanalytical operations can reveal the anamorphic properties of Kahlo's work. Psychobiography cannot explain the mysteries of such paintings, in which, as Mimi Y. Yang puts it describing *The Two Fridas*, 'the unsettled and unsettling gaze bounces back and forth, destabilizing the self in the dance of infinite mutual transformation' (Yang 2005, 323).

The mirror at MoMA hung alongside Kahlo's *Fulang Chang and I* invites the gaze of viewers in this Western New York gallery, and considered in a different light, it might offer the possibility of a more poetic questioning of the legacy of Kahlo. As Billingham suggests, there is need to reject 'determinist' models of psychoanalysis, and find instead 'generative paradigms' (Billingham 2010, 108). Such paradigms might work by turning the gaze of scrutiny back on the viewer, by activating and embracing the unreadable, recognizing that Kahlo reflects back the objectifying gaze, while asking the viewer to question their assumptions, their complacency, themselves.

Works Cited

Agosín, Marjorie. 1998. *A Woman's Gaze: Latin American Women Artists*. Buffalo, NY: White Pine Press.

Barson, Tanya. 2005. "All Art is at Once Surface and Symbol": A Frida Kahlo glossary. In *Frida Kahlo*, ed. Emma Dexter, and Tanya Barson, 54–79. London: Tate Publishing.

Betcher, Sharon V. 2007. *Spirit and the Politics of Disablement*. Minneapolis, MN: Fortress Press.

Billingham, Susan. 2010. I/legitimacy: Sexual Violence, Mental Health and Resisting Abjection in Camilla Gibb's *Mouthing the Words* and Elizabeth Ruth's *Ten Good Seconds of Silence*. In *Feminism, Literature and Rape Narratives: Violence and Violation*, ed. Sorcha Gunne and Zoë Brigley Thompson, 96–113. London: Routledge.

Branch, John. 2015. The Problem with "Strong Women", *The Huffington Post*. http://www.huffingtonpost.com/john-branch/the-problem-with-strong-women_b_8319642.html.

Brigley Thompson, Zoë. 2010. The Wound and the Mask: Rape, Recovery and Poetry in Pascale Petit's *The Wounded Deer: Fourteen Poems after Frida Kahlo*. In *Feminism, Literature and Rape Narratives: Violence and Violation*, ed. Sorcha Gunne and Zoë Brigley Thompson, 200–216. London: Routledge.

Broadman, Barbara. 2011. *The Mexican Cult of Death in Myth, Art and Literature*. Bloomington, IN: iUniverse.

Burrus, Christina. 2008. *Frida Kahlo: Painting Her Own Reality*. New York: Discoveries/Abrams.

Burton, Jane. 2005. *Achieving Equilibrium*. In *Frida Kahlo 9th June - 9th October 2005*, 27–30. London: Tate Modern.

de Caro, Frank, and Rosan Augusta Jordan. 2004. *Re-situating Folklore: Folk Contexts and Twentieth Century Literature and Art*. Knoxville TN: University of Tennessee Press.

Chadwick, Whitney. 1985. *Women Artists and the Surrealist Movement*. London: Thames and Hudson.

Cohen, David. 1993. Herbert Read and Psychoanalysis. In *Art Criticism Since 1900*, ed. Malcolm Gee, 164–179. Manchester: Manchester University Press.

Courtney, Carol A., Micahel A. O'Hearn, and Carla C. Franck. 2017. Frida Kahlo: Portrait of Chronic Pain. *Physical Therapy*, 97 (1): 91–96.

Craps, Stef. 2013. *Postcolonial Witnessing: Trauma Out of Bounds*. Basingstoke: Palgrave Macmillan.

Cvetkovich, Ann. 2003. *An Archive of Feelings: Trauma, Sexuality, and Lesbian Public Feelings*. Durham NC: Duke University Press.

Derrida, Jacques. 1995. "'Geopsychoanalysis": …and the rest of the world.' trans. Donald Nicholson-Smith, *New Formations*, 26: 141–162.

Eyres, Harry. 2005. A Celebration of Respect for Inborn Grace. *Financial Times. Business Insights: Global*.

Freixas, Erik Camayd, and José Eduardo González. 2000. *Primitivism and Identity in Latin America: Essays on Art, Literature and Culture*. Tucson AZ: University of Arizona Press.

Garland-Thompson, Rosemarie. 2002. The Politics of Staring: Visual Rhetorics of Disability in Popular Photography. In *Disability Studies: Enabling the*

Humanities, eds. Sharon L. Snyder, Brenda Jo Brueggemann, and Rosemarie Garland Thomson, 56–75. New York: Modern Language Association of America.

Gómez, Nadia Ugalde. 2006. Frida Kahlo: The metamorphosis of the image. In *Frida Kahlo: La metamorfosis de la imagen, the metamorphosis of the image*, 14–23. Mexico: Editorial RM.

Grimberg, Salomon. 2006. *I Will Never Forget You...: Frida Kahlo to Nickolas Muray, Unpublished Photographs*. München: Schirmer/Mosel.

———. 2006. *Frida Kahlo: Song of Herself*. London and New York, NY: Merrill.

Greeley, Robin Adèle. 2004. Disability, Gender, and National Identity. In *Gendering Disability*, ed. Bonnie G. Smith, and Beth Hutchison, 216–232. New Brunswick NJ: Rutgers University Press.

Harrison, Charles. 1993. Roger Hilton: The Obligation to Express. In *Roger Hilton (exhibition programme)*, ed. Roger Hilton, 16–32. London: The South Bank Centre.

Headrick, Annabeth. 2007. *The Teotihuacan Trinity: The Sociopolitical Structure of an Ancient Mesoamerican City*. Austin: University of Texas Press.

Herrera, Hayden. (1963) 2003. *Frida: A Biography of Frida Kahlo*. London: Bloomsbury.

Hooks, Margaret. 2007. The Camera and the Image. In *Frida Kahlo: Portraits of an icon*, ed. Margaret Hooks, 10–15. New York: Tumes/Throckmorton Fine Art.

Jeffreys, Mark. 2002. The Visible Cripple (Scars and Other Disfiguring Displays Included)' in Politics. In *Disability Studies*, ed. Sharon L. Snyder, Brenda J. Breuggemann, and Rosemarie Garland-Thomson, 31–39. New York: Modern Language Association of America.

Josten, Jennifer. 2006. Reconsidering Self-Portraits By Women Surrealists: A Case Study of Claude Cahun and Frida Kahlo. *Atlantis* 30 (2): 22–35.

Kahlo, Frida. 1995a. Letter to Carlos Chavez (1939). In *The Letters of Frida Kahlo: Cartas apasionadas*, trans. and ed. Martha Zamora, 104–106. San Francisco: Chronicle Books.

———. 1995b. Letter to Dr. Leo Eloesser (1932). In *The Letters of Frida Kahlo: Cartas apasionadas*, trans. and ed. Martha Zamora, 44–49. San Francisco: Chronicle Books.

———. 1995c. *The Diary of Frida Kahlo: An Intimate Self-Portrait*, trans. Sarah M. Lowe. London: Bloomsbury.

———. 2006a. *Frida by Frida: Selections of Letters and Texts*, trans. Gregory Dechant and ed. Raquel Tibol. Mexico: Editorial RM.

———. 2006b. *Frida Kahlo: La metamorfosis de la imagen, the metamorphosis of the image*. Mexico: Editorial RM.

———. 2010. *Frida Kahlo: Photographs of Myself and Others: From the Vincente Wolf Collections*. New York: Pointed Leaf Press.

Kanfo, Danielle. 1991. Egon Schiele and Frida Kahlo: The Self-Portrait as Mirror. *Journal of the American Academy of Psychoanalysis* 19 (4): 630–647.
Kettenman, Andrea. 2003. *Frida Kahlo 1907–1954: Pain and Passion*. London and Los Angeles: Taschen.
Khanna, Ranjana. 2004. *Dark Continents: Psychoanalysis and Colonialism*. Durham, NC: Duke University Press.
Kleiner, Fred S. 2006/2010. *Gardner's Art Through the Ages: The Western Perspective*, vol. II. Boston: Cengage/Wadsworth.
Kuppers, Petra. 2003. *Disability and Contemporary Performance: Bodies on the Egde*. London: Routledge.
Latimer, Joanna. 2008. Unsettling Bodies: Frida Kahlo's Portraits and In/dividuality. *Sociological Review* 56: 46–62.
Levine, Barbara. 2009. Encountering Frida Kahlo. In *Finding Frida Kahlo: In Mexico, Fifty Five Years After the Death of Frida Kahlo, in San Miguel de Allende*, ed. Barbara Levine, 7–21. New York: Princeton Architectural Press.
Lindauer, Margaret A. 1999. *Devouring Frida: The Art History and Popular Celebrity of Frida Kahlo*. Hanover, NH: Wesleyan University Press.
Mackrell, Judith. 2016. Frida Kahlo's Brush with Ballet: Tamara Rojo Dances the Artist's Life. *The Guardian*. https://www.theguardian.com/stage/2016/mar/22/frida-kahlo-tamara-rojo-she-said-sadlers-wells-english-national-ballet.
Mairs, Nancy. 2002. Sex and Death and the Crippled Body: A Memoir. In *Disability Studies*, ed. Sharon L. Snyder, Brenda J. Breuggemann, and Rosemarie Garland-Thomson, 156–170. New York: Modern Language Association of America.
McNay, Lois. 2000. *Gender and Agency: Reconfiguring the Subject in Feminist and Social Theory*. Cambridge: Polity Press.
Mencimer, Stephanie. 2002. The Trouble with Frida Kahlo. *Washington Monthly*. http://www.washingtonmonthly.com/features/2001/0206.mencimer.html.
de Meng, Michael. 2010. *Dusty Diablos: Folklore, Iconography, Assemblage, Ole*. Cincinnati OH: North Light Books.
Misemer, Sarah M. 2008. *Secular Saints: Performing Frida Kahlo, Carlos Gardel, Eva Perón and Selena*. Woodbridge: Tamesis.
Monsiváis, Carlos. 2000. *Frida Kahlo*, trans. Mark Eaton and Luisa Panichi and ed. Luis-Martin Lozano, 10–17. Boston, MA: Bullfinch Press/Little Browne.
Muray, Nickolas.1939. *Frida Painting the Two Fridas*. Nickolas Muray Photo Archives. http://nickolasmuray.com/frida-kahlo.
Nericcio, William Anthony. 2007. *Tex(t)-Mex: Seductive Hallucinations of the Mexican in America*. Austin TX: University of Texas Press.
Paz, Octavio. 1985. *The Labyrinth of Solitude/The Other Mexico/Return to the Labyrinth of Solitude/Mexico and the United States/The Philanthropic Ogre*, trans. Lysander Kemp, Yara Milos, and Rachel Phillips. New York: Grove Press.

Polizzotti, Mark. 1995. *Revolution of the Mind: The Life of Andre Breton.* New York: Farrar, Straus and Giroux.

Rivera, Juan Rafael Coronel. 2006. Frida Kahlo: The Forest of Images. In *Frida Kahlo: La metamorfosis de la imagen, the metamorphosis of the image,* 24–142. Mexico: Editorial RM.

Roberts, Veronica. 2009. A Close Look: Frida Kahlo's Fulang-Chang and I,' Inside Out: A MoMa/MoMA PS1 Blog. http://www.moma.org/explore/inside_out/2009/12/03/a-close-look-frida-kahlo-s-fulang-chang-and-i.

Rummel, Jack. 2000. *Frida Kahlo: A Spiritual Biography.* New York: Crossroad Books.

Schaefer, Claudia. 1994. *Textured Lives: Women, Art, and Representation in Modern Mexico.* Tucson, AZ: University of Arizona Press.

Siebers, Tobin. 2002. Tender Organs, Narcissism, and Identity Politics. In *Disability Studies,* ed. Sharon L. Snyder, Brenda J. Breuggemann, and Rosemarie Garland-Thomson, 40–55. New York: Modern Language Association of America.

Smith, Terry. 1993. *Making the Modern: Industry, Art, and Design in America.* Chicago: University of Chicago Press.

Souter, Gerry. 2011. *Frida Kahlo.* London: Parkstone International.

Spivak, Gayatri Chakravorty. 1999. *A Critique of Postcolonial Reason: Towards a History of the Vanishing Present.* Cambridge, MA: Harvard University Press.

Thomas, Carol. 1999. *Female Forms: Experiencing and Understanding Disability.* Philadelphia, PA: Open University Press.

Thurston, Luke. 2004. *James Joyce and the Problem of Psychoanalysis.* Cambridge: Cambridge University Press.

van der Wiel, Regina. 2009. Trauma as a Site of Identity: The Case of Jeanette Winterson and Frida Kahlo. *Women: A Cultural Review* 20 (2): 135–156.

Wright, Elizabeth. 1998/2006. *Psychoanalytic Criticism: A Reappraisal.* Cambridge: Polity Press.

Yang, Mimi Y. 2002/2005. Articulate Image, Painted Diary: Frida Kahlo's Autobiographical Interface. In *Interfaces: Women/Autobiography/Image/Performance,* ed. Sidonie Smith and Julia Watson, 314–341. Ann Arbor, MI: University of Michigan Press.

Zamora, Martha. 1995. Preface. In *The Letters of Frida Kahlo: Cartas apasionadas,* trans. and ed. Martha Zamora. San Francisco: Chronicle Books.

Zarzycka, M.J. 2007. *Body as Crisis: Representation of Pain in Visual Arts.* Dissertation, Utrecht University Repository.

The World Republic of Readers

James Procter

This chapter considers how a selection of high-profile cosmopolitan novels that converge on London are made meaningful by an internationally dispersed, non-metropolitan reading public. How does reading at a distance impact upon the production of literary meaning and value? Available scholarship has tended to approach this question by focusing upon how local literatures at the periphery have been incorporated by Western readers at the metropolitan centre (Wattie 1983; Ashcroft 1989; Huggan 2004; Brouillette 2007; Dwivedi and Lau 2014; Marx 2009; Procter 2009, 2010, 2014). In what follows, I work in the opposite direction to ask how readers outside London take up a variety of positions in relation to the literary capital. I use the notion of position taking deliberately here for its resonances with Pierre Bourdieu's (1993), and more recently, Pascale Casanova's (2004) conception of the literary field as a relational site of ceaseless struggle between capital and periphery. Contrary to certain accounts of the deterritorialized audience associated with globalization studies, evidence drawn from the audiences below will be used to suggest that reading remains a more stubbornly situated and carefully 'staked out' activity than available research has tended to acknowledge.

J. Procter (✉)
Newcastle University, Newcastle, UK
e-mail: james.procter@ncl.ac.uk

The findings that follow are drawn from the transcribed conversations of a transnational range of book groups (library based, home based or operating through the overseas offices of the British Council) located across four continents and recorded between 2007 and 2008. These groups were all based at varying distances from London, including regional and northern England (e.g., Nottingham and Liverpool) and Scotland (e.g., Glasgow and Edinburgh), India (New Delhi), Canada (Toronto), Nigeria (Kano) and Trinidad (Port of Spain and Kingston). As a sample of Anglophone readers, these various interpretive communities represent nothing more than a drop in the ocean, a fleeting snapshot that is woefully inadequate to any map of 'world reading'. In this it shares something in common with Pascale Casanova's *The World Republic of Letters*: its purpose is 'not to describe all of the world's literature', or in this case all of the world's *readers*, but more accurately 'to account for the interdependence of local phenomena' (Casanova 2004, 5). Where Casanova's substitution of 'literary lenses' proposes a shift from close to distant reading that nevertheless retains a specialized focus on textual analysis, the shift here is from professional to lay readerships.

Specifically, the chapter considers how book groups comprised of 'lay' (i.e non-academic) readers engage with London as they encounter it, via three novels: Zadie Smith's *White Teeth* (2000), Monica Ali's *Brick Lane* (2003) and Andrea Levy's *Small Island* (2004). These closely associated contemporary works of fiction have been grouped together in a variety of ways, including for their shared preoccupations with diaspora and globalization. Each is epic in scale, unfolds across a range of locations, and gives a certain thematic and aesthetic priority to questions of dislocation, movement and cross-cultural encounter. As one group said of *White Teeth*, 'there is almost like a Labrador type quality to the writing … it's boundless and, and you know um and she covers a lot a lot of ground' (Trinidad). The novels arguably exceed place in other ways too: as consecrated, or proto-canonical narratives that have been labelled 'international bestsellers'. On these grounds *White Teeth*, *Brick Lane* and *Small Island* might be said to transcend the city upon which they also converge. On the other hand they remain inseparable from the national capital, and their broader framing, promotion and reception has remained firmly fixed on this fact. A London street provides the title of Ali's novel; the city's skyline forms the backdrop of the various front covers of *Small Island*, while in *White Teeth* Cricklewood in north-west London became Smith's signature setting, a place she elevated to 'subject' in her later novel, *NW* (2011). In each case, London is more than a pure literary device internal to the narratives. It also surrounds the novels and is outside them, whether as part of the book's packaging, or the work's wider public circulation as a literary commodity.

Sarah Brouillette has argued convincingly in this context that the controversy surrounding Monica Ali's *Brick Lane* was underpinned by associations between literary property, spatial ownership and gentrification in London's East End:

> As high street and symbol for the 'new East End,' translation of Brick Lane into an array of cultural products – books and films, and their accompanying marketing and media commentary – seems to solidify its desirability as an urban frontier for exciting aesthetic experiences. (Brouillette 2009, 427)

Perhaps even more spectacularly, if less controversially, the commodification of *White Teeth* has witnessed the novel re-imagined as a piece of real estate. In 2009, for example, the 'Life and style' supplement of the *Guardian* newspaper presented readers with 'four fictional spaces', each 'featuring the season's best home buys' including Zadie Smith's debut (Powell 2009, n.p.). Above the opening line of the novel 'Early in the morning, late in the century, Cricklewood Broadway' is a photographic reconstruction of the scene in the format of a shopping catalogue, showing a decorated breakfast room complete with walls painted in 'Delhi Bazaar' Dulux paint (£19.49) and a chair draped in an African scarf from The African Fabric Shop (£23.00). Cricklewood's morning sunlight shines through a Taj Mahal tea-light fire screen (£109) placed in the window. More recently, the London *Evening Standard*'s 'Homes and Property' section opened its 'spotlight' pages on Cricklewood with the same line from *White Teeth*. The caption beside the author's prominent photo, which appears on the same pages as details of (rising) house prices, rental rates and travel costs, reads 'Ahead of the game: Zadie Smith used Cricklewood for literary inspiration' (Masey 2013, 3).

In turn, our own book group readers move seamlessly between the London between the covers of these three novels, and the London 'outside'. In what follows I focus less upon their readings of the novels in the specialist sense of that term (for example, as a mode of textual analysis), than on the framings or positionings that London as a whole offers or affords these readers in understanding the texts and their relationship to the city. Where conventional literary criticism is expected to overcome or conceal the distance between reader and text, book groups are at much more liberty to talk around books. This means that 'London' is more than a site of straight textual translation for group members (though it is that too of course), but also emerges as an opportunity for readers to position themselves near or far from the texts, put books in place, or use them to better understand their own places in the world.

When a reader in Nottingham (East Midlands, UK) makes passing reference to 'Willesden' as the home of the character Samad in Smith's *White Teeth*, she is quick to qualify her use of the proper noun by adding: 'I don't know London'. While other members of the same group are by no means unreconstructed 'locals', having either moved from elsewhere in the UK to live in Nottingham, and/or as British-born South Asians, they nevertheless concur. One reader notes how 'enormously different' London is, 'so different to other areas of the country'. Another describes London as 'like a foreign country', while yet another admits to having 'only been to London probably a handful of times in my life'. Faced with the geographical dilemma posed by reading Smith's novel—a book which the group describe at one point as 'very much a London book'—various readers transpose elements of the plot to locations closer to home. For instance, a South Asian reader notes how Samad's experiences in 1970s London 'reminded me of growing up in Huddersfield in the '70s'. Elsewhere, readers in Canada discuss *Brick Lane* by lifting elements of East London to the streets of Toronto, and comparing high-rise multicultural housing estates in the two cities. Similarly, readers in Scotland see elements of Glasgow and the working-class district of the Gorbals in Monica Ali's fictionalized map of down-at-heel Brick Lane.

It is not just the geography, but the language of place that catches the attention of these book group readers. In another Scotland-based group, participants note how in *Small Island*, both Queenie and Hortense 'posh up' (their phrase) in order to get along in the metropolis: 'you've got to think if someone speaks to you in a strong Jamaican accent you might find it difficult to understand'. The group run with this idea, and another reader responds instantly 'yeah yeah yeah true no if someone spoke to me in a strong Glaswegian accent I might have as much trouble' (Yummicks). The same group go on to imitate elevated RP English accents to foreground how 'malicious' Londoners can be to the Jamaican characters. Meanwhile, another reading group in Glasgow draws on a public reading that Andrea Levy gave in the city to foreground how English accents underpin the racialized power structures of the text:

'and y- y'know and she [Levy] did the English accents as well and it just brought it all home y'know …: on one side they knew so much, and on the other side they knew very little, and they cared even less' (SI Mitchell, S1).

In different ways these Scotland-based readers focus on accent as indices of class and regional differentiation to look at metropolitan racism through a local lens (Scotland), where accent both resonates and orientates as a powerful marker of national identity, identification and differentiation. A reader in Kano, Nigeria, makes similar observations by extending London-based prejudices to a more immediate context: 'I mean it's hate. Even in Ghana when you … talk and you have a Nigerian accent it's I mean it's the way you talk and they start looking down at you'.

Such attempts to draw parallels between seemingly incommensurate locations may appear at best naïve or wanting from the point of view and protocols of professional reading. As Derek Attridge reminds us, reading responsibly at a cultural distance involves, among other things, 'a certain kind of passivity, of being hospitably open to the otherness of the work, of being ready to be changed by what it has to offer' (Attridge 2012, 235). By translating the text into familiar terms, discourses and settings, the readers above arguably undo the otherness of the narratives, fail to see them on their own terms. Meanwhile, Rita Felski, partly arguing against such a Levinasian logic, insists on the value of everyday reading for 'recognition' as modes of forging affective connections. Andrew Smith, however, observes the pragmatic dimensions of reading for the familiar over the foreign, something which he also observes in his study of working-class readers of *Things Fall Apart* based in Glasgow:

> readers read from where they are, having no other choice. Whatever solutions can be found to that crisis of understanding posed by writings that are shaped by other kinds of social context, readers are required to find such solutions in and on the grounds of their own social and historical experiences. (Smith 2011, 2)

As one of our own reading groups based in Glasgow put it in relation to *White Teeth:*

R1: it was all the other things she seemed to know ... even about London. ...
R2: that was what one of the things I, I thought as I was reading. I don't know London I am *missing* points you know that I can't place things or ...
R1: ... she'd done her ... research there too: she knew exactly where he was walking along a certain street he would meet this group of people or there's certain shops you would see in a certain street as well which her research is, is *well* it would appear to be extremely good. (Glasgow book group)

Within this context of epistemological uncertainty about London ('I am missing points'; 'well it would appear to be') bricolage, the taking up of materials and knowledge immediately to hand becomes one way groups make imaginative connections between where they are reading about and where they are reading from.

But it is only one way. To look at book group conversation is not to encounter a thesis or argument but a series of positions that are taken up only to be modified or abandoned at a later date. If, as Andrew Smith suggests, reading at a distance generates crises of understanding, it can also become an unexpected opportunity for readers who, in encountering a string of fictional strangers, migrants and newcomers to London, start to see something of themselves and their own outsider relationship to the city. In the groups we worked with, this manifested itself as a series of indirect, unelaborated remarks rather than glib or self-aggrandizing parallels. In Liverpool, for instance, readers recalled their own disappointed first impressions of London as a smaller and shabbier city than they expected, directly after discussing the Jamaican character Hortense and her first deflated impressions of the capital in *Small Island*. Meanwhile readers in Scotland contrasted the outdoor, more open public cultures of Jamaica in *White Teeth* and Bangladesh in *Brick Lane* with their own tourist-based experiences of visiting London: 'everybody just sits there [on the tube] and there's *no* conversation'; '[they] keep their newspapers up there, oh yes'; 'yeah you don't make eye contact' (Fountainbridge BL). Participants rarely if ever reduce this to a mechanical comparison between character and reader, but such narratives clearly furnish a discursive space for elaborating experientially on some of the themes of the novels that are in other respects far away.

At the opposite end of the scale, readers who *do have* a first-hand knowledge of living in London, are those who we found are granted, or command, the most authority and power to speak during book group meetings:

> So, ... as the person ... who has lived in London, you've been there most recently, how true did it ring ... how close does she get it? (Trinidad)

> R1: ... London, England: it was so much like that in the sixties ...
> R2: oh, you were there in the sixties?
> R1: yeah yeah yeah. (Canada)
> R1: and it is something that I recognized from having to leave Oxford in the mid-sixties and come to London to get your hair done.
> R2: it was *so* much like that you know you could imagine people like that there.
> R1: oh yeah. (Jamaica)
> I mean I related to it quite positively. I liked it, but for some of the reasons I touched on before, it's set in a part of London where my grandparents lived and my mother grew up so I knew all those areas, I remember their reaction to immigrants. (Scotland)

The readers above use their London credentials on one level as a means of distinction, a way of establishing their authority as speakers. If London operates as a symbol of diasporic democratization within the novels, the same location is repeatedly harnessed in book group conversations around the books as an opportunity to display cultural capital, to establish reading hierarchies. On a small scale, there is something here of Pierre Bourdieu's understanding of the literary field as one of incessant competition, struggle and position taking.

Yet it is perhaps Pascale Casanova's recasting of Bourdieu's literary field as an international space of 'opposition between a capital, on the one hand, and peripheral dependencies whose relationship to this center is defined by their aesthetic distance from it' (Casanova 2004, 12) that resonates most in terms of the London focus of this chapter. Because the literary capital 'is equipped ... with its own consecrating authorities' (Casanova 2004, 12), Casanova argues it is core to the production of forms of literary 'prestige' which require, for instance:

the existence of a more or less extensive professional 'milieu,' a restricted and cultivated public, and an ... enlightened bourgeoisie; on salons, a specialized press, and sought-after publishers with distinguished lists who compete with one another ... respected judges of talent, whose reputation and authority as discoverers of unknown literary texts may be national or international; and, of course, celebrated writers wholly devoted to the task of writing. (Casanova 2004, 15)

The hierarchical literary relations between centre and periphery which this sort of geographical concentration consolidates is something which our readers repeatedly gesture towards: 'maybe ... [these novels]... just appealed to the London critics more' (Scotland). And:

all these writers are writing about London ... and it's very dominant culturally ... the writers come there, the bulk of the critics are down there, I'm not sure how much one could extrapolate from that experience to the rest of the country's views. (Scotland)

It is perhaps no coincidence that some of the most vocal statements in this regard come from our readers located beyond Britain and at the greatest geographical distance from London. As a reader in New Delhi puts it during a group discussion of Monica Ali, who is described as an author writing from London while 'capitalizing' on her Bangladeshi-ness in *Brick Lane*: 'so why isn't that marketing place looking for an indigenous writer?' The group go on to speculate that Monica Ali's metropolitan migrant identity is 'easier' for publishers because she appears to 'connect both societies' while at the same time appealing to current cosmopolitan British and American tastes or trends for 'so-called minority writers' (New Delhi). Exchanges like these broach the kind of inequities explored by Casanova: the global market place confers on Ali's Bangladeshi-ness a degree of symbolic capital that the 'indigenous' Bangladeshi writer can never hope for because the former occupies the 'non-national' consecrating metropolitan centre while the latter does not.

Casanova's comments also help contextualize the responses of readers in Port of Spain, Trinidad, with reference to the case of another 'indigenous writer' whose work one reader claims has been overlooked by the consecrating centres of the international publishing industry:

> S*:... I have a friend, a writer and author from Pakistan, and she lives and works there: she's from Karachi and she's quite successful within, within Pakistan, she's published two or three novels and two collections of short stories. She cannot get an international publishing deal. That's because she's constantly told that her works will not sell outside of Pakistan because she is writing about contemporary Pakistan, what's happening in Pakistan, she is not writing about oppressed women she's not writing about terrorism she's not writing about the clash of cultures East and West and so her voice is not being heard outside of her own country and the books that are selling are exactly that the ones that are about a culture clash or about you know the Brick Lanes and so on and it's all about what will sell: [...] that's what's selling so that's what being represented as the experiences of, of, of,of these cultures.

Again, the implication here is that the literary market place can only accommodate or entertain writers and works that have moved through the metropolitan centres of consecration. It is not incidental to the logic of this reader's account that the author still 'lives and works' in Pakistan, while stubbornly refusing to deal in her works with themes and issues that might be said to transcend Pakistan and pass muster or 'sell' among a metropolitan readership: 'oppressed women', 'clash of cultures' between East and West, 'terrorism'. Literary production can only claim transcendence and international acclaim when it operates on, with or through the terms of the literary centre.

This paradox, whereby the literary work's capacity to transcend its place in the world is ultimately tied to the gatekeeping capital, is what Casanova associates with the 'symbolic violence' of consecration: a process which reifies the uneven relations between centre and periphery. Precisely because the process of consecration works to confirm the *universal* and *timeless* qualities of literature, the actual provenance of the art work, or its obligatory passage through cities like Paris, London and New York, is disguised. In other words, consecration shores up, even as it masks, literary inequalities between centre and periphery, and the result is what she terms the 'Greenwich meridian of literature':

> Literary space creates a present on the basis of which all positions can be measured, a point in relation to which all other points can be located. Just as the *fictive* line known as the prime meridian, arbitrarily chosen for the determination of longitude, contributes to the *real* organization of the world... The more peripheral a literature with respect to capital, the more

belated it appears. Aesthetic distance is evaluated in this context in temporal terms, since the prime meridian dictates the present of literary creation, which is to say modernity'. (Casanova 2004, 88)

Of course, Casanova's sense of how aesthetic distance is 'measured' in time and space derives from an historical account of literary *production*. However, our data suggest that the tacit sense of a literary prime meridian may also undergird and operate at the level of literary *reception*, and in terms of the location of readers as much as books. For instance, some of our regional readers in the UK, and in other regions of the world, articulate a certain reticence, defeat even, in the face of the multicultural modernity and high-octane hybridity that have been associated with the works they encounter. Metropolitan reviewers confidently trumpeted the novelty and modernity of all three novels: *White Teeth* was described on the inside cover as a 'hip, "sassy", "street-smart" narrative' (*The New York Times*) heralding a 'new voice' (*Financial Times*). The *Guardian* reviewer said of *Brick Lane* 'I cannot think of another novel in which the politics of our times are caught with such easy vividness', while *Small Island* was celebrated in the *Washington Post* for its 'radical' use of voice that broke with traditional notions of national fixity.

Meanwhile, our readers sometimes describe the feeling of being left behind, belated in Casanova's sense, by the exceptional forms of ethnic diversity they encounter through the books and their framings:

> no city in the world can claim to be as multi-cultural as London: they have Muslims, they have Pakistanis, they have Nigerians, they have East Africans, and they have *everybody*, you understand, everybody living in this city ... and you'll not understand their mindset, except in books like this. (Nigeria)

> I read this [*White Teeth*] on the train going to London ... [I] had ... that real kind of hick in the multicultural city feeling (laughs) I was kind of going you know I've, I've very little idea of what it's like to grow up in these sorts of communities. (Scotland)

> I mean one of the things that I think [these books] made me think about was multiculturalism: ... if you live in Edinburgh, multiculturalism is something it's much [more a] London phenomenon not because you don't have a concept of cultures other than our own country ... but if you ... talk about, for example, Preston Street [in Edinburgh], lots and lots of kids from other cultures go into that school but it's not multicultural in

the way that London is ... if you're proper Scottish you really welcome them ... and all the rest of it, but it's not this idea of a multi-culture really: people are kind of expected to assimilate more here. (Scotland)

A notable exception to such expressions of spatial apartness and/or time lag emerges in the book group discussions based in Port of Spain, Trinidad. While some readers found *Small Island* 'gripping', the prevailing view was that Levy 'didn't have anything new to say': 'I kept thinking well now tell me something I don't know'; 'the publishing market is lapping it up, while the rest of us down here we're, I mean it's stuff we've heard'. One reader describes the West Indian character of Gilbert as a 'standard-issue ... West Indian to London in 1948'. Discussing *Brick Lane* during another session, a reader qualifies her sense that Monica Ali 'does write well in some cases', by adding: 'I did find that it slipped into cliché ... a lot, there was nothing—maybe as a third-world person ... a lot of it was so clichéd to me'. Similarly, of the Jamaican characterization in *White Teeth* another reader notes that: 'for those of us that actually do come from outside of Britain ... we can recognize cracks in in the characters ... for example we can see when she slips into cliché'. In these passages the readers appear to reverse the temporal logic associated with Casanova's Greenwich meridian, registering the ways in which the metropolitan fiction they encounter is ironically peripheral, belated, not up to speed.

Whether challenging its temporality (as timeless or modern), or electing to dwell on its particularity and exceptionality (as opposed to its universality), the capital is arguably provincialized through the various positions taken up by the readers above. Perhaps this has to do with the waning of universalism and timelessness associated with the consecrating capitals of Casanova's historical model; a shrinkage, fracture and dispersal of the traditional centres of power. Perhaps it speaks to what James English has termed 'a more radical *deterritorialisation* of prestige, an uncoupling of cultural prizes, and even of symbolic fields as such, from particular cities, nations, even clearly defined regions' (English 2005, 282). Or perhaps, as I see it, the book group responses represent a particular mode of *response* to these experiences of decentring and uncoupling, one that often takes the form of *reterritorialization*. Whether they align themselves with or against it, the persistent orientation of the readings above in terms of London, their apparently spontaneous use of the city as a measure or yardstick for making sense of the work, not just as an internal but an external reference point, is suggestive of the ongoing importance of place and position to making sense of contemporary literature, including diaspora fiction.

WORKS CITED

Ali, Monica. 2003. *Brick Lane*. London: Doubleday.
Ashcroft, Bill. 1989. Constitutive Graphonomy: A Post-colonial Theory of Literary Writing. *Kunapipi* 11 (1): 53–73.
Attridge, Derek. 2012. Responsible Reading and Cultural Distance. In *Postcolonial Audiences: Readers, Viewers and Reception*, ed. Bethan Benwell, James Procter, and Gemma Robinson, 234–244. London: Routledge.
Benwell, Procter, and Robinson. 2012. *Postcolonial Audiences: Readers, Viewers and Reception*. New York: Routledge.
Bourdieu, Pierre. 1993. *The Field of Cultural Production*. London: Polity Press.
Brouillette, Sarah. 2007. *Postcolonial Writers in the Global Literary Marketplace*. Basingstoke: Palgrave Macmillan.
Brouillette, Sarah. 2009. Literature and Gentrification on Brick Lane. *Criticism* 51 (3): 425–449.
Casanova, Pascale. 2004. *The World Republic of Letters*, trans. M.B. Devoise. Cambridge, MA: Harvard University Press.
Dwivedi, Om, and Larissa Lau. 2014. *Indian Writing in English and the Global Literary Market*. Houndmills: Palgrave.
English, James F. 2005. *The Economy of Prestige: Prizes, Awards and the Circulation of Cultural Value*. Cambridge, MA: Harvard University Press.
Huggan, Graham. 2004. *The Postcolonial Exotic: Marketing the Margins*. London: Routledge.
Levy, Andrea. 2004. *Small Island*. London: Headline.
Marx, John. 2009. The Marketing of Postcolonial Authors. *Contemporary Literature* 50 (4): 811–816.
Masey, Anthea. 2013. Famous Faces Help Tell Story of a Suburb With Real Sense of Community. http://www.cricklewood.net/media/uploads/es-sept-2013.pdf.
Powell, Susannah. 2009. A Room of One's Own. http://www.theguardian.com/lifeandstyle/2009/oct/10/rooms-novelists-inspired.
Procter, James. 2009. Reading, Taste and Postcolonial Studies: Professional and Lay Readers of *Things Fall Apart*. *Interventions: International Journal of Postcolonial Studies* 11 (2): 180–198.
Procter, James. 2010. Diasporic Readers and the Location of Reception. In *Diasporas: Concepts, Intersections, Identities*, ed. Kim Knott and Sean McLoughlin, 256–262. London: Zed Books.

Procter, James. 2014. *Reading Across Worlds: Transnational Book Groups and the Reception of Difference.* Houndmills: Palgrave.

Smith, Zadie. 2000. *White Teeth.* London: Penguin Books.

Smith, Andrew. 2011. First and Second Glances: Working Class Scottish Readers and Things Fall Apart. In: *Chinua Achebe's 'Things Fall Apart': 1958–2008. Series: Cross/Cultures – Readings in the Post/Colonial Literatures in English (137)*, ed. Whittaker, D. 149–160. Amsterdam: Rodopi.

Wattie, Nelson. 1983. Geographical, Historical and Cultural Distance in the Reception of Literary Works. In *The History and Historiography of Commonwealth Literature*, ed. Dieter Riemenschneider, 36–43. Tubingen: Gunter Narr Verlag.

PART II

Counternarratives of the Metropolis

Success and the City: Working in the World's Capital in Monica Ali's *Brick Lane*

Darragh Patrick Hall

There is a moment in Stephen Frears' 2002 film *Dirty Pretty Things* in which the viewer is taken through the labyrinth of a crowded market in London's borough of Hackney. The character of this lively urban space is adumbrated by the ethnic diversity of the bodies that populate it, moving through stalls filled with a smorgasbord of different kinds of meats, fruits and spices, against the sounds of different accents, languages and street beats. Within this innocuous space the viewer is afforded a glimpse into an altogether different kind of bustle than that which might be found within London's commercial centres. In a later scene, the film's protagonists—having foiled an illegal operation in which a hotel manager, Juan (Sergi López), had been issuing forged British passports to immigrants in exchange for their kidneys—meet Juan's contact in an underground car park and sell him Juan's kidney in place of the kidney he had arranged to remove from Senay (Audrey Tautou), a Turkish maid working at the hotel. Juan's contact, accepting the kidney in exchange for a brown envelope, asks: 'How come I've never seen you people before?' Okwe (Chiwetel Ejiofor), who has qualified as a doctor in Lagos

---

D.P. Hall (✉)
Bristol, UK
e-mail: darraghpdhall@gmail.com

and worked for the Nigerian government, but now works night shifts in the hotel and drives cabs by day, chewing khat to keep himself awake, responds with his material allegiance to the city's designation of the third-world migrant: 'We are the people you don't see. We drive your cabs. We clean your hotel rooms. We suck your cocks.' (Frears, *Dirty Pretty Things*). Frears's film, which follows the lives of illegal immigrants who arrive to work in London from capitalism's distant hinterlands, selling their bodies—in the sex trade, or literally their organs on the black market—in exchange for passports and the ability to remain there, registers the less than glamorous experience of city living that awaits many migrants who come to work in the World's Capital. Okwe's response both distils and suspends the tensions that constitute the migrant's relationship to the global city. In an era of globalization and neoliberal capitalism, the migrant body itself, in addition to the goods and capital garnered through dispossession in capitalism's erstwhile peripheries, now forms part of the city's geography. Simultaneously, the migrants' residence in the impoverished boroughs of the city and their working invisibly in menial factory jobs or low-paid work in the tertiary sector is both requisite and consequent of the urbanization processes of the city today. The third-world migrant, although in a sense invisible, is simultaneously everywhere: working in sweatshops, as street cleaners, sex workers, and in London's lucrative service industry as maids or hotel workers. The presence of migrants in the city both allows and mobilizes the rapid development of London's urban landscapes; but for those who supply the breath and blood to the capitalist metropolis, the shaping power over the process of urbanization in the city in which they reside is immensely limited, and the migrant is offered no position by which to challenge the neoliberal logic of the city that ensures their place outside and beyond the concentrations of wealth generated by their presence.

If the relationship between the third-world migrant and the global city is quickly becoming a topic of contestation both within the academy and social movements across the world's cities today, it also provides a basis for Monica Ali's 2003 novel, *Brick Lane*. Ali's novel, however, which narrates the life of a young Bangladeshi woman who moves to London in an arranged marriage, enacts a particular logic which tacitly coalesces participation in the neoliberal functions of the city—along the lines of particular kinds of work—with the migrant's potential to succeed in and belong to the city.[1]

On one hand, the novel can be read as a story of personal empowerment, as an allegory of a third-world migrant woman's self-liberation from the strictures of her Muslim community and marriage, where the liberal and commercial space of London offers her the tools to enable her own emancipation. On the other hand, the situation of the novel's political thrusts within the context of wider questions about the third-world migrant's relationship to the global city remains pernicious. In Ali's narrative, the neoliberal capitalist logic that the city represents is accepted because it provides the individual with the tools to actualize a relative freedom. Yet the novel, rather than positioning questions about the city's processes of urbanization as beyond its scope, posits the capitalist and commercial nature of the city as one which offers the migrant liberation from alternative and ostensibly isolated strictures. The neoliberal capitalist logic of the city, then, not only remains unchallenged, but is in fact legitimized by the parallel migrant narratives in *Brick Lane*. It is within this context that I argue that a commensurate analysis of world capital needs to be worked into an analysis of a novel that accommodates an interrogation of this kind of ideology within broader contexts of global capitalism, international migration and the capitalist metropolis.

As a city which carries a long history as the centre of British imperial wealth, London now figures as a nodal point of a networked spatio-temporal world of financial flows of surplus capital where both economic and political power has become centralized (Harvey 2003, 134). More specifically, it has accumulated this wealth through dispossession across the long modernity of the capitalist world system; and the urban geography of the city itself is, inevitably, the materialization of capitalist logic. What has now become a 'global' city, then, cannot be abstracted from its previous history as the accumulating centre of the British Empire.[2] Rashmi Varma,

---

[1] Garrett Ziegler, focusing almost exclusively on Nazneen, makes a similar point in his essay 'East of the City'. Where I depart from Ziegler's analysis of *Brick Lane* is in his reading of the nature of the equality the third-world migrant has access to, as well as the political implications of the novel's ideology, which Ziegler explicates through an analysis of Nazneen, but does not interrogate.

[2] I mean here merely to underscore the capitalist logic of the city. As I have indicated in my introduction, London should not be considered in an abstract way as a homogeneous and undifferentiated metropolitan 'centre' with a unified consciousness and functions. For a more elaborate discussion of these issues see Chrisman (2003) and McLeod (2004).

in her study of postcolonial cities, has argued that 'London's hyper-capitalist present is a reiteration as much as it is a successor to the City's accumulating imperial past' (Varma 2012, 163), while Saskia Sassen, similarly maintaining the intimate ties between the City's colonial history and its capitalist present, writes that:

> [The Global City] is the new territory where the contemporary version of the colonial wars of independence are being fought. But today's battles lack clear boundaries and fields: there are many sites, many fronts, many forms, many politics. These battles are fought in neighbourhoods, schools, court rooms, public squares. (Sassen 1996, 197)

Sassen's work on global cities,[3] in addition to demonstrating how cities function in highly strategic ways for economic globalization, demonstrates the multifaceted ways through which contemporary immigrant workforces now 'fulfil crucial functions for the centre' (Sassen 1996, 197). Libe García Zarranz's essay in this volume, on *Borderless* and its depiction of immigrants in Canadian society, raises pressing questions surrounding the political structures of power that at once subsume immigrant workers into capitalist structures and render visible only the effects of their labour. These questions affirm that patterns of international migration, while radically reconfigured over the past three decades, need to be considered within a longer history of capitalist accumulation where the city has been the receptacle of dispossessed wealth on a world scale. Jane Wills has more recently remarked that 'London now depends on an army of foreign-born workers to clean its offices, care for its sick, make beds, and serve at its restaurants and bars' and that 'in relation to its rise to global-city status, London has become almost wholly reliant on foreign-born workers to do the city's "bottom-end" jobs … this labour market is a product of [neo-liberal economic management] that [has come to] dominat[e] the global political economy' (Wills et al. 2010, 1). In the 2011 census, it was reported that 36.7% of London's population was born outside of the United Kingdom (Office for National Statistics). This influx of migrants must be regarded in terms of the fate not only of the migrants in the city, but also of the peripheries from which the majority of migrants emigrate. What is variously called neoliberalism

---

[3] See also Sassen, *The Global City* (1991).

or neoliberal globalization, which began to assume global dimensions subsequent to its recuperation in the UK under Margaret Thatcher and in the United States under Ronald Reagan, became the central guiding doctrine of economic thought and management (Harvey 2003, 134). The experimental economics instituted under Thatcher and Reagan have irreversibly altered the global economy and the ways in which corporations within capitalism's cores now source and manage their labour resources. Sub-contracting, amongst numerous other factors, has allowed multinational corporations to exploit cheaper labour sources in developing countries in the Global South. While selectively developing particular sectors in these countries, these processes have widened the gap between rich and poor, cyclically catalyzing migration to the Global North (International Organisation for Migration 2008). In these contexts, an analysis of narratives of migrancy must work in a commensurate analysis of the ways in which patterns of global migration are shaped, and how the opportunities available to the third-world subject are configured both at home and abroad. Ania Loomba has argued that this reconfigured orientation towards a global perspective has 'provided fresh grounds for examining the relevance of postcolonial perspectives to the world we now inhabit' (Loomba 2005, 213). Certainly, global neoliberalism has had its most egregious effects in the Global South, while migrants are sought to occupy bottom-end jobs in the global cities of the North in order to decrease labour costs and discipline the city's existing labour forces (Harvey 2012, 6). The relationship between urbanization and immigration is succinctly articulated by Douglas Massey and his collaborators in their 1998 study of transnational migration: 'International migration does not stem from a lack of economic development, but from development itself' (Massey 1998, 277). The presence of migrants in a city such as London is thus intimately and inextricably linked with neoliberalism on a global scale, as are the social and political forces which configure discourses of migrancy. In his work on global cities, David Harvey has argued that '[u]rbanization has always been … a class phenomenon of some sort, since surpluses have been extracted from somewhere and from somebody [usually disenfranchised minorities and the working-class majority] while the control over the disbursement of the surplus typically lies in few hands' (Harvey 2012, 5). Despite London's claims to the rank of the world's quintessential multicultural city, the dual processes of deregulation and international migration have been antecedents to a rapid and unprecedented shift in the labour market which sees the majority of non-European migrants designated to impoverished boroughs of the city and working in low-paid unskilled jobs, while racial tensions both between migrant groups and between migrants and mainstream society continue to increase.[4] It is within this context that I situate the political logic of *Brick Lane*. While ostensibly a novel of empowerment in which the city is bestowed with liberating virtues through the economic opportunities—that is, work—that are available to the migrant in the global city, the empowerment that the migrants in *Brick Lane* can achieve is afforded to them only through their fulfilling their role in the neoliberal functions of the capitalist metropolis and participating in capitalist operations.

If, as I suggest, *Brick Lane* legitimizes the neoliberal capitalism that London represents, then the novel's presentations of the city are consonant with its functions, and the city's urban space is repeatedly rendered as a hyper-capitalist one. Not only does this become apparent in the social relationships that are forged and remade within the city, but in the city's urban geography itself:

> [Nazneen] looked up at a building as she passed. It was constructed almost entirely of glass with a few thin rivets of steel holding it together … The building was without end. Above, somewhere, it crushed the clouds … Men in dark suits trotted briskly up and down the steps … Every person that brushed past her on the pavement, every back she saw, was on a private, urgent mission to execute a precise and demanding plan: to get a promotion today, to be exactly on time for an appointment, to buy a newspaper with the right coins so that the exchange was swift and seamless. (Ali 2003, 44)

The building itself is a symbol of wealth, its arrestive newness matched only by its incommensurable size. The glass renders the building transparent, while it simultaneously commands and governs the precise

---

[4] Anti-immigration sentiment has been pervasive in British media and has witnessed a substantial increase within the last decade where immigrants and ethnic minorities are increasingly cast as a threat either to the economic health of the nation or to national security. Oxford University's Migration Observatory has reported that '[d]espite uncertainties involved in measuring and interpreting public opinion, the evidence clearly shows high levels of opposition to immigration in the UK' (Blinder 2005, online). Certainly, the rhetoric used to support the 'Leave' vote in the 2016 Brexit referendum indicates that public opinion opposing immigration to the UK is still at quite a high level.

movements of those who move in and out of its rotating entrance. In contrast to the hyper-visibility of the glass building is the trope of a distorted visibility or, more frequently, *in*visibility, which consistently recurs at moments when migrant characters move through the city without participating in its commercial transit. Nazneen's first visit to the city alone, which culminates in London's financial district, simultaneously asserts the capitalist nature of the city and delineates the terms upon which the migrant can be afforded membership within it.

Nazneen's first impression of the city is one of speed where she witnesses the men and women around her hurrying to and fro either stopping to eat their sandwich in 'four large bites' or '[eating] and walk[ing] to save time' (Ali 2003, 48). The city that Nazneen witnesses on a bustling weekday afternoon is one where there is little time for activities which fall outside the convenance of profit generation. The people she sees hastily eating their sandwiches are, after all, presumably on their way (back) to work. The city permits, for Nazneen, a glimpse into a new kind of time—clocked time—where the temporality of the city is assigned a direct relationship to the production and commerce that takes place there. Even Nazneen herself, who figures outside London's commercial transit, becomes invisible to passers-by: '[T]hey were not aware of her ... They knew that she existed ... but unless she did something, waved a gun, halted the traffic, they would not see her' (45). Nazneen is invisible here because she, like the time that cannot be wasted on rooting for change or stopping to eat, is surplus to the profit-generating function of the city. There is, however, one moment in Nazneen's journey to London's financial district where she becomes momentarily visible—when she speaks English. A man 'tap[s] her on the shoulder ... [a] brown-faced man in a dark coat and tie [... and says] something' (Ali 2003, 48). Nazneen understands neither Urdu nor Hindi when the stranger tries to converse with her, but when he speaks to her in English she gains recognition: 'He spoke in English this time ... She shook her head again and said, "Sorry." ... She had spoken, in English, to a stranger, and she had been understood and acknowledged. It was very little. But it was something' (Ali 2003, 48).

The city atones for its disavowal with a fleeting moment of visibility. The recompense that Nazneen is afforded through speaking English, however, has little to do with a notion of 'Britishness' or gaining access to some hitherto recondite aspect of native culture, but rather her engagement with the global nature of the city, where English—the world's global language—acts now as a way of consolidating ethnic workers just as the material space of the metropolis has historically consolidated capital and goods (Ziegler 2007, 154). It is only by engaging with this global element of the city (speaking English) that Nazneen gains a brief moment of visibility, before her lack of knowledge of the English language sees the man '[nod] solemnly and [take] his leave' disappearing back into the motions of the city (Ali 2003, 48).

While London is presented as a highly commercial space, it is also presented as both a neutral and liberal space where the migrant, as an individual citizen, is afforded opportunities to advance themselves on commercial terms. Nazneen, who has moved to London for an arranged marriage with a Bangladeshi man described as 'at least forty years old' with 'a face like a frog' (Ali 2003, 12), is initially confined to the couple's council flat in Tower Hamlets. From the outset, Ali makes clear the undesirability of Nazneen's position, describing the council flat within which she is perennially confined as '[an entrapment], a concrete slab of entombed humanity' (Ali 2003, 61) and within it Nazneen laments her isolation from the public spaces beyond her flat, and even the 'muffled sound of private lives sealed away above, below and around her' (Ali 2003, 18). Nazneen's emancipation occurs along the lines of liberation of the patriarchal strictures of her Bangladeshi community in Tower Hamlets, sequestration from the public sphere, and in her rupture from a mode of dependence on her husband Chanu. Significantly, the liberation that Nazneen is afforded is offered through work and the commercial opportunities that the global city presents. At first, her work at home sewing garments grants her sexual freedom in that it allows her to meet Karim, a second-generation Bangladeshi, and their relationship ultimately culminates in an extra-marital affair. Their meetings through Nazneen's garment work remain for long after the only legitimate way Nazneen can see Karim, since if Chanu had found out about Karim's Bengal Tigers meetings, 'there was no question of [Nazneen] going' (Ali 2003, 194).

The city also affords a particular kind of independence to those who are willing to participate in economic exchange and commerce, and both Razia and Nazneen are willing to use the commercial space of the city in this way. The seeds of what will later become their garment-making enterprise are forged in Razia and Nazneen's observation of how much white women are willing to pay for 'ethnic' clothing:

'Fushion Fashions,' said Razia reading out the name.

> Inside, a white girl stood in front of a mirror turning this way and that in a black kameez top with white embroidered flowers and a sprinkling of pearls stitched near the top ... A similar outfit was displayed in the window ... Razia looked at the price tag. She shook her head and sighed as if all the evils of the world had been revealed to her. 'Look how much these English are paying for their kameez'. (Ali 2003, 328)

Razia's outrage at the extortionist price of the kameez is precisely what will later be converted into their own profit-generating enterprise as her vexation at commercial avarice is transformed into a commercial opportunity. The scene baldly depicts the subsumption of once-championed notions of hybridity into the language of capitalist globalization and signals its inadequacy as a means of resistance in itself. Later scenes in the novel position the independence that Nazneen will come to enjoy from her commercial links with Fushion Fashion in relation to the immobility she had much earlier been familiar with. Not only is she within the public sphere and making money, but she is also in the position to shop and spend: '[s]he checked her purse: nearly twenty pounds. Maybe she would buy some chocolate for the girls. [She] gave silent thanks' (Ali 2003, 405). Beyond this relative economic independence, the sewing business also alleviates Nazneen's feelings of isolation and connects her to other women in her community. Significantly, it is the liberal and global city of London, rather than just life in an urban space, that opens up these possibilities for Nazneen and Razia (Ziegler 2007, 148), as exemplified in Hasina's letters from Dhaka which interpolate Nazneen's story between 1985 and 2001. Despite the arguments put forward in Naila Kabeer's study of garment workers in Dhaka and London,[5] which suggests that it was Bangladeshi women in Dhaka, rather than in London, who had more labour market choices, it is Nazneen, the sister resident in London, who experiences an ostensible empowerment and new-found mobility, and the relative success that is afforded to the third-world migrant in London is not afforded to Hasina in Dhaka.

The only potential to trace the more complex facets of Nazneen's relationship to the city are figured in Hasina's letters to Nazneen in

---

[5] Ali credits Kabeer's study as a source for *Brick Lane* in her Acknowledgements (Ali 2003, 415).

which Hasina frequently imagines Nazneen as a princess living in a tower in London, or assigns Nazneen's thinness to her following the fashionable trends of the other beautiful London women. This, of course, has some purchase on the material conditions of Nazneen's life in Brick Lane when considered alongside the 'peeling red paint [which shows] splinters of pale wood', the walls covered with vulgar graffiti and 'the stairs [giving] off a tang of urine' (Ali 2003, 42–3). But Nazneen's positioning within the power relations of the city is occluded by the experiences and grim prospects that Hasina faces in Dhaka, which render Nazneen's life in London as one of privilege. It is the liberal space of the global city that affords Nazneen opportunities, and it is specifically when Nazneen begins to work that she can take advantage of these possibilities. These opportunities are furbished by Hasina's exploitation in her relationships with men and her coercion into work in the 'informal' sector. Hasina's life is presented as a foil for Nazneen's sexual freedom and relative economic opportunities.

Nazneen ultimately remains in London. Moreover, her choice to stay is detached from the potential love interests since she ends her current relationships both with Chanu and Karim, and her choice ultimately becomes a choice between cities. London, then, is rendered as a multicultural space in which the migrant can succeed provided that they fulfil their role within the city's neoliberal functions. The narrative of Nazneen's liberation becomes an essentially individualistic one, and the affirmation of the desirability of liberation on these (commercial) terms involves a necessary endorsement of the logics of global capitalism and neoliberalism that the city analogues. This, in turn, already assigns a particular (im)mobility to the migrant in terms of their ability to challenge the city's logic in a way which might enable a more collective empowerment. Thus, a city that embodies the accumulation of wealth and the dispossession of those who are disenfranchised is rendered as a liberal space in which the migrant can enjoy relative equality. The expression of the liberal and inclusive multicultural virtues of the city is consolidated and reiterated in Razia's closing lines: '"This is England" … "You can do whatever you like"' as the novel ends with a trip to an ice-skating rink where Nazneen is free to skate even 'in [her] sari' (Ali 2003, 413).

While Nazneen achieves an ostensible empowerment within the liberal space of London, her husband Chanu, who has been living there for more than thirty years by the time he returns to Bangladesh, fares less successfully in the global city. In the scene in which Chanu, Nazneen and an infant Raqib visit the home of Dr. Azad and his wife, Chanu—disillusioned with his work in the council—discusses the 'one or two ventures' that he 'has in the pipeline'. He poses the question: 'The problem is capital. If you don't have money, what can you do?' Dr. Azad, 'smiling in his peculiar way, eyebrows up, mouth down' rhetorically replies 'Make some?' (Ali 2003, 90). Dr. Azad's response to Chanu succinctly articulates the logic of the novel—that in order to 'do anything' (let alone anything you like) in the global city, the migrant must make money by working and must participate in the commercial and capitalist processes that the city embodies. At this point it is worth contrasting Chanu to characters such as Ashoke Ganguli in Mira Nair's adaptation of *The Namesake*,[6] who has moved to America with a PhD in fibre optics. Ashoke's knowledge, unlike Chanu's, is differentiated by its potential to be capitalized and instrumentalized. Chanu's background in the liberal arts—the kind of knowledge not only devalued but actively attacked by neoliberal logics—remains tacitly implicated in the narrative of his failure. Initially working for the local council and failing to secure promotions on the several occasions on which they arise, Chanu later holds a series of menial and temporary jobs in between periods of unemployment.

Chanu's failure to succeed in the capitalist and commercial space of London ultimately forecloses his possibilities of relative success or remaining in the city. Ironically, without work, the only act that affirms Chanu's self-declaration as a 'man of action' (Ali 2003, 109) is his act of leaving his employment and, later, the city when he returns to Bangladesh without Nazneen, who remains there having established a small-scale sewing business with Razia and two of their female companions. If Chanu is a failed postcolonial subject, and his failure is registered along the lines of his inability to self-make, then the novel must allow Chanu's narrative to enact a logic which accommodates his failure without imperilling the novel's underlying ideology whereby relative success and a particular kind of work remain intimated. Although an inimical system is certainly implicated in the sporadic instances showing Chanu's relationship to work (Ahmed 2010, 40),

---

[6]Ashoke Ganguli is analyzed at greater length in Guillermo Iglesias Díaz's chapter in this volume, which focuses on Mira Nair's film.

these implications are never overtly articulated and are more often overshadowed by Chanu's maladroit peculiarities.

The first insight into Chanu's relationship with work in the city is afforded through his hopes for promotion at the local council. In an earlier conversation with Dr. Azad, Chanu describes how the city has provided an altogether different experience from the one he had hoped for upon his arrival in London:

> When I came I was a young man. I had ambitions. Big dreams. When I got off the aeroplane I had my degree certificate in my suitcase and a few pounds in my pocket. I thought there would be a red carpet laid out for me. I was going to join the Civil Service and become Private Secretary to the Prime Minister ... That was my plan. And then I found things were a bit different. These people here didn't know the difference between me, who stepped off an aeroplane with a degree certificate, and the peasants who jumped off the boat possessing only lice on their heads.
> (Ali 2003, 26)

Chanu is initially hopeful that a promotion at the council will be secured. However, his assertions that '[he] is certain of the promotion in any case' (Ali 2003, 30) become increasingly conditional until he begins to realize that he will not achieve the promotion and Nazneen eventually drops it from her prayers. After apparently resigning from his job with the council, Chanu works as a taxi driver and in other low-income jobs. When the novel resumes its narration of Nazneen and Chanu's life in London after the sixteen-year interval marked only by Hasina's letters from Dhaka, we are presented with an unemployed Chanu who shows few signs of returning to work.

Chanu's outwardly visible stagnation and his abstention from the workforce conincides with his increasing lack of mobility. The first image of Chanu when the novel returns to Tower Hamlets in 2001 is one where '[Chanu] lay on the sofa in his lungi and vest ... he often spent the day prostrate on the sofa without dressing, or pinned to the floor beneath his books' (Ali 2003, 150). Having withdrawn from the workforce, Chanu becomes physically stagnant. His failure to dress signals his withdrawal from the public sphere, while the language of restriction or disorder couches references to his books and studies which are elsewhere consistently described as physical obstacles.[7] In fact, Chanu's educational ventures are rendered at least partially determinant of his poor performance in the workplace. The worth of Chanu's qualifications, which cover a gamut of arts subjects ranging from transcendental philosophy to literature and creative writing, is mirrored in the literal descriptions of his books and certificates which feature in scenes where Chanu eagerly offers his educated insights and consistently labours to trumpet his self-refinement: as '[t]he small edifice of [Chanu's] savings was reduced to dust … The number of certificates had stabilized, and were waiting in the bottom of the wardrobe until someone had the energy to hang them' (Ali 2003, 151). Here we see Chanu's finances depleted as the number of certificates he gains in literature, philosophy and history increase to the point where they occupy the same amount of space as the family's clothing.

Chanu's investment in qualifications which have little to do with profit generation and everything to do with what Chanu perceives as self-refinement by way of acquaintance with British literature and intellectual traditions leaves the family's finances decimated. Moreover, while Chanu boasts an ostensible knowledge of literature, and proceeds with a predisposition to cite Hume, his commercial awareness is synchronously figured as altogether absent.[8] This lack of commercial ability is baldly depicted in his chair-restoration business, comically punctured when Nazneen observes '[t]wo lonely hairy strings … rigged loosely across a hole' alongside 'a ball of twine and a pair of pliers' and conjectures: 'So the chair-restoring business ha[s] begun' (151). Chanu's subsequent commercial ventures amount to little more than '[e]nergetic numbers on his furiously written and rewritten business plans' while his proposals are perennially 'slighted … [b]y customers, by suppliers, by superiors and inferiors' (Ali 2003, 167). What can be discerned through these instances in the novel is that what is presented through the figure of Chanu and his inept and persistent failures in different varieties of profit generation is not a system which presents perpetual barricades to the migrant that cannot be circumvented, but rather an individual whose failures can be more readily assigned to his own ineptitudes. As Rehana Ahmed footnotes, 'the hint in the novel that Chanu got sacked

---

[7] See especially Ali 2003, 69; 114; 207.
[8] See also Ali, 28–9; 34.

from his council job remains just that' (Ahmed 2010, 40) and the claims that Chanu makes to a system with integral racism, or which affords the migrant few opportunities, consequently become drained of their legitimacy and are rendered almost deflatedly comic when juxtaposed with Chanu's idiosyncrasies. Through Chanu's narrative, the novel can thus enact a presentation which inversely mirrors the empowerment of characters who succeed in the workplace (and remain in the city), by shirking any overt suggestion of a systemic antagonism which might imperil its underlying ideology.

Contra Chanu's claims that British society is inherently racist, the novel more emphatically establishes the city as a neutral and liberal space. Nazneen's ostensible empowerment and ability to remain in London through participating in the commercialism of the city, while offering liberation within what Alistair Cormack calls 'the double bind that female migrants face, treated as alien by their host nation, and as commodities by the men in their own communities' (Cormack 2006, 700), is confined to emancipation from a set of patriarchal practices that she comes to deem oppressive, and entry into an apparently neutral multicultural space.[9]

In so far as the political logic of the narrative is apparent, that London embodies not only a multicultural centre but also an advanced capitalist hub and that the ability of the migrant to succeed in the global city is premised on their ability to participate in commercial exchange, these ideological thrusts of the novel must be considered in terms of their implications for discourses of migrancy in London and wider questions about the migrants' place in the city. This is something that has not been addressed, let alone interrogated in mainstream reviews of the novel.[10] Sukhdev Sandhu writes quite correctly, albeit in praise, that '[*Brick Lane* is] more

---

[9] The neutrality of the commercial space is further articulated in Razia's advice to Nazneen about shopping: '[I]f you go out to shop, go to Sainsbury's. English people don't look at you twice. But if you go to our shops, the Bengali men will make things up about you' (Ali 2003, 47).

[10] Perhaps the most publicized debate in the mainstream press has been the debate over issues of representation and freedom of speech in which Germaine Greer vied with Salman Rushdie over disagreements surrounding the legitimacy of the protests on Brick Lane sparked by Ali's homonymous novel. The Greer/Rushdie debate, however, is framed within issues of representation, minority rights and creative freedom rather than within the subordinate economic position of Bangladeshi migrants (see Greer 2006, Rushdie 2006 and Lewis 2006).

interested in character than it is in language or even the area from which it derives its name' (Sandhu 2003, 13), while Natasha Walter writes that she 'loved the ideal of freedom that drives the final scene' (Walter 2003, 26). Within the academy, the political logic of *Brick Lane* has proved equally unproblematic. Garrett Ziegler writes that 'the ideology that is enacted through the novel is not a problem for the novelist, or, if it is, it is not a problem that manifests in the novel ... Nazneen's experiences confirm the fundamental rightness or desirability of the mode of citizenship generated by global capitalism' (Ziegler 2007, 162). John Eade, echoing these sentiments, writes that '[t]he economic system of global capitalism is accepted because liberation can be gained through a personal politics of gendered liberation in a country where you have the power to choose' (Eade 2007, 34). Reading *Brick Lane* as a novel of individual empowerment or emancipation from localized patriarchal norms, where the path to liberation is fundamentally economic in nature, elides wider questions and a commensurate examination of the ways in which the contemporary capitalist system limits or confines the third-world migrant both within the city and beyond it in London's peripheries.

If there is anywhere within the text where wider social or political forces are given sustained attention, then it is in the mutual antagonism between the Lion Hearts and Karim's Bengal Tigers, and later in the riots. Rehana Ahmed has argued, however, that the power relations between the Bangladeshi community and wider British society are obscured in *Brick Lane*, and that the riots towards the end of the novel are symptomatic of a subordinate class position (Ahmed 2010, 25). For Ahmed, the implications of presenting the riots towards the end of the novel in terms of an internal community struggle, rather than in terms of a conflict between the Bangladeshi community and wider antagonistic forces, erases the source of the riots as a conflict between the Bangladeshi community and wider British society (Ahmed 2010, 35). If Ahmed is correct, then this likely explains why the social discord at the end of the novel appears not only to have its broader antecedents withheld, but its legitimacy undermined. In the Bengal Tigers' first meeting, the members' lack of proficiency is repeatedly emphasized for its comedic effects in their floundering through agendas and excessively bureaucratic voting. Their mission statement suggests that they have little notion of what they support or oppose. Karim asks the meeting's attendants '[w]hat are [The Bengal Tigers] against?' After one member suggests the Lion Hearts,

Karim tautologically declares that the Bengal Tigers will be 'against ... any group that opposes [them]' (Ali 2003, 199). After the 9/11 attacks, the racial tensions on Brick Lane escalate. Importantly, the later riots are a result of what becomes an intra-Bangladeshi conflict, rather than between disenfranchised migrant communities and the wider society. The riots that arise from this internal conflict are resonant of a conversation between Karim and Nazneen shortly after they had first met in which Karim laments: 'Now we's too busy fighting each other' (Ali 2003, 198). Karim describes the riots themselves as 'revenge. And revenge for the revenge ... It's not even *about* anything ... It's just about what it is. Put anything in front of them ... and they'll fight it. A police car, a shop window, anything' (Ali 2003, 398; italics in the original). Although no clear or legitimate external explanation is assigned to the riots here, a closer reading of the dynamics between the opposing groups and between these groups and the material space of Brick Lane, however, might suggest that the manifested conflict is a territorial act caused by the lack of ownership of that same space (Ahmed 2010, 34), and this relationship to space is symptomatic of the manner discussed earlier in which liberal capitalism designates these migrant workers to the city's peripheries in a microcosm of Wallerstein's capitalist world system.

Significantly, the riots also function to disrupt the same commercial space of the city in their vicinity. When Nazneen ventures to the city to rescue Shahana from the intra-Bangladeshi riot, she witnesses for the first time the absence of commercial activity:

> Nazneen looked beyond the cordon into the neck of Brick Lane. It revealed nothing. The electrical shops were shuttered, the stonemason's dark, the sandwich-shop window showed empty trays and a naked glass counter, and only the steps and the awning of the Capital City Hotel were lit up. (Ali 2003, 393)

In an antithetical presentation of London's urban landscapes, the commercial flow of the city is halted. Importantly, as the commercial space is disrupted by the riots, Nazneen again becomes invisible in a scene resonant of her initial trip into the financial district: 'The policeman looked ahead, as if she had not spoken ... "Why can't I go through?" said Nazneen. She put her face right up to the policeman's face. *Do you see me now? Do you hear me?*' (Ali 2003, 392; italics in the original). The scene reiterates the connection between commercialism and visibility, except that it is not only Nazneen who becomes anonymous here. The police wear helmets and bulging jackets and are concealed behind their shields, while the youths 'stood on the pavement and in the road, hoods pulled up, scarves around their faces, as though they had entered a manly purdah' (Ali 2003, 394). Although the riots disrupt the abstract commercial space of Brick Lane, the disruption creates a space of ambiguity at best, while the riots are assigned no cause that is external to the community in which they emerge.

The motivation for the riots, which could be further articulated and germinate some form of collective consciousness, is instead rendered as a disorganized and gratuitous disruption. Nazneen's reason for being outside on the streets while the riots are taking place is that Shahana is missing, and the narration of the riots ceases once Shahana has been found. Nazneen's (and Shahana's) individual stories here eclipse the riots which are dropped by the narrative at the crescendo of their violence. It is this portrayal of the racial tensions in Tower Hamlets and the subsequent riots coupled with the narratives of the migrant protagonists which makes the concomitant ideology of the novel difficult to ignore. The ostensible empowerment that the novel's logic avows is politically remote rather than stationed, individualistic rather than collective. At the end of the novel, despite Nazneen's work sewing garments which allows her some degree of economic independence and connects her to other women in her community, she continues to work at home and, with the exception of a solidarity with Hasina, is only connected to women *within* her community. The work that Nazneen carries out still provides her with little money relative to the amount of money that the garments that she produces will sell for, and she remains part of an invisible workforce—one of the 'people you don't see'—in the functions of the capitalist metropolis. It is worth re-emphasizing that questions of disenfranchisement on a much wider scale than that which concerns the individual protagonists are not merely beyond the novel's scope; the apparent potential to self-liberate within the city's commercial space necessitates a political positioning in relation to the city's capitalist functions—functions which cannot be abstracted from wider socioeconomic movements of immigrants and capital. While the novel opens up a critical space for thinking through the migrant's relationship to the city, it coalesces liberation with individualistic capitalist logic and stops short of any overt articulation of failure or conflict beyond internal explanation. Consequently, the text does not evade an endorsement of the neoliberal logic that the city embodies. The empowerment that successful migrants garner which procures this intrinsically individualistic quality is, moreover, consonant with discourses of freedom which structurally buttress the rhetoric of (neo)liberal capitalism. Meanwhile, the ideology that *Brick Lane* enacts within the context of global capitalism, international migration or the global metropolis is not adequately interrogated within the space of the novel.

WORKS CITED

Ahmed, Rehana. 2010. Brick Lane: A Materialist Reading of the Novel and its Reception. *Race & Class* 52 (2): 25–42.
Ali, Monica. 2003. *Brick Lane*. London: Doubleday.
Blinder, Scott. 2005. UK Public Opinion Toward Immigration: Overall Attitudes and Level of Concern. The Migration Observatory, Oxford University. http://www.migrationobservatory.ox.ac.uk/wp-content/uploads/2016/04/Briefing-Public_Opinion_Overall_Attitudes_and_Level_of_Concern.pdf.
Chrisman, Laura. 2003. *Postcolonial Contraventions: Cultural Readings of Race, Imperialism and Transnationalism*. Manchester and New York: Manchester University Press.
Cormack, Alistair. 2006. Migration and the Politics of Narrative Form: Realism and the Postcolonial Subject in *Brick Lane*. *Contemporary Literature* 47 (4): 695–721.
Dirty Pretty Things. 2002. Dir. Stephen Frears. Buena Vista International, Film.
Eade, John. 2007. Economic Migrant or Hyphenated British? Writing About Difference in London's East End. In *The Cultures of Economic Migration: International Perspectives*, ed. Suman Gupta, and Tope Omoniyi, 27–36. Aldershot, UK: Ashgate.
Greer, Germaine. 2006. Reality Bites. *The Guardian Online*. http://www.guardian.co.uk/film/2006/jul/24/culture.books.
Harvey, David. 2003. *The New Imperialism*. New York and Oxford: Oxford University Press.
———. 2012. *Rebel Cities: From the Right to the City to Urban Revolution*. New York and London: Verso.
International Organisation for Migration. 2008. *World Migration 2008: Managing Labour Mobility in the Evolving Global Economy*. Geneva: IOM.
The Power to Choose: Bangladeshi Women and Labour Market Decisions in London and Dhaka. London: Verso.

Lewis, Paul. 2006. 'You Sanctimonious Philistine'—Rushdie v Greer, the sequel. *The Guardian Online.* http://www.guardian.co.uk/uk/2006/jul/29/topstories3.books.

Loomba, Ania. 2005. *Colonialism/Postcolonialism*, 2nd ed. New York and Oxford: Routledge.

Massey, Douglas, et al. 1998. *World's in Motion: Understanding International Migration at the End of the Millennium.* Oxford: Clarendon Press.

McLeod, John. 2004. *Postcolonial London: Rewriting the Metroplis.* London: Routledge. Print.

Office for National Statistics. 2011. 2011 Census Statistics for England and Wales on National Identity, Passports Held and Country of Birth. Census 2012. http://www.ons.gov.uk/ons/publications/re-reference-tables.html?edition=tcm%3A77-301985.

Rushdie, Salmon. 2006. Letters: Brickbats Fly Over Brick Lane. *The Guardian Online.* http://www.guardian.co.uk/books/2006/jul/29/comment.letters.

Sandhu, Sukhdev. 2003. Come Hungry. Leave Edgy. *London Review of Books* 25 (19): 10–13.

Sassen, Saskia. 1991. *The Global City: New York, London, Tokyo.* Princeton and New Jersey: Princeton University Press.

———. 1996. Analytic Borderlands: Race, Gender and Representations in the New City. In *Re-Presenting the City: Ethnicity, Capital and Culture in the 21st-Century Metropolis*, ed. Anthony D. King, 183–202. New York: New York University Press.

Varma, Rashmi. 2012. *The Postcolonial City and its Subjects: London, Nairobi, Bombay.* New York: Routledge.

Walter, Natasha. 2003. Citrus Scent of Inexorable Desire. *The Guardian Online.* http://www.guardian.co.uk/books/2003/jun/14/featuresreviews.guardianreview20.

Wills, Jane, et al. 2010. *Global Cities at Work: New Migrant Divisions of Labour.* New York and London: Pluto Press.

Ziegler, Garrett. 2007. East of the City: *Brick Lane*, Capitalism and the Global Metropolis. *Race/Ethnicity: Multidisciplinary Global Contexts* 1 (1): 145–167.

Borderless (Alien) Nations: Disposable Bodies and Biopolitical Effacement in Min Sook Lee's Docu-Poem

Libe García Zarranz

> *Although neoliberal strategies of government appropriate and utilize older forms of power—sovereign power, pastoral power, and disciplinary power—biopower offers the most effective and appealing set of strategies for governing social life under neoliberalism because it finds its telos and legitimacy in its articulated capacity to maximize the energies and capabilities of all: individuals, families, market organizations, and the state.*
> Majia H. Nadesan, *Governmentality, Biopower, and Everyday Life* (2008, 3).

> *The task at hand is to establish modes of public seeing and hearing that might well respond to the cry of the human within the sphere of appearance.*
> Judith Butler, *Precarious Life: The Powers of Mourning and Violence* (2004, 147).

Foucauldian critics contend that when life becomes the object of political power, the boundaries between agency and subjection, safety and risk become blurred. It is in this crossing of borders that the liminal concepts

---

L. García Zarranz (✉)
Magdalene College, University of Cambridge, Cambridge, England
e-mail: lg516@cam.ac.uk

of biopower and biopolitics emerge.[1] In *Security, Territory, Population: Lectures at the Collège de France 1978–1979*, philosopher Michel Foucault discusses the formulation of biopower as 'the set of mechanisms through which the basic biological features of human species became the object of a political strategy, of a general strategy of power' (Foucault 2009, 1). Biopower, then, is understood not as a theory, but as a set of relations that circulate around and shape bodily and social space; a network of regulatory mechanisms that clearly demarcate the normative to the exclusion of the different. In the first epigraph to this chapter, social theorist Majia H. Nadesan discusses the emergence of biopower as a major force in controlling populations, linked to the development of liberal and neoliberal forms of governance. These neoliberal rationalities, as Nadesan and other Foucauldian critics aptly contend, privilege some individuals as autonomous self-regulating agents, while subordinating and disciplining others as invisible or dangerous. Particularly after 9/11, as I argue elsewhere, 'the strategic intensification of surveillance mechanisms, militarization, and racial profiling—all forms of biopower— has ensured the branding of certain subjects as non-desirable' (García Zarranz 2017, 62). Employing Giorgio Agamben's insights on biopolitical fracture, Nadesan claims that

> the contradictions stemming from the operations of liberal democracy are contained by a series of social and geographic exclusions. In order to maintain the fantasy of a society of self-governing individuals, the system must constantly purify itself of those persons and institutions whose very existence belies the fantasy. The 'solution' to demonstrated failures of liberal government are symbolic and/or geographic elimination and/or marginalisation of those whose presence mark the ruptures. (Nadesan 2008, 181)

Paradoxically, however, certain populations, such as illegal workers, are systematically erased from public political life, while simultaneously being exploited as productive sources of capital. In the preface to

---

[1] In *Homo Sacer: Sovereign Power and Bare Life* (1998), philosopher Giorgio Agamben discusses the state of exception in terms of 'the limit concept of the doctrine of law and the state, in which sovereignty borders (since every limit concept is always the limit between two concepts) on the sphere of life and becomes indistinguishable from it' (11). Agamben thus articulates sovereignty and *homo sacer* as 'borderline' concepts. See Agamben's *Means without End: Notes on Politics* (2000) for further reference.

Commonwealth (2009), the final piece in the trilogy begun with *Empire* (2000) and continued with *Multitude* (2004), political philosophers Michael Hardt and Antonio Negri address this paradox by claiming that '[t]he poor, migrants, and "precarious" workers (that is, those without stable employment) are often conceived as excluded, but really, though subordinated, they are completely within the global rhythms of biopolitical production' (Hardt and Negri 2009, xi). Drawing on recent interventions in political philosophy and globalization theory (Hardt and Negri 2009; Butler 2004; Sassen 1998), this chapter examines the shifting expressions of biopolitical life in the collaborative project *Borderless: A Docu-Poem about the Lives of Undocumented Workers* (2006). Depicted as a risk to society's security, the illegal workers portrayed in the docu-poem occupy a paradoxical borderline position in Canadian society.[2] On the one hand, they are invisible and disembodied forces of production, while on the other they generate visible profit for the nation, as Darragh Patrick Hall's analysis of Monica Ali's *Brick Lane* in this volume also evidences. In other words, the bodies of the undocumented workers in *Borderless* are sacrificed and consumed by both national and global capitalist structures, while often being erased from the public sphere. These 'modern outlaws', as the voiceover calls them, are thus subjected to biopolitical structures that obliterate their very existence by turning them into a paradigmatic example of alienated subjectivity, radical alterity and vulnerable embodiment. As political philosopher and queer theorist Judith Butler contends, a distinct form of normative power works through radical effacement; there never was a human, there never was a life: 'the public realm of appearance is itself constituted on the basis of the exclusion of that image' (Butler 2004, 147). The docu-poem begins to challenge these exclusionary practices by granting these *minoritized* populations (Lee 2014, 235) a voice. In doing so, *Borderless* shares the potential of docudrama, a sister genre, 'to reframe seemingly familiar events, by introducing affective "personal" counter-perspectives' (Bennett 2010, 211). At the same time, Min Sook Lee employs a series of formal strategies, such as silhouetted interviews, to expose the tensions

---

[2] The related genre of the docudrama has gained popularity in the last few years, particularly after 9/11, with titles such as *The Road to Guantanamo* (2006), directed by Michael Winterbottom and Mat Whitecross. See the collection *Docufictions: Essays on the Intersection of Documentary and Fictional Filmmaking* (2006), edited by Rhodes and Springer, for further reference on the workings of this artistic genre.

and fractures that these illegal workers face in their thorny path to gain representation. The docu-poem thus aligns itself with a body of work by other contemporary feminist, anti-racist and anti-capitalist filmmakers who seek to 'provoke their audience' (Rosenthal 1995, xii) by using socially challenging work to potentially reconfigure biopolitical and affective relations.

Released in 2006, *Borderless* is explicit in its collaborative nature. Shot on Super 8 and Mini DV, the 23-minute docu-poem is directed by award-winning filmmaker Min Sook Lee, a Korean-born, Toronto-based artist who has been looking at issues of social justice and power for the last two decades.[3] Her politically engaged work includes the documentaries *Tiger Spirit* (2008), which tackles the reunification of the two Koreas, *My Toxic Baby* (2009), which exposes the dangers of living in a chemically saturated world, and the recent *Migrant Dreams* (2016), which traces the struggles and fights for justice of a group of Indonesian migrant farm workers in Ontario.[4] The written narration in *Borderless* is placed in the hands of acclaimed Trinidadian-born, Toronto-based poet Dionne Brand. For the last three decades, Brand's poetic landscapes have exposed the dangers of racist, nationalistic and sexist structural violences within the context of Canadian society and culture. Then, the voiceover of queer Jamaican-Canadian dub poet D'bi Young Anitafrika alternates in *Borderless* with the voices of two undocumented workers, who retell the stories of their vulnerable situation in Canada in English and Spanish respectively. By doing so, the docu-poem momentarily subverts the idea of immigrant populations as translated subjects. Moreover, I would argue that this polyphonic rendering of voices not only highlights the collective purpose of the project but also suggests a renewed artistic transnationalism that would challenge received versions of official multiculturalism in Canada (Lai 2014; Bannerji 2000). Interestingly, *Borderless* was commissioned by KAIROS, an ecumenical social justice group that wanted to look at migration issues inside Canadian borders. As a result, Sook Lee explains, the short doc has been successful in the

---

[3] While being aware of the generic differences, I use the terms 'docu-poem' and 'short doc' interchangeably in my analysis of *Borderless*, following Min Sook Lee (in Michael 2009).

[4] Min Sook Lee's other works include *El Contrato* (2003), *Hogtown: The Politics of Policing* (2005), *Sedition* (2008), *Badge of Pride* (2010) and the comedy series *She's the Mayor* (2011).

post-secondary education circuit, often being used as teaching material in workshops and courses within and beyond the university classroom (Michael 2009). The docu-poem, however, has not circulated in academic circles. While acknowledging its pedagogical purpose, this essay seeks to open up the critical discussion by also considering *Borderless* as a stylized site of cultural, biopolitical and ethical intervention.

Set against a black screen, the opening captions introduce viewers to the material realities of those populations that need to cross geopolitical borders in order to find a sustainable life:

> Every year the number of people crossing borders grows. Unauthorized migration is now the fastest rising form of migration. For most, it's about survival./Half the world, nearly 3 billion people, live on less than 2 dollars a day. The others are busy reinforcing borders; but the hunger of the free market still needs to be fed.

This journey, as the docu-poem illustrates, involves fighting against the pressures of a neoliberal apparatus that increasingly tightens these borders through the intensification of surveillance and other regulatory mechanisms. *Borderless* opens up with an aerial shot of a city at night where skyscrapers and neon lights abound, including a shot of the Hilton Hotel. Initially, a general audience would not identify this as a Canadian space necessarily, but as yet another instance of a contemporary global city (Sassen 1996). The stories that the viewers are about to hear become immediately transnational, since the precarious lives of undocumented workers are a common reality today, partially as a result of aggressive capitalist and neoliberal ideologies under processes of uneven globalization. The camera then zooms into an image of a clock tower that Canadian audiences would recognize as the Old City Hall in downtown Toronto. Superimposed onto a shot of the streets, the docu-poem now shows a quotation from Angela, an undocumented worker, in white captions: 'Basically I'm here, just living here. I don't technically have any claims. Somebody could just pick me up. The only proof that I've ever been in Canada is to say I know a street here' (*Borderless*). As later explained in the docu-poem, Angela is a second-generation Caribbean woman who has been working as a domestic servant in Toronto for many years, following the example of her mother, who worked for the same family and who was thus also part of this global labour force.[5] The technique of silhouetted interviewing deployed to share Angela's story some minutes later underscores the vulnerability of illegal workers who live under risk at the service of capitalist exploitation, while simultaneously exposing their invisibility within the political dimensions of life. In her study on global cities, sociologist Saskia Sassen convincingly claims that the presence of immigrants, together with other traditionally excluded peoples, in what she calls global cities has pushed the limits of legitimacy by interrogating a key question: 'Whose city is this?' (Sassen 1998, xix). As Sassen argues, the 'global city is a strategic site for disempowered actors because it enables them to gain presence, to emerge as subjects, even when they do not gain direct power' (Sassen 1998, xxi). In this sense, Angela's productive presence in Toronto should not only grant her a sense of territorial knowledge but also allow her to participate in the public sphere of the city. And yet, this woman's life has been centred on her labour, which has forced her, paradoxically, to remain invisible and therefore excluded from the right to citizenship and political intervention.

In the next sequence, the camera is positioned inside a vehicle so that it joins the noise and movement of the city at night. As it traverses some of the streets in downtown Toronto, the audience strives to hear a phone conversation between two women where one asks the other about her day. The disruptive noises from the metropolis are intensified by the presence of non-diegetic music, which, in my view, highlights Sook Lee's deliberate commentary on the limitations ingrained in the 'presumed objectivity' of documentary filmmaking (Rhodes and Springer 2006, 6). Moreover, the decision to shoot at night-time, also an unsettling formal strategy, momentarily puts the viewers in the position of those populations who live in symbolic darkness, underground. Without much energy, Angela explains how hers has been yet another normal day where she has cooked and cleaned the house. Her everyday life consists of performing these chores for the family she works for illegally. The precarious worker's body is thus *debilitated*—which for Margrit Shildrick entails 'to never reach the putative security of corporeal, affective and cognitive

---

[5] Even though the circumstances of Angela's arrival in Canada are not addressed explicitly in the documentary, it appears that she held refugee status when she first entered the country, according to the additional educational material that is included in the DVD version of *Borderless*.

standards of flourishing' (Shildrick 2015, 14). Perhaps paradoxically from the perspective of privileged viewers, this woman is sacrificing her life as a way to secure her own existence. In his discussion of the workings of biocapital,[6] anthropologist Kaushik Sunder Rajan articulates the notion of a 'sacrificial' population:

> When this excluded population gets incorporated into logics and circuits of global capitalism ..., this population shifts away from being sacrificed to being *consumed*. The worker's body becomes available to systems of capital ... as a source of value generation, and as a source of knowledge production. (Sunder Rajan 2006, 99)

Following Sunder Rajan's argument, I argue that the bodies of the undocumented workers in *Borderless* are both sacrificed and consumed by national and global capitalist structures, while simultaneously being erased from the public sphere. As Butler cogently puts it, even though we struggle for rights over our own bodies, these very bodies are not only our own. Given that the body is formed 'within the crucible of social life' (Butler 2004, 26) and as such, always presupposes a public dimension, what happens to those bodies that are negated entry into that very public space?

In similar ways to other characters in Dionne Brand's long poems, *Inventory* (2006) and *Ossuaries* (2010), the undocumented workers in *Borderless* live anonymously, underground. As the camera approaches a high-rise apartment tower, the voiceover ponders the invisibility of certain populations in urban hubs: 'What makes a city hustle? Nothing extraordinary. It takes a lot of unknown people, unseen hands, unread

---

[6] In his analysis of genomic research and drug development marketplaces in the United States and India, anthropologist Kaushik Sunder Rajan discusses biotechnology as yet another form of enterprise inextricable from contemporary capitalism. Employing Foucauldian and Marxist theory, Sunder Rajan explains how what he refers to as 'biocapital' stands as a system of exchange, involving systems of production, circulation and consumption under current processes of techno-scientific capitalism. As he claims: 'Biocapital, like any other form of circulation of capital, involves the circulation and exchange of money and commodities, whose analysis needs to remain central and at the forefront of analysis. But in addition, the circulations of new and particular forms of currency, such as biological material and information, emerge' (17). See Hall's analysis of Stephen Frear's film *Dirty Pretty Things* (2003) in the chapter 'Success in the City' in this volume for a further examination of this notion.

hearts, borderless bodies' (*Borderless*). The shots of the building show a pattern of undifferentiated windows, which stresses the profitability of homogenization in construction at the expense of creative difference. The racialized but unseen bodies of these illegal workers are similarly rendered homogeneous and radically different from normative citizens, often reflecting residual forms of slavery and other systems of oppression. As the voiceover states, Angela earns $220 a week flat without insurance or benefits for taking care of children that are not her own, so the nation unquestionably profits from her exploitation while she is stripped of agency and exposed to risk. Notice the affective implications that this kind of labour entails, traversing other axes of differentiation such as gender, race and sexuality. In their discussion on biopolitics and materiality, Hardt and Negri argue that the contemporary scene of production has been transformed by labour that produces immaterial products such as ideas, knowledge, affects, relationships and images. As a result, other forms of material labour, together with society as a whole, are being transformed. Given her precarious status as an undocumented worker, Angela is forced to sacrifice the time with her own kids and look after other people's children instead, thus performing a kind of affective labour with political and ethical repercussions. As Hardt and Negri contend, what is common to these forms of immaterial labour is best expressed by their biopolitical character. Herein lies a paradox, given that what is being produced, the very object of production, is actually a subject: 'Living beings as fixed capital are at the center of this transformation, and the production of forms of life is becoming the basis of added value' (Hardt and Negri 2009, 132). Consequently, as Angela's case shows, the boundaries between labour and life become radically blurred.

Borderless repeatedly stresses the need to examine both material and immaterial aspects of the biopolitical structures that rule the life of illegal workers like Angela. With a travelling shot, the following sequence of the docu-poem portrays a series of houses in a suburban area of the city, which stresses the stark contrast between the visibility of these magnificent commodities and the invisibility of the exploitation that occurs behind the walls. It is not only that they contrast but rather that there is a direct relationship between the presence of these neighbourhoods and the erasure of the workforce of certain populations as one process sustains the other. In other words, without the cheap labour of invisible workers like Angela, the everyday life of privileged populations would be radically altered in the sense that their lifestyle would be unsustainable.

Significantly, the images of the row of houses remains unfocused, which points not only to the presumable need to preserve the anonymity of the people living in those neighbourhoods, but also to the idea of the universality of privilege and commodification in the suburban areas of global cities across the world. On the one hand, this is a systemic problem that extends beyond the national borders of Canada. On the other, it is also an issue that stresses class differences within the nation. As the narrator explains, there are approximately 200,000 undocumented workers who 'are a part of the third world inside Canada's borders that subsidizes our first world economy' (*Borderless*). Then, the voiceover is superimposed on a billboard that reads 'The Art of Luxury Living', depicting a heterosexual white couple drinking champagne as role models of normative behaviour. The hypervisibility of such advertisements that are part of our everyday life in magazines and TV shows, among other media, clashes with the radical erasure of non-normative populations from the public sphere. These erased communities would include illegal workers, together with other racialized subjects, such as migrants, that threaten hegemonic structures of power by their very presence—that is, what Rachel C. Lee calls the 'not-quite-person' (235); the 'disabled, diseased, or virally positive, impoverished, imprisoned, and otherwise debilitated classes' (Lee 2014, 57). It is important to point out that the implications and challenges of migration and other forms of mobility are in fact also represented in the film through the constant travelling shots of the camera.

Within the context of US conservative Christianity, particularly during the Bush administration, Nadesan discusses strategies of governmentality around biopower: 'Paradoxically, perhaps, these fears of moral malaise and social contagion coexist with a growing social anxiety about the internal threats posed by susceptible bodies, bodies with weakened immune systems, and/or susceptibility genes' (Nadesan 2008, 115). Even though *Borderless* is situated within the particular context of Canada, I believe that the term 'susceptible bodies' can be translated here in that the bodies of these undocumented workers are rendered inferior and invisible, and yet their difference is depicted as threatening to normative structures. Individuals and practices that are rendered undesirable, Nadesan further explains, are systematically subjected to surveillance and various regulatory mechanisms of control by the state and other institutional apparatuses. Geraldo, a Costa Rican construction worker in *Borderless*, discusses, in Spanish, the conditions of labour in

Canada. Shot also using the strategy of silhouetted interviewing, Geraldo explains that it is not a matter of quality but quantity. Production is therefore prioritized as the ultimate goal. The undocumented workers portrayed in the docu-poem earn less than half the money that a Canadian worker would, when they get paid at all, given that the law always supports the employer. In this sense, the risk for these undocumented workers is two-fold. The camera, on the one hand, shows a construction worker climbing on a roof, thus exposing his own physical body to a series of material conditions. Furthermore, these people work with no guarantee of even getting their wages in exchange for their labour, given that they do not exist as proper subjects under the law. In his articulation of the notion of *necropolitics*, political theorist Achille Mbembe explains his focus on 'those figures of sovereignty whose central project is not the struggle for autonomy but the generalized instrumentalization of human existence and the material destruction of human bodies and populations' (Mbembe 2003, 14). The ultimate expression of sovereignty, as Mbembe claims, thus resides in the power to dictate who may live and who must die.[7] Arguably then, the illegal workers in *Borderless* are exposed to several necropolitical mechanisms in that their lives and bodies are subjected to a kind of sovereignty capable of distinguishing who matters and who is disposable. Interestingly though, this population matters in terms of capitalist profit, while systematically being rendered disposable in terms of access to citizenship or the right to health insurance.

Along similar lines to Mbembe, Butler discusses which bodies count as having lived a liveable life, thus granting them the possibility of a grievable death:

> Some lives are grievable, and others are not; the differential allocation of grievability that decides what kind of subject is and must be grieved, and which kind of subject must not, operates to produce and maintain certain exclusionary conceptions of who is normatively human: what counts as a livable life and a grievable death. (Butler 2004, xiv–xv)

---

[7] Jasbir Puar reorients Mbembe's insights to focus particularly on how queerly racialized bodies live and die in a post 9/11 context of growing Islamophobia. In order to grasp the complexity of all the processes at play here, Puar insists on the need for 'bio-necro collaborations' (Puar 2007, 35).

Butler's insights take us back to the idea of risk in *Borderless*, given that when these illegal workers have an accident in the workplace, their rights are nowhere to be found because their very existence has not been granted. Power hence remains within the state and its regulatory mechanisms of control, which have the authority to decide to call upon the illegal status of these workers and then expel them from the nation at their convenience. As Geraldo convincingly puts it, 'no one complains because the employer could just call the police and then, you would just have to leave running' (*Borderless*). Hardt and Negri discuss the effects of the illegal status of certain populations in terms of a precarity understood as a poverty of space:

> Being clandestine not only deprives people of social services and the rights of citizenship but also discourages them from circulating in and mixing freely with other segments of the society. Just as precarity creates a poverty of time, so too geographical and social barriers intensify a poverty of space. (Hardt and Negri 2009, 148)

The lives of the illegal workers in *Borderless* are indeed rarely shared in community precisely because their very existence has been erased from all the dimensions of public life. And this is a point that Geraldo clearly refers to in the docu-poem when he claims that 'beyond the borders of Canada, Canada is Canada. And inside the borders of Canada, it's something else' (*Borderless*). In other words, Geraldo is pointing to the multicultural make-up of the nation which in fact hides a darker side when considering the conditions of illegal workers within the country. This is a complex phenomenon that not only reflects a series of concerns associated with migration, but also a mixture of racist, sexist and classist ideologies and material realities that are still very much present in the everyday life of many populations in Canada.[8]

---

[8] From the 1970s onwards, Canada has been systematically associated with the concept of the cultural mosaic, a convenient term to construct the nation as the ideal space for the development of multicultural identity. Nevertheless, even though policies such as the Canadian Multiculturalism Act (1988) recognize cultural diversity, they do so, as Smaro Kamboureli puts it, 'by practising a sedative politics ... that attempts to recognize ethnic differences, but only in a contained fashion, in order to manage them' (Kamboureli 2000, 82). As a result, numerous voices have emerged in the last three decades exploring how the rhetoric of tolerance that is intrinsic in multicultural Canada masks race, sex and class issues (Kamboureli 2000; Bannerji 2000; Brand 1994).

In *Commonwealth*, Hardt and Negri contend that certain populations are subjected to the impositions of a precarious life understood as 'a mechanism of control that determines the temporality of workers, destroying the division between work time and nonwork time, requiring workers not to work all the time but to be constantly available for work' (Hardt and Negri 2009, 146). With the lack of control over their own lives, precarity also becomes a *temporal* poverty. As I previously mentioned with regard to Angela's role as an absent mother to her own children, the precariousness of these people's lives involves a level of affective labour. Similarly, Geraldo's family pressures him on the phone to come back home soon because of a series of health-related problems in the family. His lack of resources, however, prevents him from directly helping his relatives. Instead, he can only provide a more symbolic aid by occasionally sending money, or barrels with food, as another sequence in the documentary shows. These barrels, though subjected to border controls, fully participate in the borderless system of global free trade. People, however, are increasingly subjected to more strict systems of surveillance when trying to cross national frontiers. As the docu-poem's voiceover aptly puts it, 'Border controls are an exacting science. It's no accident who gets into the front door' (*Borderless*). When Angela applies for legal status, for instance, she has to wait for two and a half years before she hears back that her claim has in fact been denied.

Borderless illustrates, through a number of narrative and formal elements, how undocumented workers in Canada are subjected to a process of dehumanization and desubjectivation by the very erasure of their existence in the biopolitical realm of society. As Geraldo explains, 'This is their country; this is their home; I am nothing more than someone who is hiding, like a rat' (*Borderless*). Dehumanization, Butler contends, 'becomes the condition for the production of the human to the extent that a "Western" civilization defines itself over and against a population understood as, by definition, illegitimate, if not dubiously human' (Butler 2004, 91). The workers depicted in the docu-poem live imprisoned lives in that they are viewed and judged in ways that deem them less than human, as having departed from any recognizable human community. These 'modern outlaws' are negated the right to voice any dissent against the biocapitalist structures that exploit them out of the liminal space they occupy between the borders of existence and effacement from the public sphere.

The idea of being negated the right to exist is intensified in the short doc by the shots taken inside an underground train that traverses the city. First, we see an extreme close-up of a black woman's mouth as she talks on the phone to her child. Then, the image fades out into a shot of the subway, which points to the idea of these populations living a precarious life underground, in darkness, without rights. I would add that the deliberate variable image quality of these sequences, a common trait in documentary style (Bennett 2010, 212), underscores the multiple and simultaneous levels of precarity that these illegal workers are exposed to. Further discussing how processes of dehumanization operate regarding representation, Butler contends that 'those who have no chance to represent themselves run a greater risk of being treated as less than human, regarded as less than human, or indeed, not regarded at all' (Butler 2004, 141). I believe that *Borderless* attempts to momentarily challenge these normative systems by providing the undocumented workers in the docu-poem with the right to voice and agency through representation, with its inherent limitations, ruptures, contradictions and paradoxes.

Borderless closes with the voice of Angela's child singing on the phone, calling from the Caribbean, as the camera zooms out of the building into a panoramic shot of the city of Toronto. After a fade-out, the last images in the docu-poem show some white captions over a black screen that pose a crucial comment on the material realities of border crossings today:

> The product of a colonial history, today's borderlines create contradictions and tensions in an age of globalization. Increasingly, borders have become opened to capital and goods, but closed to people. As a result, migrants who are forced to cross borders in order to survive have become modern outlaws. (*Borderless*)

As Hardt and Negri cogently put it, we live in a globalizing capitalist world 'whose geography is striated by old and new boundaries and cleavages' (Hardt and Negri 2009, 230). *Borderless*, however, closes with an, arguably romanticized, tone of hope: 'Despite everything, migrants continue to assert a basic human right: the freedom to move. Propelled by courage and determination, their journeys speak to us of our *common humanity* and call us to a vision of borderless justice' (*Borderless*, my italics).

I would like to conclude this essay by addressing the 'commonality' suggested at the end of *Borderless*. In the epilogue to the second part of *Commonwealth*, '*De Homine* 1: Biopolitical Reason', Hardt and Negri stress the need to explore the terrain of biopolitical reason in order to be able to experience the common not as an ontological issue but as one of production, or what they refer to as 'making the common' (Hardt and Negri 2009, 123). With regard to resistance, they insist on the need for the creation of alternatives beyond opposition: 'epistemology has to be grounded on the terrain of struggle—struggle that not only drives the critique of present reality of domination but also animates the constitution of another reality' (Hardt and Negri 2009, 121). *Borderless*, I claim, addresses this ongoing struggle by posing a critique of biopolitical structures of power that traverse the axes of gender, nation, race and class. As Judith Butler convincingly puts it in the second epigraph to this article, we need to devise alternative 'modes of public seeing and hearing' (2004, 147), together with new systems and regimes of intelligibility that would allow for voices of dissent to express themselves:

> We would have to interrogate the emergence and vanishing of the human at the limits of what we can know, what we can hear, what we can see, what we can sense. This might prompt us, affectively, to reinvigorate the intellectual projects of critique, of questioning, of coming to understand the difficulties and demands of cultural translation and dissent, and to create a sense of the public in which oppositional voices are not feared, degraded or dismissed, but valued for the instigation to a sensate democracy they occasionally perform. (Butler 2004, 151)

In this sense, I would claim that *Borderless* not only exposes the perverse functioning of several hegemonic structures of power, traversing multiple axes of differentiation, but also gestures towards the potential creation of alternative forms of socio-political and ethical relations. And this is precisely what filmmakers such as Min Sook Lee are striving to convey in their documentary work by addressing the limits of representation and by saturating the screen with voices and bodies that are rendered unrepresentable by normative structures in our unevenly globalized twenty-first century.

Works Cited

Agamben, Giorgio. 1998. *Homo Sacer: Sovereign Power and Bare Life*, trans. Daniel Heller-Roazen. Stanford, CA: Stanford University Press.

Agamben, Giorgio. 2000. *Means Without End: Notes on Politics*, trans. Vincenzo Binetti and Cesare Casarino. London and Minneapolis, MN: University of Minnesota Press.

Bannerji, Himani. 2000. *The Dark Side of the Nation: Essays on Multiculturalism, Nationalism and Gender*. Toronto: Canadian Scholars' Press and Women's Press.

Bennett, Bruce. 2010. Framing Terror: Cinema, Docudrama and the 'War on Terror'. *Studies in Documentary Film* 4 (3): 209–225.

Borderless: A Docu-Poem About the Lives of Undocumented Workers. 2006. Directed by Min Sook Lee. Toronto: Kairos.

Brand, Dionne. 1994. *Bread Out of Stone: Recollections, Sex, Recognitions, Race, Dreaming, Politics*. Toronto: Coach House Press.

Butler, Judith. 2004. *Precarious Life: The Powers of Mourning and Violence*. London: Verso.

Foucault, Michel. 2009. *Security, Territory, Population: Lectures at the Collège de France 1978–79*, trans. Graham Burchell. New York: Picador.

García Zarranz, Libe. 2017. *TransCanadian Feminist Fictions: New Cross-Border Ethics*. Montreal: McGill-Queen's University Press.

Michael, Hardt, and Antonio Negri. 2009. *Commonwealth*. Cambridge, MA: The Belknap Press of Harvard University Press.

Kamboureli, Smaro. 2000. *Scandalous Bodies: Diasporic Literature in English Canada*. Don Mills, ON: Oxford University Press.

Lai, Larissa. 2014. *Slanting I, Imagining We: Asian Canadian Literary Production in the 1980s and 1990s*. Waterloo, ON: Wilfrid Laurier University Press.

Lee, Rachel C. 2014. *The Exquisite Corpse of Asian America: Biopolitics, Biosociality, and Posthuman Ecologies*. New York: New York University Press.

Mbembe, Achille. 2003. Necropolitics. *Public Culture* 39, 15 (1): 11–40.

Michael, Joseph. 2009. Behind the Doc: Min Sook Lee. Online interview for *blogTo*. http://www.blogto.com/film/2009/02/behind_the_doc_min_sook_lee/.

Nadesan, Majia H. 2008. *Governmentality, Biopower, and Everyday Life*. New York and London: Routledge.

Puar, Jasbir K. 2007. *Terrorist Assemblages: Homonationalism in Queer Times*. Durham and London: Duke University Press.

Rhodes, Gary D., and John Parris Springer (eds.). 2006. *Docufictions: Essays on the Intersection of Documentary and Fictional Filmmaking*. Jefferson, NC: McFarland & Company.

Rosenthal, Alan. 1995. *Writing Docudrama: Dramatizing Reality for Film and TV*. Newton, MA: Focal Press.

Sassen, Saskia. 1996. Whose City Is It? Globalization and the Formation of New Claims. *Public Culture* 8 (2): 205–223.

Sassen, Saskia. 1998. *Globalization and its Discontents*. New York: The New Press.

Shildrick, Margrit. 2015. Living on; Not Getting Better. *Feminist Review* 111 (1): 10–24.

Sunder Rajan, Kaushik. 2006. *Biocapital: The Constitution of Postgenomic Life*. Durham, NC: Duke University Press.

Public Art in the Production of a Global City: Jamie Hilder's Clashing Versions of Vancouver

John Havelda

Vancouver's location on the Pacific periphery of North America along with its very brief history (the city was incorporated as recently as 1886), makes it an unlikely candidate for a centre of the international art world. Ian Wallace, an artist from Vancouver who has garnered a significant international reputation, argues that although the local population is somewhat indifferent to contemporary art, there exists in the city a 'passionate circle of collectors, exhibitors, educators, writers, architects, and poets who provided an informed and committed audience' (Wallace 2005, 53). Similarly, the poet and critic Peter Culley points out that Vancouver is 'oddly fortunate, for a city of its size, in producing and nurturing an artistic community unrivalled for international influence and prestige' (Culley 2001, 66). It comes as a surprise, he argues, that this marginal west coast city 'with its expensive property, urban sprawl, dearth of impressive bars, bookstores and museums, poor public transport, inaccessible art schools, a modest architectural heritage

J. Havelda (✉)
University of Coimbra, Coimbra, Portugal
e-mail: jhavelda@gmail.com

and conservative newspapers' should have become such an established centre of contemporary art (Culley 2001, 66). Added to this is a lack of the 'swaggering entitlement' of a city such as Calgary that draws people from the Canadian provinces. The stunningly beautiful natural setting of the city 'can feel like an ongoing rebuke, when it is not a source of vertigo or claustrophobia' (Culley 2001, 66). However, he concludes, these very disadvantages have driven many artists in Vancouver to develop 'a searching urban critique' which has spawned 'the Vancouver School' and 'Vancouver artists' (Culley 2001, 66).

Recent *public* art in Vancouver has transformed the cityscape remarkably. The Olympic and Paralympic Art Programme in 2010, despite its gagging order, ushered in a palpable renaissance in public art.[1] A prominent example is Ron Terada's *The Words Don't Fit the Picture* (Fig. 1). A light-based text piece erected outside the Vancouver Central Library injects a plethora of interpretations into a line from a Willie Nelson song, not least an implicit critique of the organizing committee. How do the words of censorship fit the picture of the Olympic ideal?

In Myfanwy McLeod's Claes Oldenberg-like, scale-shifting piece *The Birds*, installed at the Southeast False Creek Olympic Plaza in the Olympic Village, a pair of 5 m sculptures of sparrows defamiliarizes the faint relationship between urbanites and nature (Fig. 2).

Among the most prominent examples funded by the Olympic and Paralympic Art Programme is Ken Lum's iconic, irreverent re-identification of the city, *Monument for East Vancouver* (Fig. 3). Lum was brought up in the Downtown Eastside, often cited as Canada's poorest postcode. The area is the antithesis of the stereotyped, tourist image of Vancouver with its glass and steel towers against a dramatic backdrop of snow-capped mountains plunging into the Pacific. Situated just a few blocks from the site of the opening ceremony of the Winter Olympic Games, defiantly facing the economically privileged west side of the city, the text in the form of a cross outlined in LED lights demands visibility

---

[1] In a letter to the The Vancouver Organizing Committee for the 2010 Olympic and Paralympic Winter Games (VANOC), Raymond T. Grant, the former artistic director of the Salt Lake City Olympic Winter Games Arts Festival 2002, requested the withdrawal of a clause in the agreement between VANOC and funded artists. The document read 'The artist shall at all times refrain from making any negative or derogatory remarks respecting VANOC, the 2010 Olympic and Paralympic Games, the Olympic movement generally, Bell and/or other sponsors associated with VANOC' (Grant 2010).

Fig. 1 Ron Terada, *The Words Don't Fit the Picture* (2010), 1280 LED light nodes. (Photograph courtesy of the artist)

for marginalized neighbourhoods and communities. It also highlights the 'differences' that the organizing committee would rather not promote, given that economic disparity is not a marketable difference.

Vancouver has also been graced with an impressive variety of less obviously monumental works, not least *Digital Natives* curated by Lorna Brown and Clint Burnham in April 2011a (Fig. 4). An electronic billboard running ten-second tweets by First-Nations and non-First-Nations artists and writers was erected on the Burrard Street Bridge. As a note on the Digital Natives website has it, the project sought to '[interrupt] the flow of advertisements [by responding] to the location and history of the billboard, of digital language and translation, and the city itself'.

In 2011, *A Sign for the City* by Sabine Bitter and Helmut Weber reconfigured the meaning of the canon fire in the downtown Stanley Park at 9 p.m. every evening. What was once a navigation aid and a signal of the end of the fishing day was invested with political, social and cultural significance. Each day for a year, bus-shelter posters, inserts in the pages of newspapers, and pocket-size calendars indicated the event or

Fig. 2 Myfanwy McLeod, *The Birds* (2010), EPS foam with polyurethane hard coat and bronze, 5 × 1. 52 × 5 m. (Photograph courtesy of Robert Keziere, Catriona Jeffries Gallery)

the figure from local history celebrated by the report of the canon. From an empty sign an alternative history of the city was produced.

It is in this fertile context that attends to difference from counter-discursive positions, then, that Jamie Hilder's public interventions since the late 1990s have sought to alter commodifying perceptions of the city. His situationist banners hung from most of the pedestrian overpasses above highways leading into Vancouver bear apparently straightforward language. 'AESTHETICS', announces one (Fig. 5).

Hung over SE Marine Drive in 2002, it is, however, a concentration in a single word of what Susan Sontag refers to as 'the historic Western confusion about the relation between art and morality, the aesthetic and the ethical' (Sontag 1983, 143). Hilder's paragrammatic banner

Fig. 3 Ken Lum, *Monument for East Vancouver* (2010), LED lights, 18.2 m. (Photograph courtesy of visual artist Sabine Bitter)

Fig. 4 Lorna Brown and Clint Burnham (curators), *Digital Natives* (2011b), electronic billboard. (Photograph courtesy of Lorna Brown and Barbara Cole)

succinctly deconstructs the binary that has plagued much discussion of art. As Sontag puts it:

> [T]he problem of art versus morality is a pseudo-problem. The distinction itself is a trap; its continued plausibility rests on not putting the ethical into question, but only the aesthetic. To argue on these grounds at all, seeking to defend the autonomy of the aesthetic [...] is already to grant something that should not be granted – namely that there exist two independent sorts of response, the aesthetic and the ethical, which vie for our loyalty when we experience a work of art. As if during the experience one really had to choose between responsible and humane conduct, on the one hand, and the pleasurable stimulation of consciousness on the other! (Sontag 1983, 144)

Hilder's banner does all of that work in just one word.

GIVE AN F...' (Fig. 6) hung over Highway 17 in 1999 focuses on one of the least prominent elements of grammar, the indefinite

Fig. 5 Jamie Hilder, *AESTHETICS* (2002a), acrylic on canvas, 3.35 × 1.2 m. (Courtesy of the artist)

article. What any driver might expect is, of course, 'A' not 'AN', and the imperative upsets their expectations: just what is the 'F' they are being encouraged to give? In the end, it's impossible not to imagine the source text, the exhortation to be concerned. The banner nudges drivers to read what is apparently not there, a practice that would radically change the way advertising billboards, for example, are interpreted.

Again, in *TO DIE, THAT'S EASY...* (Fig. 7) the implied text is all too visible. Commuters, so it seems, are urged, to quote John Cage, to 'wake up to the very life' they're living (Cage 1973, 12). But as Hilder has pointed out in private correspondence, the piece also refers to the 1926 Mayakovsky poem, 'To Sergei Esenin', which ends: 'In this life, to die is not so difficult, /to make life is considerably more difficult', as well as the Ben Vautier text painting which reads 'Mourir, c'est facile' (Hilder 2012, n.p.).

FREEDOM THROUGH WORK (Fig. 8), hung over Nordel Way in a suburb of Vancouver in 2002, is imbued with disturbing irony. The translation of 'Arbeit Macht Frei', the slogan above the entrance to a

Fig. 6 Jamie Hilder, *GIVE AN F.....* (1999a), acrylic on canvas, 5.5 × 1.8 m. (Courtesy of the artist)

number of Nazi concentration camps, is provocatively redirected to drivers imprisoned in the suburban sprawl of the city.

The following two pieces (Figs. 9, 10), hung in September 1999, present concentrations of homonyms. These clusters of common terms, in the spirit of advertising slogans, appear to offer instantly accessible, immediate messages.

However, the homonyms disturb 'instant reading'. Anaesthetic slogans on billboards or homemade notices with the usual 'I Love You' or 'Happy Birthday' are the standard fare of highways. Such public language seeks to suppress any ambiguity and offers itself as simply part of the landscape, as 'natural' language. These two banners, however, won't keep still long enough for drivers to decipher them, even though every word is seemingly simple enough. Any fantasy that English acts as the transparent lingua franca of communication in the multicultural city is deftly punctured. The final word, when read as 'CONTÉNT', can be read as a satisfying clinch to the 'narrative' of the banner—the process

Fig. 7 Jamie Hilder, *TO DIE, THAT'S EASY...* (2002b), acrylic on canvas, 6.7 × 1.2 m. (Courtesy of the artist)

of reading leads to closure or contentment, a happy ending. Or if read as 'CÓNTENT', the banner seems to parody the idea of an ending at which we finally understand what a text is all about, its meaning, its content. Both interpretations then upset meaning as an arrival at a destination, as a reward for reading. It is impossible to be a passive consumer of these banners: the driver will have to make a choice to read them one way or another. In *The Prison Notebooks*, Gramsci argues it is necessary to '[know] thyself as a product of the historical process to date which has deposited in you an infinity of traces, without leaving an inventory' (Gramsci 1971, 324). In a sense, the choices made by a driver may provoke fleeting recognitions (the readings do after all occur at 100 km/h or so) of these traces. Why would you read 'wound' as a noun instead of the past participle of the verb 'wind', for example? Which forces led you to privilege a particular reading? All of Hilder's banners, in common with much challenging, contemporary writing, seek to slow reading down and wake a reader up, and their situation above highways where speed is celebrated is of course wittily ironic.

Fig. 8 Jamie Hilder, *FREEDOM THROUGH WORK* (2002c), acrylic on canvas, 6.7 × 1.2 m. (Courtesy of the artist)

In 2005, the joint project with Heather Passmore and Anne Lesley Selcer *Banlieusard*, which might be translated as 'suburbanite', was exhibited at the Artspeak Gallery in Vancouver. In wall drawings, Hilder maps his trajectory through the city over the course of a year—the thickness of the line indicating the frequency of a route taken. Such documentation transforms the mundane business of getting from A to B into a long-duration performance piece (Fig. 11).

This remapping of Vancouver gestures towards Guy Debord's psycho-geographic map of Paris in which the city has been cut up into distinct ambient areas, with red arrows marking routes generated by *dérive* or drifting around, which the situationists encouraged, as opposed to habitual, mechanical movements. More specifically, Hilder's drawing references Paul-Henry Chombart de Lauwe's 1952 map of a young woman's movements for a year through the XVIth *arrondissement* of Paris.

Hilder's map, like Chombart de Lauwe's and Debord's maps, reveals a very limited and repetitive use of the city. Guy Debord argues that such maps are 'examples of modern poetry capable of provoking sharp emotional reactions (in this case indignation at the fact that there are people

Fig. 9 Jamie Hilder, *TEAR WIND LEAD READ LIVE BASS* (1999c), acrylic on canvas, 6.7 × 1.2 m. (Courtesy of the artist)

who live like that)' (Debord n.p.). Hilder's re-inscription is likewise an example of 'modern poetry' in Debord's terms in that it too represents a rather banal life of student, worker, artist and consumer, which produces sharp emotional reactions of, as Hilder has it, 'guilt, shame and despondency' (Hilder 2012). These situationist mappings reconfigure the city as text to be interpreted and written, or perhaps more accurately performed and contested. The authoritarian grid is erased by such tactics. Rather than presenting urban *structures*, these maps chart urban life and energy flows. Or maybe *lack* of energy flows, as there is in Hilder's work a deliberate attempt to subvert the classed, raced, gendered glamour of the *dérive*. Indeed Hilder's re-inscription of the situationist tactic is an implicit critique of the call to creative arms. As he put it in a talk about

Fig. 10 Jamie Hilder *DOVE BOW WOUND CLOSE SOW CONTENT* (1999a), acrylic on canvas, 6.7 × 1.2 m. (Courtesy of the artist)

his art, 'I didn't want my work to be an example of how to improve your travels through the city, because the best way to do that is to be rich, and have a lot of free time, and the freedom to be imaginative' (Hilder 2009).

Throughout 2006 Hilder undertook a second year-long performance piece called *Miracle Mile* in which he sought to reach a level of fitness that would allow him to match Roger Bannister's 1954 sub-4-minute mile.[2] The project, which references Tehching Hsieh's *One Year Performance* of 1980–1981 and Eleanor Antin's *Carving: a Traditional Sculpture*,[3] was first exhibited in 2007 at the Charles H. Scott Gallery in Vancouver.

---

[2] Hilder's title refers to the race, dramatized as 'The Miracle Mile,' between the only two men to have run the mile in less than four minutes, Roger Bannister and the Australian John Landy, at the 1954 British Empire and Commonwealth Games in Vancouver.

[3] Hsieh punched a time clock in his New York studio every hour for one year, while Antin documented a 10-pound weight loss over 37 days in 148 black-and-white photographs.

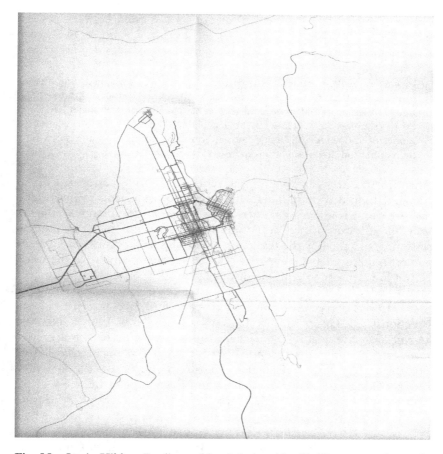

Fig. 11 Jamie Hilder, *Banlieusard* book jacket (detail) (Vancouver, Artspeak, 2005; print.)

It was comprised of extensive photographic, video and text documentation, including a notarized pledge stating that Hilder would make a serious attempt to run a mile in under four minutes. The performance turns Hilder into a type of living public sculpture as he repetitively runs through the streets of Vancouver. The transformation of the body is central to the project, as attested by the daily photographs, though to read this narrative as a lengthy border crossing of geek to jock would obscure the classical Greek understanding of the bond between art and sport. Debra Hawhee in *Bodily Arts: Rhetoric and Athletics in Ancient Greece* argues that:

> In ancient Athens, athletic and rhetorical practices overlapped and nurtured each other in many ways: culturally, they were founded upon joint values of agonism and *aretē*, and they came together in the ancient festival to combine the visible with the articulable. Pedagogically, they shared modes of knowledge production, an attention to timing, and an emphasis on habituation, imitation and response. (Hawhee 2004, 6)

Rhetoric was seen as an art that required *physical* performance and training. Indeed sophists taught in, among other places, gymnasia and *palestrae* or wrestling arenas.[4] Hilder's *Miracle Mile* presents athletics training as performance art. Indeed the discipline of daily training sessions is matched by the discipline of keeping daily records. Both sport and art require feats of endurance. Hilder's documentation *is* a rhetorical act: as inducement to continue it is 'dramatistic'.[5] The video documentation ends with footage of Hilder's attempt to run the sub-4-minute mile. However, everything suggests that the final race against the clock is fictionalized. Hilder runs alone in what appear to be leather spikes on an uneven gravel track, yet manages to just scrape inside the 4-minute mark by 5/100ths of a second. It's *Chariots of Fire* on Balaclava Park, but there is no grand celebratory gesture as he breaks the 4-minute barrier: Hilder just walks off camera and that's it. Did he really do it? The video seems to suggest that such curiosity, such yearning for closure is beyond the point. Devoting himself to the performance for a whole year is surely what matters, not any kind of final achievement. In an interview with Charlotte Higgins, the British artist Richard Long argues that 'A work of art can be a journey' (Higgins 2012, n.p.). Among Long's many walks is the 1030 miles in 33 days from the southernmost to the northernmost point of mainland Britain. Although he walks in the rural or wilderness and Hilder runs in the urban, both are acts of endurance which focus more on the activity and documentation than

---

[4] *Palestra* in Portuguese means 'lecture', highlighting this powerful link between rhetoric and the body.

[5] 'Dramatism' is a term coined by Kenneth Burke to refer to a mode of analysis that focuses on language as action rather than communication.

achieving goals. Both implicitly argue that simply *movement* and its documentation can be a work of art, and raise the question as to whose bodies are allowed to move and what bodies register within both artistic discourse and the urban landscape.

Since 2005, the web-based project www.invisiblevenue.com, independently produced and curated by Christian L. Frock, sidesteps the neoliberal hegemony by offering a space for work situated outside the market-driven, commercial dealer/gallery system. In *(Meant to be) Lost and Found*, a collaboration by Anthony Discenza, Charles Gute, John Herschend and Jamie Hilder with Invisible Venue in 2009, each artist produced a text which appeared to be authentic correspondence. One hundred reproductions of each piece with: 'This is public art. www.invisiblevenue.com' printed on the back were left in various locations in New York and Brooklyn. The modest form seeks to challenge assumptions about the monumentality and funding of public art.

Hilder's instruction leaflet for the performance *Open Source: Instructions for Intervention in Public Space*, published on the website, begins 'Find someone you believe is damaging public dialogue. Try to replace them.' He goes on to explain:

> I do not want to suggest that you attempt to replace somebody by getting them fired, although if it's possible to get people fired from jobs they're performing to the detriment of a wider social sphere don't hesitate on my account. By replacement I mean mimicking or masquerading as: operating alongside but with opposing goals. So if you become a security guard, this would mean providing access to property. If you become a tourist guide, it means offering information that gives some insight into power structures and representation. (Hilder 2011, n.p.)

In 2008, Hilder trained as a Downtown Ambassador for Genesis Security. These red-and-black-clad figures are employed by the Downtown Vancouver Business Improvement Association, whose stated goal is 'to champion a vibrant, healthy and *diverse* downtown so that … Vancouver will be recognized as having North America's #1 *business-friendly downtown* core and be a premier destination for Lower Mainland residents for business, shopping and entertainment' (DVBIA 2010, n.p.; my italics). Speculating on the city's global potential, the DVBIA claim that 'Downtown Vancouver will provide an enriched urban experience that cannot be matched' (DVBIA 2010, n.p.). Downtown Ambassadors exist primarily to 'provide hospitality, help and information'. However, their purview does officially stretch to what the DVBIA refer to as 'crime prevention services' (DVBIA 2010, n.p.). Their mission is to clear the streets of undesirables in a 90-block area, which the DVBIA euphemizes as 'assist[ing] street homeless and other disadvantaged individuals wherever possible'. Indeed, their altruism extends to 'check[ing] on the welfare of street involved people between 50 and 150 times per month. They direct homeless people to resources and shelters and provide snacks. They provide warm clothing in the winter and hydration during hot weather' (DVBIA 2010, n.p.). Despite having debatable legal authority to do so via the Safe Streets Act and the Urban Trespass Act which became enforceable in 2005, Downtown Ambassadors make the lives of the (mostly racialized) homeless and impoverished more difficult by encouraging them to move beyond the range of the tourist gaze. Panhandling or begging within 5 metres of ATM machines and 'squeegeeing' may be punished with fines of up to 115 CAD, and repeat 'offenders' imprisoned. New rules on sleeping in public spaces have been imposed. Apart from such interventions, the very presence of the Downtown Ambassadors implicitly argues that the citizens of Vancouver do not need to help visitors out. Social interaction thus becomes *work* carried out by uniformed personnel. This repositioning of casual social relationships as the business of a service industry takes its place in the neoliberal moulding of identities through language. Visitors to Vancouver are interpellated as customers or consumers of the designer 'diverse' city.

For four days, dressed in a replica of the Downtown Ambassador uniform, Hilder patrolled the streets of downtown Vancouver offering tourists versions of local history which focused on political and economic issues. The performance/public art project *Downtown Ambassador* fills in the gaps left by the commercialized image of Vancouver fed to tourists; however, Hilder is not so much concerned with historical hygiene, but rather with the empowerment of tourists to see beyond the city's spectacularization. In video footage of the project, a tourist approaches and asks 'What do Downtown Ambassadors do?' to which Hilder replies: 'Talk to people, inform them about the city'. The tourist's next enquiry 'Getting ready for the Olympics?' receives an unexpected response: 'The Olympics funding comes at a time when education is being slashed, so we'll look good on TV but we won't be any smarter' (Hilder 2010, n.p.). He was arrested during his performance for 'personation with intent to deceive', after a Downtown Ambassador spotted that his uniform was lacking the Genesis Security badge. Later he wrote an affidavit which included a journal of his training for Pivot Legal Society, United Native Nations and the Vancouver Area Network of Drug Users who filed a Human Rights Tribunal complaint against Genesis and the Downtown Ambassadors.

Another element of Hilder's *Downtown Ambassador* project, published as 'Special Advertising Section' in *Public Art Dialogue*, is a number of full-page faux 'Beautiful B.C.' adverts using photography and text that succinctly point up the distorted histories and dubious politics of the Downtown Ambassadors. A photograph of a uniformed Hilder presiding over an inuksuk that seems to have wandered a bit too far south bears the caption 'Take in our spectacularized aboriginalities' (Fig. 12). He informed tourists that the likewise geographically anomalous totem poles in Stanley Park were erected on land from which local First Nations groups were illegally evicted (Hilder 2010, n.p.).

The ambiguous 'See our hospitality come out in force', and 'Look out' point up the ominousness of all this uniformed, institutional intercourse (Figs. 13, 14). They also highlight the way in which a carefully curated First Nations diversity is mobilized to 'market' the city.

Above the advertising jingle 'A city designed with you in mind' (Fig. 15), Hilder beams a smile for a shot with tourists. It is all so wonderfully coherent: a fake Downtown Ambassador stands on the fake 'ye olde towne' cobbles of Gastown in the vicinity of a steamclock running on electricity, bought in 1977 as a tourist attraction.

In the unannounced performance *After the Fact: Question and Answer*, Hilder again uses the fake/impersonation strategy, this time to mock standard institutional discourse in academic circles. His pretend response after a lecture at the College Art Association's 100th Annual Conference in Los Angeles in 2012 catalogues the conventions in academic Q&A interventions:

> the initial flattery before a criticism; the vocalization of doubt or insecurity in the process of inquiry; the isolation of a peripheral word or phrase within a presentation to shift discussion towards an only slightly related field; the mention of the most popular thinkers or cultural producers of the day as a way to test the presenter's alignment within contemporary discourse; the mention of an obscure thinker or cultural producer as a way to disqualify the presenter's conventional, conservative approach to a topic; and the long, rambling speech that terminates in a banal, vague question or comment, a speech that denotes physical presence more than intellectual engagement. (Hilder 2012, n.p.)

Fig. 12 Jamie Hilder, 'Take in our spectacularized aboriginalities' *Special Advertising Section, Public Art Dialogue* (2011). (Courtesy of the artist)

Fig. 13 Jamie Hilder 'See our hospitality come out in force' *Special Advertising Section, Public Art Dialogue* (2011). (Courtesy of the artist)

Fig. 14 Jamie Hilder, 'Look out' *Special Advertising Section* (2011). (Courtesy of the artist)

Fig. 15 Jamie Hilder, 'A city designed with you in mind' *Special Advertising Section* (2011). (Courtesy of the artist)

This incisive performance might appear to criticize standard institutional discourse, however, as in the above-mentioned public interactions in the guise of Downtown Ambassador, Hilder's interests seem instead to be directed towards examining 'a style of performing knowledge, and of the affective relationship that develops in a crowd of witnesses' (Hilder 2012, n.p.). Hilder's public art politically engages his audience to ask the crucial question 'Who has the power to control the language and movement of citizens in globalized urban spaces and why'?

Works Cited

Brown, Lorna, and Clint Burnham (eds.). 2011a. *Digital Natives*. Vancouver: Other Sights for Artists Projects Association.

———. 2011b. *Digital Natives*, website. http://digitalnatives.othersights.ca/.

Cage, John. 1973 (1961). Experimental Music. In *Silence*, 13–17. Hanover, NH: Wesleyan University Press.

Chombart de Lauwe, Paul-Henry. 1952. Trajets pendant un an d'une jeune fille du XVIe arrondissement. *Paris et l'agglomération parisienne*, vol. 1, 106. Paris: Presses universitaires de France.

Culley, Peter. 2001. Out of the Blue: Three Works on Vancouver. *Border Crossings* 20 (2): 65–70.

Debord, Guy. 1957. *Guide psychogéographique de Paris: Discours sur les passions de l'amour,* lithograph on paper. http://arttattler.com/archiveatlas.html.

Debord, Guy. n.d. Theory of Dérive. *Situationist International Online*. http://www.cddc.vt.edu/sionline/si/theory.html.

Downtown Vancouver Business Improvement Association. 2010. https://www.downtownvancouver.net/.

Gramsci, Antonio. 1971. *The Prison Notebooks: Selections*, trans. and ed. Quintin Hoare and Geoffrey Nowell Smith. New York: International Publishers.

Grant, Reymond T. 2010. Restricting Artists is not an Olympic Ideal: An Open Letter to VANOC. http://www.artsmanagement.net/index.php?module=News&func=display&sid=1218.

Hawhee, Debra. 2004. *Bodily Arts: Rhetoric and Athletics in Ancient Greece*. Austin: University of Texas Press.

Higgins, Charlotte. 2012. Richard Long: 'It was the Swinging 60s. To be Walking Lines in Fields was a Bit Different', *The Guardian Online*, June 15. http://www.guardian.co.uk/artanddesign/2012/jun/15/richard-long-swinging-60s-interview.

Hilder, Jamie. 1999a. *DOVE BOW WOUND CLOSE SOW CONTENT*, acrylic on canvas.

———. 1999b. *GIVE AN F......*, acrylic on canvas.

———. 1999c. *TEAR WIND LEAD READ LIVE BASS*, acrylic on canvas.
———. 2002a. *AESTHETICS*, acrylic on canvas.
———. 2002b. *TO DIE THAT'S EASY...*, acrylic on canvas.
———. 2002c. *FREEDOM THROUGH WORK*, acrylic on canvas.
———. 2005. *Banlieusard*, Vancouver: Artspeak, book jacket (detail).
———. 2009. Unpublished Notes for Talk in "Im/perfect Bodies" Series, University of British Columbia.
———. 2010. *Downtown Ambassador*, video. http://invisiblevenue.typepad.com/invisible_venue/2011/02/special-advertising-section-downtown-ambassador-by-jamie-hilder.html.
———. 2011a. *Open Source: Instructions for Intervention in Public Space*. http://invisiblevenue.typepad.com/invisible_venue/2011/11/open-source-instructions-for-intervention-in-public-space-now.html.
———. 2011b. Special Advertising Section. *Public Art Dialogue* 1 (1): 113–118. http://dx.doi.org/10.1080/21502552.2011.537116.
———. 2012a. *After the Fact: Question and Answer*. Live Performance. http://invisiblevenue.typepad.com/invisible_venue/2012/05/after-the-fact-question-and-answer-by-jamie-hilder.html.
———. 2012b. Private correspondence with the author, 14 June 2012, e-mail.
Lum, Ken. 2010. *Monument for East Vancouver*. http://vancouver.ca/files/cov/public-art-brochure-monument-for-east-vancouver.PDF.
McLeod, Mafanwy. 2010. *The Birds*. http://vancouver.ca/files/cov/public-art-brochure-the-birds.PDF.
Sontag, Susan. 1983 (1982). On Style. In *A Susan Sontag Reader*, 137–155. New York: Vintage.
Terada, Ron. 2010. *The Words Don't Fit the Picture*. http://vancouver.ca/files/cov/public-art-brochure-the-words-dont-fit-the-picture.PDF. Accessed 7 Dec 2016.
Wallace, Ian. 2005. The Frontier of the Avant-Garde. In *Intertidal: Vancouver Art and Artists*, 52–62. Antwerp and Vancouver: Museum van Hedendaagse Kunst and the Morris and Helen Belkin Art Gallery, the University of British Columbia.

A Nation Goes Adrift: Subaltern Inter-Identity in José Saramago's *The Stone Raft*

Maria Sofia Pimentel Biscaia

A strong bias continues to be apparent in conventional studies on the Portuguese imperial past which frequently disregard or are unaware of the complexities which Postcolonial Studies have sought to bring to light. This approach fails to explain cultural, societal and political configurations of both present and past. Though this discourse of imperial pride still reverberates within the walls of major political and academic institutions, there have been artistic and critical attempts to interrogate the construction of the past and consider how it affects national identity today.

José Saramago, winner of the 1998 Nobel Prize for Literature, dedicated much of his life to posing questions about Portuguese identity, to the country's internal controversies, and to producing and circulating in the literary and political markets a conceptualization of the national character which, far from its portrayal in mainstream discourses, appears variously fragmentary, multiple, ambivalent and even weak. Such features are inconsistent with the construction of a glorious nation which was

---

M.S. Pimentel Biscaia (✉)
University of Vigo, Vigo, Spain
e-mail: msbiscaia@ua.pt

© The Author(s) 2017
B. Martín-Lucas and A. Ruthven (eds.), *Narratives of Difference in Globalized Cultures*, New Comparisons in World Literature, DOI 10.1007/978-3-319-62133-3_9

once crowned with an empire. In 1992, the Prime Minister of the right-wing government, Aníbal Cavaco Silva, demanded that Saramago's *The Gospel According to Jesus Christ* be removed from the European Literary Prize shortlist on the grounds of offending the nation's religious character. The affair prompted Saramago's self-exile to Spain, where he died in 2010. Saramago always resented the government's decree, comparing it to a fascist act (Saramago 2005).

In this chapter, I use the example of José Saramago's *The Stone Raft* (1986) to demonstrate the role of literature in the production and marketability/commodification of a given national identity that is not only consumed by its people, but also produced in circulation beyond its borders. I propose that the construction of a national identity is a specific cultural product with various materializations, including literature. Moreover, since there can be more than one producer, several products compete among themselves. In *The Stone Raft* national identity is written considering two distinct markets: the identity produced by official entities to satisfy the local market of imperial sympathy; and the external market represented by the British, Europe and the world at large which seek to construct a subalternized Portuguese identity.[1] Saramago sets out to organize creative resistance to both and to expose the complex hybrid identity that has always been part of Portugal's character by strengthening cultural associations with Spain. Interestingly, his work earned him the recognition of his genius in the global literary market and the hostility of official domestic bodies.[2] In this novel, as generally in his work, Saramago

---

[1] The use of the raft as a metaphor for a nation sailing in turbulent waters has been popular in contemporary art. Consider *The Raft of the Medusa* by Hu Jieming (2002), the fabulous *The Raft of G. W. Bush* by Joel Peter Witkin (2006), and *The Raft of the Medusa (100 Mile House)* by Adad Hannah (2009). They obviously draw inspiration from Théodore Géricault's *Le Radeau de la Méduse* (1818-19).

[2] The amount of work being produced on Saramago is astonishing and the Saramago Foundation keeps an updated bibliography on the author on its webpage. However, frequently the material itself can be quite difficult to come by. It is noteworthy as well that despite his global status, the material in English is sparse, especially when compared to the dozens of books written in Portuguese and, even more rarely, in other languages. In recent years Harold Bloom edited *José Saramago* (2004), Adriana de Paula Martins Alves and Mark Sabine edited *In Dialogue with Saramago: Essays in Comparative Literature* (2006) and David G. Frier published *The Novels of José Saramago: Echoes from the Past, Pathways into the. Future* (2007). These works pay little attention to *The Stone Raft* as they are meant to introduce critical material on Saramago to the English-speaking world or due to their comparative purposes.

is committed to producing a discourse of cultural contestation which can be viewed as what Homi Bhabha has called a 'counter-narrative of the nation' which 'evok[es] and eras[es] totalizing boundaries and essentialist identities' (Bhabha 1994, 149). Saramago thus carries out a critical process of dissemination anchored in the idea of split: 'the problem is not simply "selfhood" of the nation as opposed to otherness of other nations. We are confronted with the nation split within itself, articulating the heterogeneity of its population' (Bhabha 1994, 148). The nation thus 'becomes a luminal signifying space that is internally marked by the discourses of minorities, the heterogeneous histories of contending peoples, antagonistic authorities and tense locations of cultural difference' (Bhabha 1994, 148).

The narrativization of a hybrid identity in *The Stone Raft* and the theorization of Portugueseness as inter-identity in the manner elaborated by Boaventura Sousa Santos follow suit with ideas discussed in Globalization and Postcolonial Studies with respect to the metropolis. In European tradition, the metropolis has been regarded as the centre of the empire, with this concept being apposite to the imperial relation. The term is interchangeably used as a reference to both the mother countries and their capital cities, the latter often used as metonyms. In *The Stone Raft*, the focus is on the mother countries, Portugal and Spain, and their conflict with European powers which have continuously tried to subalternize them. In European thought, a binary hierarchy was constructed where the metropolis was placed at the centre and the colonies were located on the periphery. The binarism has been critically deconstructed, for the notional centre cannot be precisely traced and, therefore, the line of demarcation between the centre/metropolis and the colony/periphery is illusionary. I contend that the dismantling of the idea of the metropolis in Saramago's novel in the geological separation of Iberia from Europe demonstrates this quality; theoretically it is discussed by Sousa Santos as Portugal's semi-peripheral status.

The underpinning allegory of *The Stone Raft* is brilliantly simple. The established social, political and economic order is overrun by an inexplicable geological phenomenon: the Iberian Peninsula separates itself from Europe and floats off into the Atlantic. The narrative describes the journey of Iberia, now an island, a stone raft, as well as the journeys made within it, in the style of an Iberian road movie in which the five protagonists try to make sense of the new space and their new individual and collective identities. This is a book of questions: Why did the peninsula break away? Where is it floating to? Who or what forces are pulling it? How are the Iberians affected? In *The Stone Raft* José Saramago transforms Portugal (as well as Spain) into a floating island pulled in different directions, in order to allegorize the various forces which participate in constituting national identity.

The story is developed in a magic realist tone which differs from the Latin American, African and postcolonial varieties in the scarcity of the extraordinary qualities/events as well as of spectacularity and cheerfulness. Each magical manifestation is associated with one of the protagonists: thousands of starlings follow José Anaiço; Pedro Orce (as well as the dog travelling with the group) feels the earth moving; Joaquim Sassa is able to throw a stone farther into the sea than is humanly possible (already alluding to future events and to the peninsula drifting in the ocean); Joana Carda draws a line in the dirt which cannot be erased (a split within the nation); and Maria Guavaira unravels a blue sock with a seemingly endless thread. Only one event—the breaking apart from Europe—is truly stunning, and even that is described sombrely. The three men, the two women and the dog—a recurrent animal in Saramago's novels—finally reach the chasm where the Pyrenees were divided:

> [T]hey could hear their hearts beating with fear and uneasiness, their bodies sweating profusely despite the intense cold, asking themselves whether they would be brave enough to reach the edge of the abyss, but none of them wished to appear cowardly and almost in a trance they found themselves looking out to sea at an altitude of about one thousand eight hundred metres, the escarpment a sheer vertical cut and the sea shimmering below, the tiniest waves in the distance and white spume where the ocean waves thrashed against the mountain as if trying to dislodge it. Pedro Orce cried out, exalted in jubilant grief. The world is coming to an end, he was repeating Joana Carda's words and they all repeated them. My God, happiness exists, said the unknown voice, and perhaps that's all it is, sea, light and vertigo. (Saramago 1994, 234)

For most of the novel, the characters' roaming is conditioned by this abyss, conditioned by a factor *in absentia*, which is why, once the group is established, seeing the abyss becomes their goal: seeing is believing. It is, in fact, more than that: seeing is existing. Roque Lozano's character is introduced to make this point alone: as what is shown on television cannot be trusted, he and his donkey are off to see Europe disappearing in the distance; if the new island sails off too far in the meantime, then Europe has simply never existed, he posits (Saramago 1994, 53 and 243). The sight of the abyss therefore becomes a necessary encounter which is described briefly but where we witness the most extreme reactions from the group. For the most part, the men and women face their new situation with a characteristically magical-realistic banality.[3] Consider when the group learns the newborn island is en route to collision with the Azores: '[i]t will be the greatest catastrophe in history, Perhaps, perhaps not, ... all this would be absurd if it weren't happening, now let's go and eat' (Saramago 1994, 101). Saramago intertwines this magical-realistic element with the quality which has repeatedly been described as a quintessential Portuguese trait: a people of gentle ways (*gente de brandos costumes*). This is a 'peaceful race', it is said (Saramago 1994, 79). Historically, this depiction of the Portuguese was promoted by Salazar's regime as a way to discourage the nation from actively fighting against the 1933–1974 dictatorship. Saramago uses it ironically to suggest instead a tendency by the Portuguese to submissiveness in the face of adversity. At the same time, he depicts the Portuguese as a brave people: '[e]verything arrives in Portugal and we arrive everywhere' (Saramago 1994, 59). Where does the truth lie? How to deal with this intrinsic ambivalence? The underlying queries posed by the novel are therefore attempts at revealing what constitutes the Portuguese identity and what in their turn constitutes Iberian and European identities.

Boaventura Sousa Santos has postulated a highly influential theory of Portuguese identity which I believe is most constructive for a reading of cultural products such as literature.[4] He argues that the Portuguese identity has remained fairly cohesive since the seventeenth century, throughout the colonial period and recently as a member of the European

---

[3]The coalition of the extraordinary with the commonplace has characterized magical realism since its inception and is attested by Franz Roh, Alejo Carpentier and Angel Flores (1925, 1949 and 1955 respectively) along the lines of the mundane, the common and the everyday. For a discussion which uses the approach of the fantastic instead, see Cristiana Sofia Monteiro dos Santos Pires's *O modo fantástico e A Jangada de Pedra de José Saramago* (2006).

[4]This discussion focuses on selected aspects of Boaventura Sousa Santos's theory. For reasons of relevance I do not cover the whole range of his vast and complex argument here.

Union: it is a semi-peripheral country in the capitalist world system. The core features of this condition are described as follows:

> an intermediate economic development and a position of intermediation between the center and the periphery of the world economy; a state which, being both product and producer of that intermediate position, never assumed fully the characteristics of the modern state of the core countries, particularly those consolidated in the liberal state since the mid-nineteenth century; cultural processes and systems of representation that do not adjust well to the typical binarisms of western modernity – such as culture/nature, civilized/uncivilized, modern/traditional – and may therefore be considered originally hybrid, even if ultimately merely different. (Sousa Santos 2002, 9)

Portugal's original hybridity gives rise to several sub-hypotheses which find themselves fictionalized in *The Stone Raft*. First, Portuguese colonialism was semi-peripheral as the country was semi-peripheral to begin with; Sousa Santos describes it as subaltern colonialism (Sousa Santos 2002, 9). Portuguese colonialism was marked both by a deficit of colonization resulting from the country's inability to colonize efficiently and by an excess of colonization: in other words, by a double colonization, as Portuguese colonialism was subject to the influence of colonialisms generated by core countries and, in particular, England. Portugal could be seen, as Sousa Santos says, as England's 'informal colony' (Sousa Santos 2002, 11). The reason for this dependence was that England was able to create a capitalist attachment to Portugal not unlike what it established with its colonies, based on unequal credit deals and old international treaties (Sousa Santos 2002, 11). Second, Portuguese colonialism was not only reflected at an economic level in the colonies; it produced and continues to produce social, political and cultural re-enactments in the heart of Portuguese society, generating what could be termed a form of internal colonialism.

The third sub-hypothesis refers to Portugal's place in the European Union which, as with the colonial experience, reinforces the nation's semi-peripheral condition. The fourth sub-hypothesis is that a borderland zone results in a borderland culture which is dictated by form but lacks content since the state has failed to provide a sense of national homogeneity. Sousa Santos terms Portugal's unique characteristic 'undecidability'. The country's inter-identity means that Portugal is a

Calibanized Prospero in the eyes of fellow colonizing nations—especially the British—and a Prosperized Caliban for the territories it annexed. These sub-hypotheses can be seen at work in Saramago's novel. *The Stone Raft* allegorizes a crisis of national identity, foreign representations of the national character and control over the circulation of that character in domestic as well as external markets which discursively contribute to that representation. The novel fictionalizes these complexities but is in itself also a cultural product of resistance to hegemonic (international, European and national) discourses.

THE PORTUGUESE, THE SPANISH AND THE BRITISH

Sousa Santos correctly argues that Portuguese colonialism need to be considered in the light of its 'specificity' against the 'norm' of British colonialism (2002, 11). Portuguese colonialism is subalternized by British practices and by the hegemonic discourse which Portugal has to use to make representations of itself and of its colonies. Portuguese colonies thus face a double problem of representation. Portuguese colonial specificity is translated into differences of postcolonial conditions. Though postcolonialism has advocated ambiguity between the colonizer and the colonized, Portuguese colonial practice was already ambivalent, interdependent and hybrid; Anglo-Saxon colonial relations, on the contrary, emerged from an acute polarization between colonizer and colonized, between Prospero and Caliban, the Shakespearean characters Sousa Santos uses as his conceptual and discursive hubs (Sousa Santos 2002, 17). A second major difference refers to skin colour and the concept of 'race'. For the British the skin constituted the limit to mimicry whereas the phenomenon of miscegenation in the Portuguese realm, though far from being non-racist as is often claimed, especially by Lusotropicalist advocates, negates mimicry itself. Portuguese colonialism puts forward quite specifically Homi Bhabha's point on mimicry: to mimic is emphatically not to be that subject. Therefore Portugal was already experiencing being colonized and, unlike the stereotype of British imperialism, it feared colonization from its own colonized territories, given its incompetent colonizing practices. In Sousa Santos's words, '[t]he identity of the Portuguese colonizer does not simply include the identity of the colonizer as in turn himself colonized. The Portuguese Prospero is not just a Calibanized Prospero; he is a very Caliban from the viewpoint of the European super-Prosperos' (Sousa Santos 2002, 17).

Portuguese colonialism is therefore marked by the 'stigma of undecidability' (Sousa Santos 2002, 19) which lies at the heart of how Europe, as a political identity, as well as other contemporary imperialistic powers in the novel (Britain, the United States and even the Soviet Union) react to Iberia's sailing off. Portuguese postcolonial analyses must consequently carry historical specificities, taking into consideration the factor of undecidability to construct a 'situated, contextualised colonialism' (Sousa Santos 2002, 20).

Identity, as a mode of representation, is also a mode of domination and a prime goal for Saramago is to act out its complexities. Saramago's thesis in the novel is unquestionably a take on Portugueseness. For Saramago, though, Portugueseness is intrinsically connected to Iberianness. The territorial split creates a profound alteration in the relationships between Portugal and Spain; as the novel puts it, there is a 'revival of fraternity' between the two countries (Saramago 1994, 70). But the land gash also triggers reactions on the part of Europe which emphasize aspects postulated by Sousa Santos: subalternization, calibanization, stigmatization and even racism. Sousa Santos himself compares, though stressing the specificity factor, Portuguese to Spanish colonialism (Sousa Santos 2002, 11, 12 and 26).[5]

The Gibraltar affair in the novel exemplifies British subalternization of other colonialisms. Listening to the news during their voyage, the travellers hear the British Prime Minister referring to Iberia as a peninsula (which the author does throughout as well), a mistake which is humorously received by the Leader of the Opposition who replies that it is an island, 'although by no means as solid as our own, of course' (Saramago 1994, 37). Every member of the House of Commons laughs, united in a common nationalistic interest: British sovereignty over Gibraltar. The Gibraltar affair highlights the literal and metaphorical fracture between Iberia and Europe. A radio reporter describes in a sentimental tone how it affects Spain:

> El Peñon [the cliff] may end up isolated in the middle of the sea, if this should happen there is no point in blaming the British, we are to blame, yes, Spain is to blame for not having known how to recover in good time

---

[5] For further information see a comparative overview of Portuguese and Spanish colonialisms by Claire Taylor (2007, 46–58).

this sacred piece of the fatherland, now it is too late, El Peñon itself is abandoning us. (Saramago 1994, 34)

Iberia's voyage rekindles imperial networks of territorial influence, European battlegrounds where a losing nation still mourns its subalternization to another European country and the victor still relishes its win. 'Her Majesty's government' quickly orders a new fortification to be built on the north side of Gibraltar and suspends discussions on the transfer of sovereignty (Saramago 1994, 34). Spain's rebellious act of floating away gives England the opportunity it has been waiting for to reinstate its hegemony by transforming Gibraltar into a 'proudly isolated [fortress] in the middle of the now widened Atlantic, as a symbol of the enduring power of Albion' (Saramago 1994, 34). Put as simply as José Anaiço did, '[t]here are still no signs of the British Empire coming to an end' (Saramago 1994, 34). To appease the sense of defeat by the British, the Iberians rewrite this historic moment in their hearts in quite a different manner:

> they see Gibraltar [on the television], not simply separated from Spain, but already at a considerable distance, like an island abandoned in the middle of the ocean, transformed, poor thing, into a peak, a sugarloaf, or reef, with its thousand cannons out of action. Even if they should insist on opening new loopholes on the northern side, *perhaps to gratify imperial pride*, they would be throwing their money into the sea, both in the literal and figurative sense. (Saramago 1994, 70–1; my italics)

Of course, becoming an island is what has just happened to Iberia (they are moving, not Gibraltar) but pride, imperial pride, blinds them to this parallel: 'If Gibraltar is not going to be ours, we who have become part of these waters, then why should it go to the English' (Saramago 1994, 67). Clearly, European imperialisms are a thing of the past as much as of the present, a thing as much internal as external. Eduardo Lourenço has referred to this phenomenon as the simulacrum of an eternal mythic present which drives societies to project themselves in time. Some have, at a point in time, been fixed on an archetypical moment of their past history and their future only makes sense by repeating that mythified moment. For Portugal, as for Spain, that was the imperial enterprise of the fifteenth and sixteenth centuries (Lourenço 1998, 21–2).

For the British also, that moment is imperialism, but repeated, even reinstated, quite differently. The aggressive imperial British attitude and the Spanish cockiness are contrasted with the Portuguese approach in the novel:

> And we end up watching the ships, a Portuguese commented, the others took him to mean the ships that would be passing through the new channel, but we Portuguese know perfectly well that the ships to which he was referring are altogether different, they carry a cargo of shadows, longings, frustrations, delusions and deceptions, their holds filled to the brim, Man overboard, they shouted, but no one went to his assistance. (Saramago 1994, 31)

'To watch ships pass by' is a Portuguese expression meaning to miss out on a chance while others take it. As the narrator notes, there is a circumstantial reading, but the idiom recalls the Portuguese trait of inaction. Portuguese 'ships' carry, to use a very apt expression by Margarida Calafate Ribeiro and Ana Paula Ferreira, imperial ghosts, unburied ghosts, longings for past glories and disappointments for their loss (2003). Similarly, Eduardo Lourenço speaks of the Portuguese people as an imaginary and phantasmatic being (Lourenço 1988, 85). Present-day Portuguese national identity is based on an imperial premise which has become this dark cargo. Portugal will not help itself and Europe is certainly not coming to its assistance. Portugal could be compared to that other ghost ship, *The Flying Dutchman*, invoked throughout. Haunted, Portugal is a 'country going adrift' which, like the ship of the seventeenth-century maritime tales, is doomed to sail into eternity (Lourenço 1988, 75). The imagery is repeated towards the end in Galicia where Pedro Orce finds a stone ship, a phantom ship, in a cave which in a single night suffers the erosion of a thousand years, suggesting the time for conquering navigations is over (Saramago 1994, 161).[6] To use Eduardo Lourenço's apt description, Portugal suffers from a feeling of unconscious and

---

[6] The imagery must be inspired by the legend of the stone ship which carried the body of Saint James to Galicia. After the martyrdom in Jerusalem, Saint James's body sailed for seven days, guided by angels, until it reached Iria Flavia (Padrón, Spain). After 800 long years, the body was miraculously found, starting the legend at the root of Santiago de Compostela as a religious, cultural and touristic centre. I want to thank Belén Martín-Lucas for pointing out this important aspect to me.

intimate fragility (Lourenço 1988, 76). Though he acknowledges the weight the 'vessel-nation' (Lourenço 1998, 18) carries, he nevertheless stresses its exceptionality and that of its passengers:

> To a certain extent, our journey towards the future is a simple one. As a group on the edge of Europe as well as its eccentric centre, we have already been in the Future. Never has such a small sailing-vessel taken so much future time on board, for we sailed once upon a time at the heart of a History that began when we put out to sea. (Lourenço 1998, 26)

Saramago's oscillation between revealing a country both great and small, lethargic and intrepid is therefore the symptom of the 'schizophrenic polarisation' of Portuguese culture (Lourenço 1988, 70).

Apocalypse, Migration, Tourism and the Media: Culture and Identity from the Borderland

In Prospero's imagination, Iberia becomes the realm of Caliban in Europe with matching social, political and cultural re-enactments across the society. First the peninsula suffers a blackout, a symbol of the future ahead: Iberia's invisibility and the end of the world (Saramago 1994, 26). The ensuing reaction is revealing of an expected identity: 'pandemonium was truly peninsular, demons on the loose, cold fear, bedlam' (Saramago 1994, 26). The immediate impact invokes apocalyptic fears:

> It is night, the beginning of night, ... but it soon becomes clear just how much this terror means, this pitch darkness, this ink-stain which has dropped on to Iberia. Do not take away the light, oh Lord, let it return, and I promise you that until my dying day, I shall ask for nothing else ... There were lots of women shouting, lots of men were shaking, as for the children, all one can say is that they were all crying their hearts out. (Saramago 1994, 26)

The rupture and the magical events that follow are presented as a sign of the universe approaching its end (Saramago 1994, 1); significantly, the novel opens with literary elaborations on Cerberus who guards the gates of hell. Iberia seems to be that place; the Greeks have rightly located hell in the region (Saramago 1994, 16). It is even claimed that this has always been hell on earth, the devil's first home: 'his were the hooves that scorched the ground and trampled the ashes, amidst mountains which shivered with fear then and continue to do so to this day, the ultimate desert where even Christ would have allowed Himself to be tempted by the same devil' (Saramago 1994, 61). The crack is then the gaping hole giving entrance to hell (Saramago 1994, 42), a sign of the end of the world approaching. Terrified, tourists flee to airports, train stations and ports. Crowds engage in a 'furious Babel of gestures' (Saramago 1994, 28). The scene created is nearly apocalyptic with hundreds of thousands of people trapped on the floating island, desperate to escape, creating chaotic traffic jams and abandoning their cars anywhere; exploitation systems are quickly installed, stampedes take place, people are crushed, shots are fired. Tourists are helplessly caught 'between the devil and the deep blue sea' (Saramago 1994, 29). These become the first refugees who leave behind empty hotels and apartments (Saramago 1994, 29). Massive migrations take place: to get out of Iberia, to see Gibraltar, to escape the coast when it is on a collision course with the Azores. Soon enough, all Iberians become refugees in their own land. These are not the marks of Prospero; this is Caliban and his lack of command, disorganization and even mayhem: '[t]here were few abandoned cars on the roads, and those they saw invariably had parts missing, having been stripped of their wheels, lamps, rear-view mirrors, windscreens, a door, sometimes all the doors, the seats' (Saramago 1994, 111). The world that emerges from the chaos is plausibly characterized by primitiveness. Due to the shortage of fuel, the travellers encounter 'incongruities': from chaotic, traffic turns thin so they witness carts pulled by donkeys as well as cyclists on the motorway (1994, 111). Eventually their Deux Chevaux ('two horses' Citroën) is also literally replaced by two donkeys, and the group develops a quiet though nomadic routine, travelling during the day, sleeping in the wagon or abandoned houses, cooking under the stars. As Sousa Santos shows, primitiveness is a characteristic long attributed to Portugal by its Northern fellow countries (Sousa Santos 2002, 23). To continental Europe, Iberian nomadization is a sign of their intrinsic instability and, therefore, their bodies embody a political threat which the spontaneous act towards insularity comes to relieve. Their homelessness is unsettling as they clearly do not know where they are heading; they simply travel at an aimless pace (Saramago 1994, 244). Joana poses the question, where is home? (Saramago 1994, 245); and the answer is sought in and by the novel.

If there is a magical-realist element whose magnitude approaches that of the geological rupture, it is the collective pregnancy of Iberian women which provides a second example of threatening bodies. The ex-peninsula achieves a certain degree of stability towards the end of the novel but for one chief difference. Clearly addressing the desertification problem in many 'real' peninsular regions, Saramago imagines an Iberian community where people find new partners because they have been dislocated. This is 'the inevitable outcome of all great wars and migrations' (Saramago 1994, 244). It also recalls the construction of a Portuguese identity which is highly sexualized, even promiscuous. The outbreak of pregnancies awakens repressed fears regarding the Calibanized form of Portuguese identity and its attested tendency to cafrealize the body[7]; hence also the stigmatization of the Portuguese given their miscegenating past, in Africa in particular. In addition, it fictionalizes 'the possibility of an original hybridization, a kind of autophagic self-miscegenation that precedes and makes possible all others' in the eyes of those Europeans who locate Portuguese racial background with the Moors, the Jews and the Africans (Sousa Santos 2002, 20). Homi Bhabha's anti-essentialist hybridity is therefore the source of the stigmatization of the Portuguese at the same time as the novel describes the colonial anxiety of that people, reveals paradigms of cultural imperialism and asserts the interdependent construction of national subjectivities. The paternity of the raft children, as with Joana and Maria, is meaningfully uncertain: maybe the floating land, maybe the sea. The attribution of paternity to the new generation of Iberians remains purposefully ambivalent. Though considerably less menacing than the multitude which step Saleem to death in Salman Rushdie's *Midnight's Children*, this multitude is a characteristic of 'uncivilized', colonized countries and therein lies the reason why it embarrasses its leaders (this fertility is inappropriate before the sterility of the Western world): 'the demographic explosion ... would be evident in the Peninsula nine months hence, twelve or fifteen million children born

---

[7] 'Cafrealisation' is a nineteenth-century term which refers to the social process and stigmatization experienced by Portuguese men that consisted of waiving their status and culture in favour of *cafre* customs. The term is impregnated with offensive nuances as the word *cafre* was meant to invoke black 'savagery' and 'primitiveness'. In Sousa Santos' theoretical terminology, the process is akin to being Calibanized. In postcolonial critical production, a close but not fully identical term is 'going native'. See Sousa Santos for historical textual evidence.

almost at the same hour, crying out in chorus to the light, the Peninsula transformed into maternity' (Saramago 1994, 254).

The main way that this Calibanized identity reaches a global market is the media. The radio and television (remember that if one cannot see something it does not exist) are not the only channels through which, quite literally, Spanish and Portuguese learn where they are in the world, but also who they are: clueless migrants, deterritorialized rioters, refugees in their homeland and uncontrollable procreators: '[j]ournalists only had to catch a woman in the street and they were shoving a microphone into her face and bombarding her with questions, how and when did it happen, what name was she going to give the baby, poor woman, with the camera devouring her alive, she blushed and stammered' (Saramago 1994, 254). The process of creating an identity is shown to be cannibalizing to Caliban himself. Today's economic-media-cultural power, claims Eduardo Lourenço, is so overwhelming that it is comparable to a theocracy without God (Lourenço 1998, 123).

THE EUROPEAN UNION AND THE WORLD

The disruption which causes the peninsula to transform itself into an island is the result of a pre-existing state of isolation. This 'displacement' merely confirms it (Saramago 1994, 31)[8]; Iberia is not part of the *community* of the European Community, whose Commission illuminatingly claims that 'if the Iberian Peninsula wished to go away then let it go, the mistake was to have allowed it to come in' (Saramago 1994, 31). Portuguese and Spanish leaders fail to see the joke and, naturally, mysteriously, Iberia floats further away like 'a ship drawing away from harbour and heading out to an unknown sea once more' (Saramago 1994, 32). They leave Europe and the security it offered as well as the sense of a collective identity which they had borrowed. Notice the novel came out in 1986, when Portugal and Spain became members of what was then the European Economic Community. The EEC advocated homogenizing measures on politics and economics but many wondered whether historic and cultural specificities were to be preserved or crushed

---

[8] Andreia Aparecida Silva Donadon Leal describes this aspect of travelling in *The Stone Raft* as displacement. Insightfully, she draws attention to the dialectic tension between the movable and the immovable, the latter made to move, made to travel, with the displacements of the narrative (2012, 231).

under the weight of this transnational institution. Having always already been in the margins, the Portuguese and the Spanish embark once again on a journey into the unknown, as they had done as the first European imperialistic forces. In other words, the Portuguese and the Spanish are retrieving a past when they were European champions of courage and leadership, and the other European countries followed their lead. On becoming an island, they are also asserting their identity at sea and discarding temporary alliances on land which only emphasized their liminality. At a time when Iberians asked themselves what the peninsular fate would be, Saramago suggests it is away from Europe. Can the ensuing fracture lead to new glories?

The novel displays a feeling of imperial nostalgia and throughout the author offers the reader eulogistic evocations of the past, a place in the national memory where Portugal was greatest and where its spirit was most notable:

> Let's go and see the rock [Gibraltar] as it passes, and they got to their feet, eager for adventure, they don't even feel the scorching heat, like children given their freedom, they run laughing down the slope, Deux Chevaux is like a burning cauldron, within seconds the three men [Pedro, Joaquim and José] are bathed in sweat, but they scarcely take any notice of their discomfort, for from these southern parts, men set out to discover the New World, and they too, rugged and fierce, sweating like pigs, advanced in armour, steel helmets in their heads, sword in hand, to fight the naked Indians, clad only in feathers and war-paint, an idyllic image. (Saramago 1994, 64)

The mocking description of the adventurers is unmissable, as they are portrayed, in a nutshell, as piggish children. Infantilization was, of course, an effective tool of colonial disempowerment. Sarcasm is, in addition, applied to emphasize the 'exotic' perspectives of indigenous peoples. But what is noteworthy is that the Portuguese and the Spanish shared this audacious spirit so that in one go they are brought together and in terms of identity separated from the rest of Europe. 'A nation is nothing other than one big family', and this family of the Portuguese and the Spanish who have been thrown together by common hardships also shares an identity which is symbolically and geographically distant from the European centre (Saramago 1994, 176). The physical break-up is thus a strategy to narrativize cultural difference.

In his article, Sousa Santos claims that Portugal's semi-peripheral condition has not only developed on the basis of the colonial system but also continues to be reproduced in the country's relation with the European Union (Sousa Santos 2002, 9), a relationship that is just as clear, or even more poignantly so, in the current state of economic affairs. Furthermore, the novel cannot be understood without considering what was then viewed as globalization: the Americanization or marketability of the world (Lemos Martins 2008, 59). It is in these contexts that the debate over the Iberian fate unravels. Not surprisingly, the *topos* of fate pervades the novel (Saramago 1994, 2, 11, 29, 30, 109), traditionally seen as an intrinsic constituent of Portugueseness (the national musical genre, *fado*, literally means 'fate'). Relevantly Eduardo Lourenço posits that a 'people is what it is for the sole reason it has a concept of itself as a destiny and nothing else … This conviction confers what we call "identity" on every people and on every culture' (Lourenço 2002b, 109). As Lemos Martins recognizes, Saramago fictionalizes Iberia's fate as a catastrophe (Lemos Martins 2008, 59). He sees in *The Stone Raft* a saturated idea of identity which had been made to converge with a sense of universalism. Saramago offers instead lococentrism and multiple identifications as a form of resistance against the ethnocide of the fetishization of unity (Saramago 1994, 62). Iberism is, therefore, Saramago's proposal, no doubt influenced by his well-known affiliation with communist ideologies. Hence the diverse origins of the characters: Joana from Ereira (Santarém) and Coimbra, José from the northern Portuguese coast, Joaquim from Ribatejo, Maria from Galicia (Northwest Spain), Pedro from Venta Micena (Southern Spain), and even the dog from the Spanish/French border. They travel through Iberia investigating the new cartography based on the re-collocation of the peninsula as its own centre, reinstating Portugal and Spain as metropolises, but as they find one another they come to represent the multiple identities of Iberia which are not reducible to Spanishness and Portugueseness. Iberism is presented as an entity embodying one people, its differences and similarities realizing Saramago's 'metaphoricity of the peoples of imagined communities' (Bhabha 1994, 141). In 1990, Saramago wrote about his belief in Iberism based on the evidence of a relationship between the two states beyond the formal and formatted official dialogues and on the pursuit of the harmonization of common interests, intercultural exchange and intensification of knowledge. More recently, Salman Rushdie has reflected on the permeability of national borders in this age of migration:

'Is the nation a closed system? In this internationalized moment, can any system remain closed? Nationalism is that "revolt against history" which seeks to close what cannot any longer be closed. To fence in what should be frontierless' (Rushdie 2002, 61). This is why, according to Homi Bhabha, our time, the time of migration, is also a time of gathering (Bhabha 1994, 139). A nation is a family, after all.

The idea of Iberian federalism has, however, never been popular in Portugal (or in Spain, for that matter), which throughout its history has been haunted by the ghost of colonial victimization in the form of a Spanish invasion. In "Mi iberismo", Saramago describes how in his formative years he learnt that Spain was Portugal's 'natural' enemy, as it turned a blind eye to a history abounding with invading enemies such as the French and exploiting allies like the English (Saramago 1990). Now as then, the Portuguese still promote that grudge, viewed as a patriotic imperative which aims to consolidate a sense of national identity.[9] The complicity which the Portuguese and the Spanish share in the novel, represented in the romantic relationships between Joana and Joaquim, and Maria and José, could be argued to be an Iberian utopian fate made credible by the magic realist quality of the exceptionality of the circumstances. But the fates of Joana's and Maria's children remain unknown as, in fact, their paternity could be either Portuguese or Spanish. Saramago envisions a dynamic, locally determined future for the Iberians but as to their destinies together, the reader is left to wonder, for the weight of history when it comes to the nations' relationships might be overwhelming.

Several passages highlight the indeterminacy, utopianism and incompleteness of Iberia's future. The novel ends with the travellers being left behind by the dog because the 'journey continues' (Saramago 1994, 263); although Pedro dies because he no longer feels the earth moving, the elm branch on his grave, Joana's branch, is green and hopefully it will bloom the following year (Saramago 1994, 263); when Pedro Orce volunteers to leave the group on account of the embarrassment caused by the dubious paternity, Maria Guavaira replies, reverberating the problematic relationship between individuals of the two countries: 'Don't

---

[9] On the construction of nationhood on the basis of the ambivalent identification love/hate, see Homi Bhabha (1994:149) who, based on Sigmund Freud, uses Spain and Portugal as an illustration.

go ... for if you leave, it's almost certain that we'll all separate, for the men won't be able to stay with us nor we with them, not because we don't love each other, but because we don't understand each other' (Saramago 1994, 229). A similarly ambivalent and utopian example is that of a Spanish television announcer describing Portuguese migration: 'All those Portuguese who were staring at the sea, stared and saw nothing, and we do not want to be like them', but this announcement is precisely what makes Pedro Orce travel with the two Portuguese men (Saramago 1994, 72). Moreover, the same announcer simultaneously denigrates the Portuguese shame for their deficit of colonialism and identifies them with the Spanish: 'Look at the Portuguese, all along their golden beaches, once but no longer the prow of Europe, for *we* have withdrawn from the European quayside to sail once more the Atlantic waves, which admiral will guide us, which port awaits us' (Saramago 1994, 71–2; my italics).

What distinguishes the Portuguese from the others is that 'this race is swarthy' and in the novel, the use of the word 'race' aims to invoke a people's pungency but, and equally important, to emphasize its place as a separate people (Saramago 1994, 71):

> [T]he villages through which the Deux Chevaux passes have that sleepy air which is said to be characteristic of the south, the people here are accused of being indolent by northern tribes, facile and arrogant remarks of racial disparagement made by those who have never had to work with the sun beating down on them. But it is true that there are differences between one world and another, everybody knows that on Mars the inhabitants are green, while here on earth they are every colour except green. (Saramago 1994, 52)

This cultural difference is materialized in a European construction of the southern peoples based on racial and deeply rooted national precepts which Saramago ridicules in favour of ethnic multiplicity, making the comparison with alien beings. But the difference is nevertheless there and the Iberians themselves rejoice in the partition as the passage quoted previously reveals: they are elated to see 'the rock' go (or rather, to stay behind as they sail off).

Sousa Santos indicates 'race' as one of the elements which characterize Portuguese inter-identity; the features used by the Portuguese in this passage to construct a representation of 'savage' and 'primitive' peoples are the same as those used by Northern Europeans to describe the Portuguese: 'underdevelopment and precarious life conditions, sloth and sensuality, violence and affability, poor hygiene and ignorance, superstition and irrationality' (Sousa Santos 2002, 21). Sousa Santos gives an extensive list of records by all sorts of European travellers whose impressions confirm the creation on the part of the European centre of a degraded Portuguese identity. Lord Byron, for instance, reproaches Portugal for its subalternization to the French enemies and the English allies as well as for the people's overall unpleasant appearance and 'uncivilized' behaviour. In Lisbon he sees them as miserable slaves, reared in dirt, unconcerned with cleanliness and the African diseases they have contracted (Sousa Santos 2002, 22). Once, Portugal was even labelled by foreigners as the Realm of Stupidity (Lourenço 2002b, 121).

This is the subjectivity attributed to the Portuguese who once cherished dreams of ruling the world. In *The Stone Raft*, Portugal stands in a place in between, a limbo which reawakens its imperial desires. Accordingly, the ex-peninsula stops moving at the moment when the travellers reach the gaping mouth dividing the Pyrenees, as it stands precisely between America and Europe. Immediately the newspapers offer headlines which translate the strategic position achieved on the political world stage: 'The Birth of a New Atlantis, A Stone Has Moved on the Universal Chessboard, A Link between America and Europe, An Apple of Discord between Europe and America, A Battlefield for the Future' (Saramago 1994, 235). But the most popular was the one that did away with the past ghosts and turned the Iberians into champions of the world once again—'The Need for a New Treaty of Tordesillas'—for indeed the island stopped on the line 'which in those glorious days had divided the world into two parts, one to me, one to you, one to me', though the relationship between the two nations is here suggested to be less than honourable (1994, 235). The countries do not need to imagine themselves in the centre of the world (or rather, their world), as they actually move to that spot. Old metropolitan ambitions are inflamed and proposals emerge to make Portugal and Spain 'a pointer on the scales of world politics' (Saramago 1994, 235). Just as quickly, some parties propose political strategies where one country subdues the other; can Iberism succeed when both nations aspire so ardently to new imperialisms?

Saramago wants the reader to apprehend the irony lying in the condition of a country which was once great, maybe even so great it can never aspire to reach that point again, and which today is ruled by the will of others. The world has new leaders; Portugal, like Spain, is disputed by the great world powers, the Soviet Union (also now extinct) and the United States, demonstrating that the Iberians fail to understand the boundaries of the geopolitical game they had given birth to: globalization. Indeed, as it comes to be acknowledged later on, '[w]e're already travelling on a stone raft. But it's much too big for us to feel like sailors ... How true, nor has travelling through space above the world turned us into astronauts' (Saramago 1994, 248). Others went to space, others rule the world. The time for intrepid sailors seems to be gone; the island is instead inhabited by impoverished refugees. But when the government of national salvation is questioned by the American ambassador Charles Dickens, the Portuguese react rabidly: 'Just because the Ambassador has written *David Copperfield* doesn't entitle him to come and give orders in the land of Camões and *The Lusiads*' (Saramago 1994, 237). Portuguese ignorance is thus comically exposed as is Saramago's sense of humour—and the foundational narrative invoked, the book where all things Portuguese are admired, the peninsula starts to move again. The peninsula rotates on its own axis and halts upside down, completing the representation of a topsy-turvy world (this is one of the few carnivalesque elements), 'two countries with their legs up in the air' (Saramago 1994, 250). It is moving southwards between Latin America and Africa. Portugal stands still in the middle of the watery territory where it was happiest, surrounded by its most beloved former colonies in South America and Africa. But it is also halfway between Europe and the United States, those who moulded late twentieth-century globalization, and they have their views on Iberia. The United States is not willing to 'abdicate its responsibilities to civilization, freedom and peace' and because Portugal and Spain had 'penetrate[ed] contested areas of influence', they will not benefit from 'aid equal to that which awaited them when it seemed likely that their future would become inseparable from that of the American nation ... If they were to become stranded in the Antarctic our worries would be over' (Saramago 1994, 255). Eduardo Lourenço explains that the United States is a cultural superpower as no other before it because its hegemony relies on classic economic factors as well as on the culturization of all related consumer goods through radio, television and civilization itself as a permanent planetary spectacle (Lourenço 1989, 22). All is cultural and nothing is cultural, he adds (Lourenço 1989, 23). The Americanization of culture transforms the latter into an asset meant to produce profit, into an object of appropriation, which has only become possible through multimedia (Lourenço 1989, 22).

Not so different from the United States, Europe had cried anarchy and social chaos when the population took over the hotels following the exodus of the tourists (Saramago 1994, 80) but found such behaviour emblematic of Iberianness: 'whenever they spoke of the ancient Iberian Peninsula, they would shrug their shoulders and say to each other, What can you do, they're like that, you can't change human nature' (Saramago 1994, 80). This mirrors the opinions of some Europeans for whom the Iberian nations destabilized or even endangered a cohesive construction of a European identity. Indeed Europe felt 'shaken from top to bottom by a psychological and social convulsion of nature which seriously endangered its identity, deprived at that decisive moment of its very foundations, of those individual nationalities so laboriously created throughout hundreds of years' (Saramago 1994, 124). Nonetheless, 'Europeans, from top leaders to ordinary citizens, soon became accustomed, one suspects with an unspoken sense of relief, to the lack of any territories to the extreme west' (Saramago 1994, 124). Iberianness is, in fact, undesirable for the European social body which feels entitled to criticize Iberia:

> Although it might not be very polite to say so, for certain Europeans, to see themselves rid of baffling Western nations, now sailing adrift on the ocean, where they should never have gone, was in itself an improvement, the promise of happier times ahead, like with like, we have finally started to know what Europe is, unless there still remain some spurious fragments which will also break away sooner or later. Let us wager that ultimately we shall be reduced to a single nation, the quintessence of the European spirit, simple and perfect sublimation, Europe, that's to say, Switzerland. (1994, 125)

The ironic, even reproachful tone rapidly changes to defence of the Portuguese, their adventurous spirit and even their right to Europeanness:

> However, if there are such Europeans, there are also others. The race of the restless, ferment of the devil, but not so easily extinguished, however much the soothsayers may tire themselves out with prophecies. It is she who watches the train passing and becomes sad with longing for the journey she will never make, it is she who cannot see a bird in the sky without feeling the urge to soar like an eagle, it is she who upon seeing a ship disappear

over the horizon, gives a tremulous sigh from the heart, in her rapture she thought they were so close, only to realize it was because they were so far apart. (1994, 125–126)[10]

But most of all, the Iberians are a bad influence, spreading instability throughout the European continent. Or, at least, that is how it is ironically presented. '*Nous aussi sommes ibériques*', a slogan of solidarity towards Iberians which recalls that other famous phrase by John F. Kennedy, starts to appear on walls all over Europe. It is thought to be vandalistic behaviour by anarchists but, instead, it evokes the French revolutionary spirit, perhaps last witnessed in the 1960s: 'hundreds of thousands, millions of youths throughout the Continent have taken to the streets, armed not with reasons but with clubs, bicycle chains, grappling-irons, knives, awls, scissors, as if driven insane with rage, as well as with frustration and the sorrow of things to come, they are shouting, We too are Iberians' (Saramago 1994, 128).

The Stone Raft reads like a road movie, first on Deux Chevaux, later on two donkeys. It is also in the Portuguese literary tradition of the shipwreck narrative (Blackmore 2002) and travel writing (Ventura Souza 2009; Seixo 1999) as Portugueseness is fictionally invented as a raft floating in the directions the currents take it: Europe, Africa and the American continent. It is a hybrid, nomadic inter-identity, simultaneously a flaw and the cornerstone of Portugal's post-imperial identity, undecidedly a European consciousness reaching out to the European Union as its beacon and stubbornly driven to territories of its imperial past. In *The Stone Raft* José Saramago narrativizes the country's attempt to hold onto its continuously invoked 'glorious' past as first globalizing 'civilizers' which is encumbered by the overwhelming feeling of fragmentation *and* multiplicity. The nation is caught in a whirlwind of complex dependences, particularly of historical and cultural types. The country is born and torn between Atlanticity, Iberianness and Europeanness while marketing itself as a nation with a global mission and as a proud metropolis. Unable to reconcile the past and the present, imperial nostalgia and marginalization by its supposed peers, an external rupture takes place as well. The country cracks away under the pressure of

---

[10] Notice that in the Portuguese text the only subject who sees the ships leaving is clearly female.

conflicting cultural narratives and markets of national discourses which reveal the irony of having once been the prow of Europe but other nations having taken the lead.[11] In 'Mi iberismo', Saramago does not deny a fate to the Portuguese nation which is global but he rejects the imposition of a homogenizing European identity which subalternizes Portuguese specificity, even at the expense of inflating back to life calibanizing preconceptions, perhaps because, as Eduardo Lourenço has alluded to, Portugal has a vocation towards the infinite and wandering (Lourenço 1989). As he also reminds us, the United States are now the producers of *the* hegemonic culture (Lourenço 1989 and 2002a) which obeys a multimedia logic and which transforms culture into a commodified asset (Lourenço 1998, 24). That being the case, it is not just Portugal or Spain which are products of American representational domination. The question one has to pose, therefore, is whether Europe is not being subalternized as well. We must, as Eduardo Lourenço has put it, continue to review, renovate and suspect images and myths which are incarnated in our relationship with the homeland which we were, are and will be (1988, 71). Saramago did just that.

Works Cited

Alves, Adriana de Paula Martins and Sabine, Mark, eds. 2006. *In Dialogue with Saramago: Essays in Comparative Literature*. Manchester: University of Manchester.

Bhabha, Homi. 1994. *The Location of Culture*. London and New York: Routledge.

---

[11] A key discourse and a case in point is that of soccer: for the 2010 World Cup in South Africa, the national team was nicknamed 'the Navigators'. The purpose was to symbolically relive the Portuguese maritime journeys to Africa, a re-experience felt by most as invigorating and only by an unhappy few as uncomfortable. With the victory in the European Championship in France in 2016, the symbolic experience was reinterpreted as a victorious return to Europe, a vindication of Portugal's 'rightful' place among the powerful nations which humiliated Portugal in the past. The team was welcomed back in Lisbon by President Marcelo Rebelo de Sousa. In his tribute to the Navigators, who were given the Order of Commander, the President did not fail to refer to the Portuguese diaspora and the former colonies. Such sporadic and exhilarating triumphs contribute to the irony of successes hiding the aforementioned crack, 'once but not longer the prow of Europe', as economically and politically victory belongs to others (Saramago 1994, 71).

Blackmore, Josiah. 2002. *Manifest Perdition: Shipwreck Narrative and the Disruption of the Empire.* Minnesota: University of Minnesota Press and Camões Institute.

Bloom, Harold. 2004. *José Saramago*, Harold Bloom, ed. 2004. Philadelphia: Chelsea House.

Frier, David G. 2007. *The Novels of José Saramago: Echoes From the Past, Pathways into the Future.* Cardiff: University of Wales Press.

Lourenço, Eduardo. 1989. A cultura na era da mundialização. In *O esplendor do caos*, 13–24. Lisbon: Gradiva.

———. 1992 (1988). *O labirinto da saudade: Psicanálise mítica do destino português.* Lisbon: Dom Quixote.

———. 1998. *We the Future.* Lisbon: Assírio e Alvim.

———. 2002a. Chaos and Splendor. In *Chaos and Splendor & Other Essays*, ed. Carlos Veloso, 25–29. Dartmouth, MA: University of Massachusetts Press.

———. 2002b. Portugal and its Destiny. In *Chaos and Splendor & Other Essays*, ed. Carlos Veloso, 109–171. Dartmouth, MA: University of Massachusetts Press.

Martins, Moisés de Lemos. 2008. A ideia ibérica como recusa da "*reductio ad unum*". A propósito de *A jangada de pedra* de José Saramago. In *Comunicación y desarrollo cultura en la Peninsula Ibérica. Retos de la sociedad de la información. Actas del III Congreso Ibérico de Comunicación*, ed. Francisco Javier Gómez Pérez, Moisés de Lemos Martins and Francisco Sierra Caballero, 57–65. Seville: Universidad de Sevilla.

McLeod, John. 2004. *Postcolonial London: Rewriting the Metropolis.* New York: Routledge.

Pires, Cristiana Sofia Monteiro dos Santos. 2006. *O modo fantástico e* A Jangada de Pedra *de José Saramago.* Porto: Ecopy.

Rushdie, Salman. 2002. *Step across this Line.* London: Vintage.

Saramago, José. 1990. Mi iberismo. Preface in *Sobre el iberismo, y otros escritos de literatura portuguesa*, edited by César Antonio Molina, 5–9. Madrid: Akal.

———. 1994 (1986). *The Stone Raft*, trans. Giovanni Pontiero. London: The Harvill Press.

———. 2005. La religión se alimenta de la muerte. Interview with Miguel Mora, *El País*, 12 November. www.elpais.es/articulo/elpporcul/20051112elpepicul_1/Tes.

Seixo, Maria Alzira. 1999. *Lugares de ficção em José Saramago: O essencial e outros ensaios.* Lisbon: Imprensa Nacional—Casa da Moeda.

Silva Donadon Leal, Andreia Aparecida. 2012. A viagem: estudo comparativo de *Macunaíma* e *A Jangada de Pedra*. *Memento* 3 (1): 230–237.

Sousa Santos, Boaventura. 2002. Between Prospero and Caliban: Colonialism, Postcolonialism and Inter-Identity. *Luso-Brazilian Review* 39 (2): 9–43.

Taylor, Claire. 2007. The Spanish and Portuguese Empires. In *The Routledge Companion to Postcolonial Studies*, ed. John McLeod, 46–58. London and New York: Routledge.

Ventura Souza, Ronaldo. 2009. A Viagem pela Barca de Pedra. *Desassossego* 1: 1–10.

PART III

Disruptive Genders

'Something Terrible Happened': Spectacles of Gendered Violence and Nadine Gordimer's *The House Gun*

Sorcha Gunne

'Something terrible happened' is the opening line of Nadine Gordimer's first post-apartheid novel, *The House Gun* (1998), sounding what in hopeful times was perhaps a somewhat discordant note. 'Something terrible happened' is a refrain that echoes through the novel, but in the opening line it primarily refers to how the quiet, mundane lives of Harald and Claudia Lingard are shattered by the news that their only child, their son Duncan, has been arrested for shooting dead his friend and, it is subsequently revealed, former lover Carl Jespersen. 'Something terrible happened'. A refrain that is, however, equally apposite to the reporting of the real-life events of February 2013 when the world's media was dominated by the headline that Paralympic champion and Olympic athlete Oscar Pistorius had been arrested for shooting dead his girlfriend, model Reeva Steenkamp. The couple's high-profile public personas and their budding romance seemed idyllic, and certainly added to the sensational and salacious nature of the media coverage of the

S. Gunne (✉)
NUI, Galway, Ireland
e-mail: sorcha.gunne@nuigalway.ie

shooting which predominantly focused on Pistorius—his actions leading up to the shooting, his actions after, his arrest, his behaviour in court. In other words, the story told in the media charted his catastrophic downfall from global athletic superstar to being on trial for murdering his girlfriend. Similarly, in Gordimer's novel, it is Duncan's arrest and trial that is the main driver of the narrative. It seems to me that both *The House Gun* and the Steenkamp/Pistorius case are incidents of violence that were ultimately fatal because, at an obvious level, in each case there was a gun that 'happened to be there'. Moreover, though, they evidence how violence is an integral part of the production and circulation of constructions of gender and sexuality in South Africa and worldwide. Obviously, these two incidents—one fictional, the other arguably stranger than fiction—are radically different; nonetheless there are some striking resonances between the two that, following the general trend of using the personal to index the social in Gordimer's writing (Medalie 1999, 634), relate to the broader context of social constructions of class, race and gender that are manifested in the morbid symptoms of economies of violence in post-apartheid South Africa. In September 2014, Pistorius was cleared of the charge of murder, but was instead convicted on a lesser charge of culpable homicide (equivalent to a charge of manslaughter). After serving less than a year in prison, Pistorius was released on house arrest. In December 2015, however, the Supreme Court of Appeal overturned this ruling and found Pistorius guilty of murder. When reading the revised verdict, Judge Eric Leach described Steenkamp's murder as 'a tragedy of Shakespearean proportions' (Allison 2015).[1] Regardless of the charge or the conviction, the shooting constitutes intimate partner violence which is a form of gendered violence.

In a striking coincidence, coinciding with Steenkamp's death, the *Mail and Guardian* newspaper ran a five-part series on rape and gendered violence. The first in the series was an article by Heidi Swart, the Eugene Saldanha Fellow in Social Justice Reporting, which unpacked the links between two other high-profile cases of rape and murder, one in South Africa and one in India. The significance of this

---

[1] This statement was reported by Simon Allison in *The Guardian* on 3 December 2015. In July 2016, Pistorius was sentenced to six years in prison. The prosecutor deemed the sentence 'shockingly lenient' (Burke 2016, online). At the time of writing, appeals are ongoing.

comparative approach is important because it suggests that while historical specificities maintain differences in manifestations, gendered violence nonetheless occurs worldwide. The article begins: 'The two women will never know each other but their names are now inextricably linked—Anene Booysen and Jyoti Singh Pandey' (Swart 2013, online). Swart goes on to highlight that on a variety of levels these two women led very different lives. For example, they come from different geopolitical regions and even different classes: Booysen, who had never finished school, was a 17-year-old cleaner from a small town nearly 200 km from Cape Town; Pandey was a 23-year-old physiotherapy student studying in New Delhi. They are, however, connected in torture and death, as Swart reports: 'each was repeatedly raped by a group of men. Both were disembowelled and both died from the wounds their attackers inflicted on them' (Swart 2013, online). Swart contends that although there was public outcry in South Africa and India, South Africa's response had been relatively 'muted' whereas the intensity of the protests in India were much stronger with Pandey even being 'dubbed "India's daughter"' (Swart 2013, online).[2] Furthermore, at the level of international reporting, Pandey's rape and death was covered in far more detail, whereas Booysen's rape and death received sparse international coverage by comparison.[3] Addressing the relatively muted response to Booysen's case, Swart cites Lisa Vetten, a former senior researcher at Tshwaranang Legal Advocacy Centre, who posits that 'the issue of rape had become commonplace in the media, and that people simply heard about it too often to be shocked' (Swart 2013, online). Vetten speculates that 'sensitised by what happened in India … the media was looking to see how South Africa would respond. But, if India hadn't happened, would people in South Africa have reacted as strongly?' (Swart 2013, online). By posing the question, Vetten is implicitly answering it: the two

---

[2] Identifying Pandey as 'India's daughter' is problematic because it implies that her worth is relative to her value in a patriarchal system of exchange.

[3] This is not to suggest that Booysen's death did not make international headlines—it did. But the case did receive less coverage than Pandey's. Following Beth E. Richie's study (2000), Lisa M. Cuklanz and Sujata Moorti assert that 'recent studies of news coverage of gendered violence including rape and wife battering have repeatedly shown that cases involving victims of color routinely receive less coverage than cases involving white victims, with the possible exception of celebrity cases, in which either the victim or the accused is well known before the violent incident in question' (Cuklanz and Moorti 2009, 12–13).

incidents are more deeply connected because worldwide media attention to one case had an effect on media coverage of the other.

Certainly, there are many more horrific sex attacks and deaths that are not covered by the media, a point echoed by Jean Seaton: 'There are many violent and unnecessary deaths that receive no attention. Only a few become news' (Seaton 2005, 184). What was it about these two cases in particular that brought them to the attention of the media? One could speculate that it was Pandey's position of privilege—specifically as a young middle-class student—that so offended the sensibilities of the media around the world and, as a consequence of ubiquitous reporting, the public. It is also important to register that media coverage in this context is not necessarily an indicator of social justice or a universal drive for equal rights. Reporting cases of gendered violence may momentarily raise awareness, but it does not address the structural causes of gendered violence in the first place, nor does it result in systemic change. This is related to the fact that, as Cuklanz and Moorti point out, media coverage often conforms to gender stereotyping and rape scripts that perpetuate women's victimization and the inevitability of rape. 'The media as the exemplary institutions of democratic societies', they argue, 'reiterated the gender binaries foundational to the Western project of modernity and our understandings of the liberal subject. Consequently, media coverage either highlighted the feminine characteristics of the victims or the violent masculinity of the perpetrators; sexual violence itself was reduced to a biological drive' (Cuklanz and Moorti 2009, 3).

In another *Mail and Guardian* article, titled 'Gender-based violence: Three dead bodies, zero safe space', Jos Dirkx, founder and director of the NGO Girls and Football South Africa, identifies how gendered violence is a structural phenomenon by linking the cases of Booysen and Pandey to that of Reeva Steenkamp.[4] At first glance, Steenkamp's inclusion might appear anomalous because, of course, she was not raped and disembowelled. Nonetheless, Dirkx insightfully perceives all three to be cases of gendered violence that 'shocked' the world. She postulates that: 'These three atrocities have headlined world news over the last two months, yet they are by no means rare or unusual. Violence against women—sexual, physical and often residing in a domestic space—has become so normalised in South Africa and worldwide, that

---

[4] This connection was also made by Adam Haupt (2013) writing in *The Guardian*.

it has taken centuries of abuse topped by three global tragedies for us to speak' (Dirkx 2013, online). Dirkx is, I think, correct in assessing how violence against women has been normalized, but I am not as optimistic as she that these three cases will effect change. The nature of the reporting of the Steenkamp/Pistorius case evidences the contrary: the focus on Oscar Pistorius as the fallen tragic hero reinforces the cult of celebrity and, as Sapa argues, 'shifts attention from gender-based violence' (Sapa 2013, online). In other words, placing Pistorius at the centre of events detracts from the structural nature of gendered violence and what Bourdieu calls masculine sociodicy. In *Masculine Domination* (2001), Bourdieu contends that 'masculine sociodicy *legitimates a relationship of domination by embedding it in a biological nature that is itself a naturalized social construction*' (Bourdieu 2001, 23, italics in the original). Sapa quotes Mfanozelwe Shozi, the chairperson of the Commission for Gender Equality:

> The consequence of this style of reporting is to present Ms Steenkamp's death as an unfortunate aberration, rather than as part of a broader pattern of gender-based violence in South Africa [and I would add the world ...] Gender-based violence has reached alarming proportions in our country and such cannot be allowed to go unabated. Women and children are bearing the brunt of our violent society and Ms Steenkamp's death is no exception. (Sapa 2013, online)

Media coverage that always already renders the female as the inevitable victim or posits a celebrity case as exceptional often obscures the structural level at which gendered violence operates. 'Gender violence is commonly defined as violent acts (real or threatened) perpetrated on females because they are female,' explains December Green (1999, 1). She continues: 'Whether gender violence operates as direct physical violence, threat, or intimidation, the intent is to perpetuate hierarchical gender relations. It is manifested in several forms, all serving the same end: the preservation of male control over resources and power' (Green 1999, 2).

Gendered violence is not exceptional. The World Health Organisation reports that gendered violence 'accounts for more death and disability among women aged 15–44 than cancer, malaria, traffic injuries and war combined' (Cuklanz and Moorti 2009, 1). Nor is it a problem confined to India, South Africa and 'Other' places, as proven by a 2013 World Health Organisation study which estimates that globally one in three women will be affected by gendered violence at some stage in their life.[5] Gendered violence does not occur in a vacuum and the pervasiveness of tropes of rape and gendered violence has long been evidenced in popular culture, as Joanna Bourke highlights: 'Western society is deluged by a glossolalia of violence, particularly sexual violence. Nineteenth-century Penny Dreadfuls recounted stories of lust and violence in gruesome detail. Romances lovingly depict their heroines being "ravished" against their will. One in every eight Hollywood movies includes a rape scene … Newspapers increasingly and routinely describe horrific sex attacks' (Bourke 2007, 14).[6] There is a plethora of contemporary newspaper articles, academic studies and even YouTube channels highlighting and contesting how, as a consequence of structurally unequal social relations, gendered violence continues to be ubiquitous.[7] These studies analyze various aspects of gendered violence including: persistent rape myths that blame the victim; the under-reporting of rape to police and lack of successful prosecutions; and rape and HIV/AIDS.[8] Recent history shows, however, that high-profile news cases make little difference at a structural level, as one article by Andisiwe Makinana notes: 'When I

---

[5] Released in June 2013, a World Health Organisation study in partnership with the London School of Hygiene & Tropical Medicine and the South African Medical Research Council revealed that globally 35% of all women will experience either intimate partner or non-partner violence. The study also found that intimate partner violence is the most common type of violence against women, affecting 30% of women worldwide.

[6] There is important work that remains to be done on contemporary manifestations, and the popularity thereof, of gendered symbolic violence in the Bourdieusian sense, for example in recent years the success of E.L. James's *Fifty Shades of Grey*, a novel that not only perpetuates the cult of the virgin myth, but is clearly less about sexuality and more about total domination. Such a critique is, however, outside the scope of this article.

[7] Anita Sarkeesian's (2009) website and YouTube channel 'Feminist Frequency: Conversations with Popular Culture' is an excellent example.

[8] See Pamela Scully's (2009) article on Jacob Zuma's 2006 rape trial. In this article Scully outlines the details of the trial and argues that both the trial and its news coverage 'exposed deep fault lines in South Africa at the juncture of ethnic mobilization and women's rights. Zuma's defence proved so adeptly how mobilization around ethnic solidarity could silence criticisms of women's rights, and how defence of bodily integrity and the right to say no could be an affront to a man's sense of himself' (171). This argument is not unique and is reflective of, for example, Chicano criticisms of Chicana feminism. Similarly, in the literary world, there is a long tradition of a backlash against perceived negative portrayals of masculinity, including accusations of treason against women writers who challenge troubling constructions of masculinity, for example Alice Walker and Edwidge Danticat.

heard about the brutal rape and murder of 17-year-old Anene Booysen last week, I thought, I have heard this before [in the case of Valencia Farmer]. The two cases have many similarities. Both stirred a national debate on rape. Alas, 14 years later, we are still here' (Makinana 2013, online).[9] In resonance with Gordimer's novel: 'Violence is a repetition we don't seem able to break' (Gordimer 1998, 294). These cases of rape and death—and gendered violence, more broadly—in the world's media do not map comfortably or neatly onto Nadine Gordimer's novel *The House Gun*. Nonetheless, it is useful to consider them together because Gordimer's insightful analysis of violence, in this instance grounded in a specifically South African context in *The House Gun*, is both a commentary on the political by telling the personal *and, at the same time*, moves beyond treating gendered violence as simply metaphor or national allegory. Gendered violence must be analyzed as more than just a metaphor if we are to recast rape as a crime committed against the person—a human rights violation. As Bourke asserts: 'Rape is not a metaphor for the ruin of a city or nation ... It is not an environmental disaster ... It is the embodied violation of another person' (Bourke 2007, 6).

In her influential nonfiction work *The Essential Gesture* (1988), Gordimer, drawing on Antonio Gramsci, describes the condition of apartheid South Africa as 'living in the interregnum' where '[h]istorical co-ordinates don't fit any longer; new ones, where they exist, have couplings not to the rulers, but to the ruled ... "The old is dying, and the new cannot be born, in this interregnum there arises a great diversity of morbid symptoms"' (Gordimer 1988, 263). Over her long and distinguished career, Gordimer has been one of South Africa's most astute social commentators. Although she was a prolific critical writer and social activist, as Stephen Clingman notes, it is in the realm of fiction where her work really excels. 'To many she has, through her fiction, become the *interpreter* of South Africa', he comments. 'Inside that tragedy', he continues, 'Gordimer has been a voice of conscience, of moral rigour, and of a clarified hope—the kind of hope that writing of brilliance can bring with it, no matter what kind of social distortions it is forced to survey' (Clingman in Gordimer 1988, 1). Gordimer's invocation of Gramsci in her description of the interregnum is testimony to why she is held in

---

[9] Valencia Farmer, a 14-year-old girl who, in 1999, was gang raped and then stabbed 53 times before her throat was slit and she was left for dead.

such esteem as a social commentator: her ability to depict and assess the inherent contradictions—the morbid symptoms—not only of apartheid, but of what came after. It is no wonder then that following *None to Accompany Me* (1994), her novel of the lead-up to the first democratic elections, her first post-apartheid offering should be a complex and enduring critique of the issues facing the future of South Africa. So much so that, in how it deals with violence at the intersection of race, class, gender and sexuality, *The House Gun* demonstrates a relevance that not only endures but intensifies in the twenty-first century.

The House Gun tells the story of Harald and Claudia Lingard, a middle-class white couple—he's a top-level executive in an insurance company and she's a doctor—whose lives have remained relatively unchanged since the end of apartheid. That is until one night a knock at the door of their townhouse reveals Khulu, a friend of Duncan's, and that 'something terrible happened'. Duncan has been arrested for shooting dead his friend and former lover, Carl Jespersen. He shot him with the gun that communally belonged to the household. Gordimer asserts that this is not a detective novel. In other words, Duncan's innocence or guilt is not at stake. Rather, the point of the story is the trial. As the trial unfolds, Gordimer captures some of the most salient issues facing post-apartheid South Africa—most prominently the interconnectedness of gender, sexuality, race and class with violence. In doing so she registers a critique of what Cuklanz and Moorti call the 'the limited grammar within which violence was portrayed' (Cuklanz and Moorti 2009, 3). Moreover, by drawing on modernist literary strategies, such as shifting narrative perspective and drawing on intertextual allusions to writers such as Dostoevsky, Gordimer suggests that her novel is a commentary on what is specific to South Africa and also to how that relates to an interconnected world system. In its content, the novel reaffirms this worlded context: just before Khulu knocks on the Lingards' door they are watching the news where many terrible events around the world are being depicted.

In contemporary South Africa the dominant imagining of 'rainbow' prioritizes race over sexuality. Critics such as Brenna Munro (2012) and Cheryl Stobie (2007), however, both comment on the numerous depictions of non-normative sexualities in South African writing that coincide with the transition from apartheid to post-apartheid. Munro credits Gordimer with being the first heterosexual writer to embrace the question of fluid sexualities in her fiction (Munro 2012, 173). For her, in Gordimer's writing 'the emphasis on the intersection of whiteness and class … offers a vital critique of the marriage of race and sexuality in post-apartheid South Africa, even as "rainbow" nationalism is brought into fuller imaginative life' (Munro 2012, 196). Stobie is perhaps more critical of Gordimer's depiction of Duncan as both bisexual and a murderer, interpreting this as a problematic and troubling depiction of a sexuality that does not conform to the hetero-normative status quo. Setting aside Stobie's own caveat that 'it might be considered to be stretching a point to suggest that one sexual act implies bisexual behaviour' (Stobie 2007, 69), her article recognizes that 'Gordimer's concern is not with the lived texture of bisexual experience, but its structural and symbolic resonances' (Stobie 2007, 69). Whether or not one agrees with Stobie's assessment, Duncan's bisexuality—or perhaps more accurately, non-heteronormative sexuality—is useful in exploring the morbid symptoms of a post-apartheid interregnum where, despite the end of apartheid, the old is still dying and the new still cannot be born.

In this regard, the novel has also been read as a commentary on the pervasiveness of violence in post-apartheid society as evidenced by the eponymous house gun itself (Medalie 1999). At various points in the novel this critique is unequivocal and is articulated by a range of characters including Harald—who speculates that the culture of violence 'gives licence to a young man to pick up a gun that's to hand and shoot in the head a lover' (Gordimer 1998, 142)—both prosecution and defence counsels and the judge during his ruling. Echoing Harald's earlier musings, the judge, in his summation, highlights the consequences of having a gun to hand:

> the gun *happened to be there*, on the table. If it had not been there, the accused might have abused the deceased verbally, perhaps even punched him in the usual revenge of dishonoured lovers of one kind … But that is the tragedy of our present time, a tragedy repeated daily, nightly, in this city, in our country. Part of the furnishings in homes, carried in pockets along with car keys, even in the school-bags of children, constantly ready to hand in situations which lead to tragedy, the guns *happen to be there*. (Gordimer 1998, 267)

In her article, Stobie draws on Jacklyn Cock's work to contend that 'guns are a crucial signifier of masculinity for both white and black men in South Africa' (Stobie 2007, 68). This symbolism is problematic because it imagines a scenario where to be masculine is to be both protector and perpetrator: 'in general a gun "combines two contradictory images: it is a means of both order and of violence; and paradoxically it is believed to provide protection from violence through the potential threat of violence"' (Stobie 2007, 69). It is the high profile of the gun, that 'happened to be there' and its ambiguity as simultaneously protective and lethal that most overtly suggests a connection with the contemporary case of the shooting dead of Reeva Steenkamp by her partner Oscar Pistorius in 2013.

At the bail hearing in February 2013, Pistorius's defence team revealed that, like Motsami's defence of Duncan in the novel, they would not contest that Pistorius shot Steenkamp. What they did argue, however, is that the circumstances were mitigating. In short, he thought she was a burglar. Writing in *The Guardian,* David Smith reported that 'Pistorius said he was "acutely aware" of violent crimes committed by intruders. He had received death threats in the past and had been a victim of violence and burglary. For that reason he kept a 9 mm Parabellum pistol underneath his bed when he went to sleep at night' (Smith 2013, online). These details were conveyed in the affidavit read out in court by Pistorius's advocate. The remainder of Smith's article went on to outline how Pistorius was 'filled with horror' at the potential intrusion and acted to protect himself and his girlfriend. This line of defence chimes with Duncan's circumstances and the house gun in Gordimer's novel. Duncan, who the previous night had witnessed his girlfriend Natalie and his former lover Carl having sex in the living room, returns to find Carl sitting on the same sofa. Carl plays down the incident, calling Duncan '*bra*' in the process. At which point, Duncan picks up the gun and shoots Carl in the head. Motsami, Duncan's lawyer, builds the case on mitigating circumstances: the house gun that 'happened to be there' and Natalie's promiscuous behaviour that provoked Duncan to an altered state of mind rendering him capable of murder. In both the fictional and real-life cases, the presence of a gun is contextualized by the endemic nature of violence in South Africa: the shootings were not premeditated, but were instead made possible by the presence of a gun. In this formulation, both Pistorius and Duncan are, to some degree, positioned as victims of circumstance. In the novel, equating hi-fi equipment with life, the narrator posits: 'A house gun. If it hadn't been there how could you defend yourself, in this city, against losing your hi-fi equipment, your television set and computer, your watch and rings, against being gagged, raped, knifed. If it hadn't been there the man on the sofa would not be under the ground of the city' (Gordimer 1998, 157).

In *The House Gun* the repeated references to the fact that the gun 'happened to be there' are made in the passive voice which is suggestive of the complex set of factors that contribute to this crime and mitigate Duncan's personal responsibility. Gordimer's narrative comments on how the extremity of violence permeates the everyday; how 'a daily tally of deaths was routine as a weather report' (Gordimer 1998, 49); how Duncan 'like everyone else breathed violence along with cigarette smoke' (Gordimer 1998, 267). In other words, violence, in a very real sense, perpetuates violence. Gordimer, in her assessment, relates the contemporary climate of violence to the violent history of apartheid: 'taxi drivers shot one another in rivalry ... quarrels in discotheques were settled by the final curse-word of guns. State violence under the old, past regime had habituated its victims to it. People had forgotten there was any other way' (Gordimer 1998, 50). Furthermore, towards the end of the novel during the hearing where Duncan is to be sentenced, she explicitly considers the debate between personal responsibility and mitigating circumstances. Presenting topical debates through exchanges between characters is a technique characteristic of Gordimer.[10] In this exchange, neither prosecution nor defence dispute that the climate of violence and the eponymous house gun contributed to the shooting of Carl Jespersen. They do, however, disagree on the degree to which it should be considered a mitigating circumstance. The prosecution argue: 'Yes, the gun was there; the crime of vengeful jealousy with which it was committed is by no means *excused by*, but belongs along with the hijacks, rapes, robberies that arise out of the misuse of freedom by making your own rules' (Gordimer 1998, 270). Conversely, Motsami argues:

> Duncan cannot be brought to account for encouragement of robberies, hijackings and rape so regrettably common in this time of transition from long eras of repression during which state brutality taught violence to our people ... The climate of violence bears some serious responsibility for the act the accused committed, yes; because of this climate, the gun was there. The gun was lying around the living-room, like a house cat; on a table,

---

[10] For example, Gordimer notably uses this technique in *Burger's Daughter* (1979) to discuss the merits and limits of the Black Consciousness movement.

like an ashtray. But the accused bears no responsibility whatever for the *prevalence* of violence. (Gordimer 1998, 271; italics in the original)

As a literary strategy, this technique of debating and presenting both sides of the issue—of raising the questions rather than providing an answer—suggests that although both sides make some valid points, neither is wholly convincing. This, it seems to me, is Gordimer's nuanced approach to registering the complexity of social relations.

The media coverage of Pistorius's trial has been called a media circus by Franny Rabkin (2013). She writes that: 'After an initial brief gasp of collective stunned silence, South Africans have talked of little else than *the death of Oscar Pistorius's girlfriend*, Reeva Steenkamp. We simply can't get enough of the story and our voracious appetite for more, and yet more, gory detail seems only to feed on itself' (online; my italics). The compulsion to cover every aspect of the story is characteristic of contemporary 24-hour news media. Part of the worldwide obsession with the Steenkamp/Pistorius case is the privilege and celebrity of those involved, echoing the point made by Cuklanz and Moorti that '"it could happen to anyone" has meant "it could happen to those in power"' (Cuklanz and Moorti 2009, 12). This resonates with a central dilemma in Gordimer's novel: Claudia and Harald's struggle to come to terms with the intrusion of violence into their sphere of privilege. Both the Lingards struggle to make sense of the incident because they don't belong to the 'criminal classes'—things like this are supposed to happen to other people—but with the intrusion of violence the gap between rich and poor propagated by a neoliberal hierarchy collapses. Their recurring motif, their signature tune if you like, is the idea that their nice safe quotidian life has been shattered by this violent act perpetrated by their son. The violence of apartheid did not affect them. The transition to democracy did not affect them. They built security gates and they adapted, but they did not change. Gordimer's point, it seems to me, is that the Lingards were removed from the atrocities of apartheid and separate from the violence of transition, but they cannot be so any longer. The violence has irrevocably intruded. Duncan's violent act, furthermore, challenges their benign or neutral liberalism: 'many compromises with stereotype attitudes easily rejected in their old safe life were coming about now that the other values of that time had been broken with. Once there has been killing, what else matters?' ... Hamilton responded with zest to the new attitude he sensed in them as if he had been coaxing it all along, ah-hêh, ah-hêh, nice decent white couple from their unworld' (Gordimer 1998, 145). With that one word, 'unworld', the Lingards' safe everyday life where atrocities only happened elsewhere to other people is revealed to have been an illusion. Claudia and Harald's lives, which had not changed significantly since the end of apartheid, have been shattered by the murderous act of their son. Duncan's imprisonment acts as a leveller, drawing Claudia into the same orbit as many of her patients at the clinic, something that was previously unfathomable despite the end of apartheid.

Framing the narrative in terms of Harald and Claudia's experience allows Gordimer to demonstrate that 'violence is the common hell of all who are associated with it' (Gordimer 1998, 143). The narrative point of view, consistent with a modernist style often favoured by Gordimer (Medalie 1999, 635), at times delves into Harald's consciousness and at other times it offers insight into Claudia's thoughts. Occasionally, the two are combined, indicated by the use of 'he/she', or 'it doesn't matter whether the thoughts are Claudia's or Harald's' (Gordimer 1998, 78) and the narrator is not wholly reliable, as evidenced by the speculative 'probable' on their first court visit: 'It is probable that neither of the Lingards had ever been in a court before' (Gordimer 1998, 6). Twice, the narrator asks why Duncan is not in this story that is partly about him. And only twice does the narrative focus offer insight into his consciousness. Thus, Duncan is and is not at the centre of the narrative. By distancing Duncan, Gordimer refuses to afford him the privilege of the fallen tragic hero. This is somewhat complicated because both Claudia and Harald, nonetheless, think about the murder 'in terms of happening *to* the perpetrator, not the victim' (Gordimer 1998, 78). It seems to me that this strategy runs the risk of silencing and erasing the humanity of the murdered or violated person. Far from excluding Carl Jespersen, though, this move resists reducing the murdered to 'mere spectacles of victimization' (Bourke 2007, 7), because, following Bourke, violence, especially gendered violence, should not be explored by focusing on the wounded because this serves to perpetuate the 'blame the victim' myth.[11]

---

[11] Making a similar point in relation to the difficulties of depicting rape and gendered violence in film, even if such depictions aim to challenge the dominant rape script that disempowers women because of the potential for rape narratives to be misappropriated, Jyotika Virdi argues that 'we are caught between a rock and a hard place: the erasure of rape from the narrative bears the marks of a patriarchal discourse of honour and chastity; yet showing rape, some argue, eroticizes it for the male gaze and purveys the victim myth.

'It [is] astounding', writes Bourke, 'how quickly the move is made away from male responsibility to focusing on female responsibility' (Bourke 2007, 47), a move that constitutes a fundamental part of the 'blame the victim' myth. This move from male responsibility to female responsibility is evidenced in Motsami's defence strategy where he attempts to put Natalie on trial, not Duncan. Natalie/Natashya, as she is often referred to in reference to Dostoevsky, is the third character in the love triangle, the other two coordinates being Duncan and Carl, and she is brutally treated by Motsami in his defence of Duncan. Motsami's strategy is to attribute blame to Natalie—her promiscuous behaviour pushed Duncan beyond the edge of reason to a state of mind where he could not be held fully accountable for his actions. Although the narrative holds back Natalie's point of view, other characters, including Motsami and Claudia, depict her as a wily and manipulative sexual predator (Gordimer 1998, 83, 113, 123). Even Duncan himself implicates her: his act of killing was something that was 'made possible by her' (Gordimer 1998, 181). Harald is seemingly repulsed by Motsami's 'patronizing generalization about women' (Gordimer 1998, 73) with regard to Natalie (and women like her in general) and his gesture of collusion that implicates Harald as a co-conspirator. This, however, contradicts Harald's earlier revelation that mirrors Motsami's depiction of Natalie: 'Man, she provoked him beyond endurance, drove him beyond reason, not only that night, with her exhibition, but for over a year or so preceding that night' (Gordimer 1998, 58). Far from reinforcing gender stereotypes, Gordimer draws attention to the systemic inequality of the sexes. By complicating Motsami's, Claudia's and Harald's attitudes to Natalie, Gordimer perceptively pinpoints that problematic social constructions of women and femininity cannot be divorced from problematic social constructions of men and masculinity, the like of which would later be evident in Jacob Zuma's 2006 trial for the rape of Khwezi (Scully 2009).

The Lingards' privilege—their professions, their townhouse, their comfortable lifestyle—Natalie's perceived culpability for Duncan's action and the thinly veiled racism that circulates around Motsami

---

How do we refuse to erase the palpability of rape and negotiate the splintering of the private/public trauma associated with it?' (2006, 266).

are all indicative of the same critique. They create uncomfortable sympathies that expose shallowly buried prejudices towards race, class, sexuality and gender: 'A murder trial, out of the common criminal class, with a privileged son in the professions accused of murder has provided the Sunday papers with a story of a "love triangle" calling up not only readers' concupiscence but also some shallow-buried prejudices' (Gordimer 1998, 182)—a sentiment that clearly resonates with the Steenkamp/Pistorius case. Where Gordimer's novel really excels, though, is in how, in numerous ways, she disrupts the gendered violence script. The expectation with domestic and gendered violence is that the victim will be female: 'Why should it be unexpected that it was a man? Was not that a kind of admittance, already, credence that it could have been done at all? To assume the body would represent a woman, the most common form of the act, *crime passionel* from the sensational pages of the Sunday papers' (Gordimer 1998, 10; italics in the original). By depicting Duncan's sexuality as not strictly heterosexual and the victim as male, *The House Gun* disrupts the hetero-normative script of gender-based violence. Anti-rape activists and academics are correctly weary of positioning women as inevitably rapeable (Cahill 2001), but in this constellation it is unfathomable to Natalie that she could be the victim: '*She* could not have been the one to die. Why not? She doesn't even consider it? Why not?' (Gordimer 1998, 74) muses Motsami. Motsami's words, however, only serve to highlight how Gordimer's text plays on the expectations of domestic and gendered violence as she creates a tension between Natalie's refusal of inevitable victimhood and circulating myths of promiscuity. This, then, is left for Motsami to reconcile with patriarchy in court as he saves Duncan 'at the cost of her. Natalie/Natasya. He has opened her up and exposed her, dissected her womb with a baby in it, held out for all to see her mind and motives and body whose force and contradictions a lover knew only too well' (Gordimer 1998, 243). By initially repositioning Natalie in the schema of gendered violence and then subsequently depicting how Motsami symbolically disembowels her on the stand, Gordimer disrupts the gendered violence script, therefore, emphasizing the sociodicy or structural dynamic of women's victimhood in a patriarchal world system. The implication is that until the under-lying reasons, the root causes, of gendered violence are interrogated, disrupted and deconstructed, we are doomed to repeat the atrocities committed against Valencia Farmer, Khwezi, Anene Booysen, Jyoti Singh Pandey and Reeva Steenkamp.

Atrocities that do not happen only in African or Asian countries, but across the globe including in the Middle East, Europe and the United States, and to a plethora of women whose cases were not, are not, and will never be reported by the world's media or granted justice in the world's courts.[12]

Works Cited

Allsion, Simon. 2015. Oscar Pistorius Guilty of Murder as Court Overturns Previous Conviction. *The Guardian Online,* December 3. https://www.theguardian.com/world/2015/dec/03/oscar-pistorius-conviction-reeva-steenkamp-upgraded-murder.

Bourdieu, Pierre. 2001. *Masculine Domination,* trans. Richard Nice. Stanford: Stanford University Press.

Bourke, Joanna. 2007. *Rape: Sex, Violence, History.* Washington: Shoemaker and Hoard.

Burke, Jason. 2016. Attempt to Appeal Against "Shockingly Lenient" Pistorius Sentence Rejected. *The Guardian Online,* August 26. https://www.theguardian.com/world/2016/aug/26/south-african-prosecutors-attempt-to-appeal-oscar-pistorius-sentence-rejected.

Cahill, Ann J. 2001. *Rethinking Rape.* Ithaca and London: Cornell University Press.

Cuklanz, Lisa M., and Sujata Moorti. 2009. *Local Violence, Global Media: Feminist Analyses of Gendered Representations.* New York: Peter Lang.

Dirkx, Jos. 2013. Gender-based Violence: Three Dead Bodies, Zero Safe Space. *The Mail and Guardian,* February 19. http://mg.co.za/article/2013-02-19-gender-based-violence-three-dead-bodies-zero-safe-space.

Gordimer, Nadine. 1979. *Burger's Daughter.* London: Jonathan Cape.

———. 1988. *The Essential Gesture.* 'Introduction' by Stephen Clingman. London: Jonathan Cape.

———. 1994. *None to Accompany Me.* New York: Farrar, Straus and Giroux.

———. 1998. *The House Gun.* London: Bloomsbury.

---

[12] High-profile cases from other regions include the Norwegian woman who was sentenced to a 16-month jail term for adultery after reporting her own rape in Dubai in 2013; the woman who had fled her own country after being raped in 2014, but who became suicidal when she discovered she was pregnant and was forced to give birth because of Ireland's abortion laws; and the woman who was attacked in 2016 in the United States in what became known as the Stanford rape case, which made international headlines because of the leniency of the sentence handed down to the perpetrator.

Green, December. 1999. *Gender Violence in Africa: African Women's Responses*. Basingstoke and London: Palgrave Macmillan.
Haupt, Adam. 2013. Oscar Pistorius Case: South Africa is a Country at War with its Women. *The Guardian Online*, February 22. http://www.guardian.co.uk/commentisfree/2013/feb/22/oscar-pistorius-south-africa-war-women?INTCMP=SRCH.
Makinana, Andisiwe. 2013. Fight Rape as we Fought Aids. *The Mail and Guardian*, February 15. http://mg.co.za/article/2013-02-15-00-fight-rape-asthe-country-needs-more-than-condemnation-of-rapists-we-fought-aids.
Medalie, David. 1999. "The Context of the Awful Event": Nadine Gordimer's *The House Gun*. *Journal of Southern African Studies* 25 (4): 633–644.
Munro, M. Brenna. 2012. *South Africa and the Dream of Love to Come: Queer Sexuality and the Struggle for Freedom*. Minneapolis: University of Minnesota Press.
Rabkin, Franny. 2013. The Oscar Pistorius Media Circus May Test South Africa's Contempt Laws. *The Guardian Online*, February 19. http://www.guardian.co.uk/commentisfree/2013/feb/19/oscar-pistorius-mediaMedia-south-africa-contempt?INTCMP=SRCH.
Richie, Beth E. 2000. A Black Feminist Reflection on the Antiviolence Movement. *Signs* 25 (4): 1133–1137.
Sapa. 2013. Women Protest Outside Oscar Pistorius Bail Hearing. *The Mail and Guardian*, February 19. http://mg.co.za/article/2013-02-19-women-protest-outside-oscar-pistorius-bail-hearing.
Sarkeesian, Anita. 2009. Feminist Frequency: Conversations with Popular Culture. https://www.youtube.com/user/feministfrequency.
Scully, Pamela. 2009. Media Constructions of Ethnicized Masculinity in South Africa. In *Local Violence, Global Media: Feminist Analyses of Gendered Representations*, ed. Lisa M Cuklanz and Sujata Moorti, 160–180. New York: Peter Lang.
Seaton, Jean. 2005. *Carnage and the Media: The Making and Breaking of News About Violence*. London: Allen Lane.
Smith, David. 2013. Oscar Pistorius: "I Thought Reeva Steenkamp was a Burglar." *The Guardian*, February 19. http://www.guardian.co.uk/sport/2013/feb/19/oscar-pistorius-trial-reeva-steenkamp?INTCMP=SRCH.
Stobie, Cheryl. 2007. Representations of "The Other Side" in Nadine Gordimer's *The House Gun*. *Scrutiny 2* 12 (1): 63–76.
Swart, Heidi. 2013. Will Anene Booysen's Brutal Rape and Murder Shake the Nation into Action? *The Mail and Guardian*, February 15. http://mg.co.za/article/2013-02-15-00-will-anene-booysens-brutal-rape-and-murder-shake-the-nation-into-action.

Virdi, Jyotika. 2006. Reverence, Rape—And then Revenge: Popular Hindi Cinema's "Women's Film." In *Killing Women: The Visual Culture of Gender and Violence*, ed. Annette Burfoot and Susan Lord, 251–272. Waterloo, ON: Wilfrid Laurier University Press.

World Health Organisation. 2013. Global and Regional Estimates of Violence against Women. http://apps.who.int/iris/bitstream/10665/85239/1/9789241564625_eng.pdf.

Alternative Modernities and Othered Masculinities in Mira Nair's *The Namesake*

E. Guillermo Iglesias Díaz

Mira Nair is renowned for re-creating Indian diasporic communities in film, with racial, ethnic and gender issues as key features. She was also one of the first to encounter controversy with this kind of sub-genre: filmmakers dealing with Indian diaspora end up facing harsh criticism for 'selling out' (or even debasing) their home nation and its traditions in market-oriented films intended for the pleasure of Western audiences. As a consequence, the circulation and reception of representations related to the Indian diaspora in the transnational cultural market has been the object of intense analysis in recent decades and, although the approaches are numerous, when gender issues are at stake the focus has generally been on the treatment of women and/or non-hetero-normative sexualities, with little attention paid to male normativities. Hence, this chapter focuses on the circulation of shared fictions about othered masculinities and, in view of Nair's reputation as a feminist filmmaker, on the male characters portrayed in *The Namesake* (Nair 2007).

The film, an adaptation of Jhumpa Lahiri's novel, tells the story of Ashoke and Ashima Ganguli and their experience as immigrants in the

---

E.G. Iglesias Díaz (✉)
International University of La Rioja, Logroño, Spain
e-mail: egid262@gmail.com

USA. While some reviews underscore the anxiety that their American-born son Gogol feels about not fitting in because of his parents' traditional ways (IMDB 2006, online), others such as Roger Ebert (2007, online) or the Rotten Tomatoes website (2006) highlight the fact that the Gangulis had an arranged marriage and must deal with the consequences of leaving their home town Calcutta, namely, the difficulties of adapting to life in New York. In any case, the discourse articulating most plot summaries and reviews of *The Namesake* is that of the Indian family and their struggle to fit into US society, a story of 'upwardly mobile immigrants torn between tradition and modernity as they are absorbed into the American melting pot' (Holden 2007, online). Following this line of argument, it is not surprising that the film has met with some sarcasm from mainstream Indian reviewers who, ironically, point out how, 'after six years of *Monsoon Wedding*, [Nair] asks us to save our heritage because the next Gen that is so accustomed to western influence, finds it too hard to accept the age-old traditions' (Shukla 2006, online).

As stated above, *The Namesake* deals with the life of a West Bengali first-generation immigrant family in the United States. If I insist on the origins of the main characters it is because of the frequent metonymic use of 'Indian' to refer to 'South Asian': we should bear in mind that 'South Asia' is frequently used in the context of a liberal Western discourse which suggests a homogeneous geographical area often represented by an Orientalized version of India, leaving other nations (Sri Lanka, Bangladesh or Bhutan, to name but a few) in a subaltern position, if not completely elided. In addition, many specialists stress the Eurocentric vision of the South Asian diaspora as monolithic and homogeneous, portrayed on most occasions as an enclosed community whose lives are marked by a strict observance of traditions, and represented as hopelessly nostalgic for their homeland, a 'condition of homesickness' (Desai 2004, 31–2) which ultimately provokes the alienation of the diasporic individual: South Asian diasporas are 'transnationalities that are disjointed, heterogeneous, and hybrid rather than stable, unified, or coherent' (Desai 2004, 4). Accordingly, bearing in mind that the family in the film is Hindu from West Bengal, the representation of the male characters in *The Namesake* may or may not share some of the features common to other representations of (diasporic) South Asian men, but in no way should these characters stand for South Asian masculinities in general terms.

As Judith Butler argues, 'gender is not always constituted coherently or consistently in different historical contexts [and] intersects with racial, class, ethnic, sexual, and regional modalities of discursively constituted identities' (Butler 1990, 3). Reina Lewis seems to share the same point of view when she affirms that 'without the recognition that gender, race and subjectivity are complex, plural and contingent, it is difficult to find strategies with which to contest the present naturalization of past power relations' (Lewis 1996, 1). Additionally, when gender issues are under scrutiny the focus has traditionally fallen on women, as if gender studies were a synonym of 'women's studies':

> To study 'gender' is not just to study women, who are marked as gendered by their oppression (traditionally, women are '*the* sex'). To let the study of gender be equivalent to the study of women is to leave men as unmarked by gender and hence normatively human. But the unmarkedness of the superordinate is precisely the mark of their dominance. (Brod 2002, 166)

When analyzing diasporic South Asian films from a gender perspective, attention has usually been drawn to 'women [and] arranged/forced marriages, domestic violence, runaway girls, etc. as an expression of the crises of cultural conflict' (Kalra 2009, 115), while male characters and their depictions have passed relatively unnoticed, leaving them 'as unmarked by gender', with one exception: male characters only occupy a central position in the analysis of South Asian public culture when they are at a far remove from hetero-normative models or behave as strict (often violent) observants of patriarchal values (as was the case in Stephen Frears's *My Beautiful Laundrette* (1985), or in Ayub Khan-Din's *East is East* (1999), respectively).

Taking into account that the main characters in the film are Hindu, in order to unpack South Asian diasporic masculinities we should start by highlighting the radical difference between contemporary understandings of religious affiliations, 'where the "good" non-Muslim is part of the ever popular dynamic of Bollywood and the "bad" Muslim is a "home grown terrorist"' (Kalra 2009, 116). Since the 9/11 attacks in New York, Muslim communities have been criminalized in the media and suffered racist violence in several countries of the so-called 'first world'. Indeed, as recently as February 2017, American President Donald Trump signed an executive order revoking travel visas for nationals from seven predominantly Muslim nations and prohibiting their entrance into the United States based solely on the notion of a 'perceived threat'. Back in India, although Muslims have inhabited the country for several centuries, Hindu nationalist collectives and political parties such as the Bharatiya Janata Party (BJP, one of the two major political parties in India, in power from 1998 to 2004 and again since 2014) continue to impose Hinduism as the only truly Indian identity. However, we need 'a broader historical brush ... which can focus on continuities between colonial subjects and immigrant subjectivities' (Kalra 2009, 115) in order to understand current ethno-religious and racialized hierarchies.

In this sense, although the British might have imagined the Indian nation as 'the domain of passive spirituality juxtaposed against superior and practical Christianity, India did not emerge in this discourse as just romantic and beautiful but also as foreign and barbaric' (Said, quoted in Badruddoja 2008, 184). The British opposed Christianity to 'foreign' and 'barbaric' Muslims who, in the race-relations narrative of Western discourse, are still framed between emasculation and hypermasculinity. According to British classifications, Sikhs were loyal warriors, although childish and irrational, while Hindus were considered effeminate and tame (Basu and Banerjee 2006, 480). Thus, if we are to analyze present-day categorizations,[1] we should turn our attention to the colonization era and the resistance initiated by Indian nationalism: in an effort to emulate European nation-building processes, Indian nationalist ideology assumed as true their weakness and lack of vigour and repudiated the emasculated archetype of the bookish and effeminate individual who was unable to fight for his nation, embracing the modern model of masculinity imported from Eurocentric and enlightened rationale:

> The effete image of Bengalis portrayed by many British colonial officials impinged on the consciousness of Bengali Hindus who from the late nineteenth century engaged in a political project of recovery of physical prowess through a physical culture movement. This project was intimately linked with notions of competing masculinities within the colonial milieu. (Basu and Banerjee 2006, 477)

---

[1] These pervasive categories surface in popular culture; as an example, consider the character Raj (played by Kunal Nayyar) in the television series *The Big Bang Theory*: after several seasons making more or less explicit jokes about his sexual tendencies, in episode 21 of the 6th season he realizes that everyone believes he is homosexual.

According to George L. Mosse (1996), the concept of modern masculinity was introduced in parallel with the ideology of nationalism, and the imperial project, which '[m]odern masculinity helped to determine' (Mosse 1996, 4), set the foundations for the ideals both of nation and masculinity: in opposition to a wide variety of so-called 'depraved' colonial subjects (ranging from the effeminate to the hyper-sexualized, from the ignorant to the uncivilized and savage), the European male, apart from establishing strict gendered divisions between men and women, created an image of himself whose main features, among others, were his willpower, honour, courage, self-control, coherence and rational thinking.

The ideal of a European modern masculinity needed an antithesis, namely, women, racialized men and those with any gender variance or a sexuality that breaks with hetero-normativity. Thus, when nationalisms of resistance took root in colonized territories they adopted, paradoxically, most of the foundations established by the modern nation in Europe, including their male normativities based on physical strength and prowess, and values such as courage, honesty or endurance. Thus, despite having introduced the 'modern man' and hetero-patriarchal normativity in their colonies, the imperial discourse managed to lay 'the burden of sexual and gender oppressions ... at the feet of patriarchal and feudal "traditions"' in India (Desai 2004, 134). Precisely for this reason, more and more specialists claim the necessity of 'queering' the concept of home and, by extension, that of national identities as a way of vindicating the diversity inside the nation, but also in order to establish a distance from (neo)colonial discourse and normativities.

Turning to class issues, there is an assumed division between Indian migration occurring before and after independence: the first wave of migrants took place under the British Empire in the form of indentured labour sent to other colonies wherever this was needed (Africa, the Caribbean). After independence, there were bright young students and/or professionals (like Ashoke Ganguli, the father of the main character in the film) and low-skilled workers. While the first group participated more or less actively in the national project of 'modern' India and represented the pride and joy of the Indian nation-state abroad, the diasporic individuals belonging to the lower classes (both those who had to leave as indentured workers and the unskilled workforce who emigrated after independence) came to question India's future as an economic world power and remind us of the extreme inequalities of the Indian nation-state.

Bakirathi Mani and Latha Varadarajan have analyzed the new relationship between India and its diasporic populations after the neoliberal turn of the Indian government in the late 1980s and early 1990s. Examining the 2003 conference organized by the Indian government in Pravasi Bharatiya Divas, they point out that it was described as 'the largest gathering of the global Indian family' (Mani and Varadarajan 2005, 45), concluding that it shows the importance of diasporas for the Indian nation-state today:

> By rhetorically evoking an unbroken link between 'Mother India' and her 'children abroad,' the conference ... foregrounds the emergence of a newly important group of 'national' subjects: the *pravasi bharatiya*, or 'Indians abroad.' Marking the culmination of a series of neoliberal economic reforms first instituted by the Indian government in 1991 – including proposals for dual citizenship and tax incentives for NRI [Non-Resident Indian] and PIO [Person of Indian Origin] groups – the 2003 Pravasi Bharatiya Divas conference signifies the growing importance of diasporas to the domestic and global ambitions of the postcolonial Indian state. (Mani and Varadarajan 2005, 45–6)

However, not all the 'children abroad' are treated in the same way by 'Mother India': after the 1990s, the term Non-Resident Indian (NRI) became associated exclusively with 'upper-middle to upper-class men who are seen as positioning India in global flows of capital and possibly also participating in local-global politics' (Rajan 2006, 1107–8). This excludes not only low-skilled workers and women, but also third- and fourth-generation immigrants whose forebears had left the Indian subcontinent during the period of colonial occupation (known as People of Indian Origin or PIOs). The Indian state shows a growing interest in establishing strong links with members of the first group, in particular, with 'the American high-tech NRI [who] plays a pivotal role in legitimating a relatively new technocratic development agenda in India ... initiated in the 1980s and codified in the 1990s [that] appeals to the symbolic power of postcolonial technological nationalism with a new emphasis on the meritocratic logic of the global marketplace' (Chakravartty 2000, 5). The attachments of these diasporic individuals to their home nation are multiple, from family ties, to tourism, remittances or investment: whatever form it takes, the Indian nation-state welcomes them. Meanwhile, individuals who belong to the second category must content themselves with occupying a subaltern (even folkloric) position: '[at the meeting in Pravasi Bharatiya Divas] the relationship between descendants of indentured labourers and the modern Indian state was primarily represented in "cultural" rather than economic terms – for example, through the profuse display of Indo-Caribbean music and dance during the evening cultural show' (Mani and Varadarajan 2005, 22).

While PIOs in India have scarcely any political influence, rendering them practically invisible, more and more specialists point out the link between NRIs (in particular, those upper-middle class professionals living in the USA, Canada or Great Britain) and Indian nation-state policies, especially after the political turn initiated by Rajiv Gandhi (called by the media the Ronald Reagan of India) after he became Prime Minister in 1984. In recent decades, one of the most significant priorities of the Indian state has been maintaining the relationship between American NRIs and the Hindu right in order to establish a direct connection between the success of Indian entrepreneurs, Hindu traditional values and essentialist features of the ethno-religious sort. Thus, as Chakravartty has pointed out:

> Indian competence in the Internet economy is associated with the web of interrelations that ties together Indian families across national borders. More common is the argument that Indians have a long history of excelling in abstract thinking useful in writing computer code. This line of reasoning is almost always followed by the assertion that the concept of zero was developed by Indians ... and therefore Indians are naturals for software development. (Chakravartty 2000, 25)

Some specialists suggest there is no such thing as 'racialized masculinity', because the concepts of 'masculinity' and 'race' will always hinge on hegemonic (that is, 'white') definitions. As a consequence, whatever remains outside the norm is liable to be considered deviant or abject. Julia Kristeva's definition of the term seems to fit diasporic bodies like a glove: it is 'not lack of cleanliness or health that causes abjection but what disturbs identity, system, order. What does not respect borders, positions, rules. The in-between, the ambiguous, the composite' (Kristeva 1982, 4). According to Butler and her use of the concept applied to gender(ed) bodies, the 'abject' is that sexual or gender identity which falls outside 'the heterosexual matrix ... that grid of cultural intelligibility through which bodies, genders, and desires are naturalized' (Butler 1990, 151). Virinder S. Kalra applies a similar argument to Muslim men, but I believe we can extrapolate it to other non-white identities when he points out that,

> to talk of [racialized] masculinity or femininity is always to be producing an insurmountable difference away from a normative white stable formation. This provides a theoretical justification for the apparent mutability of [a] discourse that can oscillate between 'dangerous/violent' and 'passive/bookish' without stating the normative masculinity that provides the measure of judgment. (Kalra 2009, 120)

These categories (linked as they are to understandings of 'the modern') were created at a time when the imperial quest was at its peak. Since then, public culture and the never-ending re-telling of (neo)colonial narratives populated with colonial types has perpetuated the discursive categories deeply rooted in our societies. Accordingly, I agree with Paul Gilroy when he asserts that 'the imperial and colonial past continues to shape political life in the overdeveloped-but-no-longer imperial countries' (Gilroy 2004, 2).

Far from affecting Orientalist constructions exclusively, these colonial categorizations have their impact on the communities they attempt to classify due to the 'loop effect' (Warnke 2008, 64), a process which involves individuals interiorizing external (racial, class, gender, national, etc.) identifications as part of who they are, in many cases contributing to their perpetuation. Warnke's 'loop effect' is reminiscent of Stuart Hall's (1990, 226) 'inner expropriation of cultural identity'. Hall, in turn, quotes Franz Fanon when he claims that this expropriation produces 'individuals without an anchor, without horizon, colourless, stateless, rootless – a race of angels' (in Hall 1990, 226). After all, it was the African thinker who, as Derek Hook explains, introduced for the first time the concept of 'internalization' in order to explain 'the process by which external, socio historical reality is assimilated into "internal" and subjective reality' (Hook 101). We will return to these processes of 'identity expropriation' when we come to analyze the main character, Gogol, and how his lack of success in fitting into heterosexual normativity is symptomatic of his (in Homi K. Bhabha's words) liminal position.

The Bengali, Hindu, (upper-) middle-class, heterosexual male characters in *The Namesake* oscillate between colonial and postcolonial shared constructions of South Asian masculinities and, in this sense, Desai points out that diasporic 'cultural production and circulation may present oppositional politics' (Desai 2004, 9), by placing right at the centre of the narrative those who usually occupy a subaltern position. However, that diasporic public culture may at the same time 'traffic in normativities and self-commodification to access production and circulation' (Desai 2004, 9).

In Nair's *The Namesake*, Ashoke Ganguli's masculinity moves between apparently opposing categories: on the one hand, as a professor with a PhD in 'fibre optics' he embodies the ideal NRI, the kind that 'Indian national and regional governments have embraced, enticed and tried to formalize networks with' for the last twenty years (Chakravartty 2000, 4). Very early in the film (0:07:50) he is introduced as one of those bright professionals who find their upward mobility by engaging with transnational flows of technology and means of communication, well-known features of late capitalism going global. In this respect, Ashoke may be considered an example of the alternative modernity Dilip Gaonkar (2001) refers to as a way to dismiss the classic dichotomy of tradition vs. modernity which pervades many of the films with South Asian characters as protagonists. Although gender roles in the Ganguli household are delimited in quite conventional terms and Ashoke is the breadwinner, he is sweet and tender with his wife and children and never shows any kind of intolerant or violent hyper-masculinized behaviour.

At the same time, Ashoke's alternative masculinity resembles in many ways a well-established discursive position[2] in the construction of the colonial male subject: his character may seem too close to the stereotype of the bookish, effeminate Bengali who 'comes to stand for the Indian' (Kalra 2009, 121). As mentioned above, the concept of modern masculinity involves an added complexity in a postcolonial context: if the modernizing male elite intended to break with the colonial order, they had to repudiate 'proper' masculinity roles because 'to be properly modern and masculine is to be subjugated to colonial values' (Menon, qtd. in Bose 2008, 43). Further, the nationalist Bengalis adopted British hegemonic definitions of masculinity as a way to fight back against imperialism and assumed as true the depiction of the Bengalis as effeminate and weak. Within the 'discourse of hegemonic

---

[2] For the difference between 'stereotype' and 'discursive position' see Colin McArthur's *Scotch Reels* (1982, 68).

imperial masculinity, the most potent symbol of the "effeminate, native, other" was the Bengali ... the Bengali babu, or government clerk, as the archetypical effeminate figure constructed in opposition to the hardy, masculine, imperial British ruler' (Basu and Banerjee 2006, 480). This tension between competing masculinity models is still evident in contemporary Indian diasporic flows: 'dominant white Western heteronormativity and South Asian diasporic heteronormativity – properly married, intraracial, intrareligious, bourgeois, and intranational heterosexuality' (Desai 2004, 29) are crucial for the connection between diasporas and the continuance of nationalist projects, both in the diaspora and on the subcontinent (in the case of *The Namesake*, in the USA and India respectively).

Thus, in terms of tradition, Ashoke Ganguli is 'properly' married to Ashima, as their marriage accomplishes each and every prerequisite in Desai's quotation above: Ashoke and Ashima's parents arrange their wedding according to tradition and theirs is an 'intraracial, intrareligious, bourgeois and intranational' heterosexual coupling. They embody the perfect model for an NRI family, with a loving wife who lives by gender and sexual normativities, while the head of the household works as a professor at an American university in such a leading-edge field as fibre optics. The Gangulis fit into the kind of well-off NRI ideal family that 'plays a pivotal role in legitimating a relatively new technocratic development agenda in India [which appeals] to the symbolic power of postcolonial technological nationalism' (Chakravartty 2000, 5).

On the other hand, despite his portrayal as the ideal NRI model, Ashoke Ganguli participates in feminized activities or attitudes according to gendered standards and (neo)colonial discursive positions. For instance, the first time we see him (0:01:20) not only is he reading fiction (a mode of leisure associated with women, like the one sitting by his side, who is reading too), but he also rejects the idea of such a male-related activity as 'travelling around the world'. The setting for the opening sequence is that of a train coach (in Bahktinian parlance, a chronotope for India if there has ever been one) and Ashoke is travelling to visit a relative.[3] A passenger starts a conversation with him and affirms that every young man in India should take the chance to travel abroad.

---

[3] By the end of the film, there will be another scene on a train, this time his son Gogol being the one who travels, although the context, as will be discussed later, is completely different.

His attitude, marked by a gendered sense of adventure and an obvious Westernising drive,[4] contrasts with Ashoke's, who retorts that he has no particular interest in travelling: he'd rather stay home reading a good book. The division of space into gendered categories (public-male / private-female) gained another dimension in Indian nationalist ideology, which established a link between modernity and Westernisation for men (in this case, the passenger on the train) and tradition and home nation for women (hence Ashoke's feminization). In addition, for Ashoke the significance of the act of reading goes far beyond the level of leisure: his life will be saved, literally, by a collection of short stories by Nikolai Gogol (1:02:20); his first-born will bear the name of the Russian author (0:23:35); and, in a metafictional twist, he will tell his son that they all came from Gogol's overcoat (0:39:40). Ashoke has no interest whatsoever in 'discovering the world' or in that common trope of travelling as a narrative and vital process for self-knowledge.

Soon after the opening sequence, we witness the meeting for the arranged marriage with Ashima (0:06:40). Due to length restrictions it is impossible to discuss in depth Ashima's role as the keeper of family values and traditions, but it is significant that the first and last times we see her in the film she is singing Hindu classical music and, in order to impress Ashoke's parents, her parents ask her to recite a poem by one of the most important romantic authors, William Wordsworth ('her best subject is English', they say proudly: 0:08:05)[5]: right from the first moments of the film, Ashima stands for 'Mother India in the late twentieth century', aware of and respectful of her roots and background and, at the same time, portrayed as the modern Indian woman, cultivated (in English, too), with a strong personality, and ready to fly to New York with her husband-to-be. While she seems eager to meet her future husband and is portrayed as a bold young woman (she even dares to try Ashoke's shoes while no one is looking), Ashoke plays the

[4] When he asks Ashoke if he has 'seen much of this world', Ashoke says he's been 'to Delhi once and every year I visit my grandfather in Jamshedpur'. The passenger tells him, laughing, that he is not talking about 'this world' and he adds: 'I mean England, America. I was in England for two years. It was like a dream: sparkling clean streets, nobody spitting on the road' (0:02:05).

[5] For the implications regarding gender constructions of sequences in which a woman carries out some kind of performance inside a film and their endorsement of the subordinate role of women in classic cinematographic representations, see Kaja Silverman (1988, 56–7).

(feminized) role of an extremely shy man, looking down and feeling uncomfortably nervous at the meeting. Later, during the preparations for the wedding, the camera will focus on the elaborate ornamentation of Ahsoke, the groom, all dressed up for the occasion (0:09:25), instead of following, as is the norm in cinematographic portrayal of weddings, how the bride gets dressed.

It is the train accident that almost kills him that gives Ashoke the impulse to leave his country but, paradoxically, not 'home': in spatial terms, the dominant setting in the film is the private space of home, the space which is inexorably linked to women and, in a diasporic context, the place where national identity is 'safe' from foreign contamination:

> Frequently, home is defined in opposition to those spaces marked as public, political, and unsafe. Home is constructed not only as the private (space of the patriarchal family or homogeneous ethnocultural community) but also as a site of consumption and (re)production, of domesticity and familiarity, as a womb of safety and containment. In addition, home is created through the productive and reproductive labor of women. (Desai 2004, 134)

In a diasporic context, home may well be understood as the site for nostalgia or 'homesickness' and the Gangulis are no exception: their social life is mostly within the South Asian community, Ashima speaks regularly with her family, paints elaborate postcards with Indian motifs and scolds their children for answering back and becoming Westernised, understanding the West as 'threatening in terms of contamination and corruption' (Desai 2004, 127).

Most of the action in *The Namesake* takes place at home and Ashoke is never seen at work, men's 'natural place' according to hetero-patriarchal discourse. In this sense, the film can be considered a celebration of 'the private female space, autonomously opposed to the public, male-centric spaces' (Bose 2008, 52), especially if we take into account that whenever there is a reference to Ashoke's job, the images always shift to scenes of desolation. The first time, we see him through the window as Ashima says goodbye from inside the house, with his figure becoming smaller and smaller in freezing cold New York (0:13:56); the only other time we see him in a scene related to his job he has been invited to Cleveland and we see him as he arrives at his rented apartment, with rooms painted all in white and naked walls, projecting feelings of loneliness and emptiness

(1:08:00): indeed, Ashoke never returns from this trip and dies soon after this scene.

If Ashoke fits, at least partially, colonial and postcolonial discursive categories, Gogol Ganguli is a perfect example of what has been recently labelled an ABCD ('American Born but Confused Desi'). The polarity between his pet name, Gogol, and his real name, Nikhil, is 'almost too perfect a metaphor for the experience of growing up as the child of immigrants, having a divided identity, divided loyalties, etc.' (Lahiri 2004, 6), a confrontation between identities at his innermost level which are deeply distressing for Gogol. This is one of the reasons why the label ABCD is understood in some quarters as 'a pathologizing term portray[ing] urban youth of color as part of a maladaptive culture' (Badruddoja 2008, 161), and although Nair affirms in the extras included in the DVD (Nair 2007) that 'the core of this film' (0:03:40) is the fluidity between different individual and collective identities, that fluidity is not to be seen in the film. The difficulties of adapting to life in the USA and the classic 'tradition-versus-modernity' dilemma are foregrounded from the beginning, most especially in the character of Gogol. This character experiences as traumatic the fact that he inhabits that liminal space between worlds, and some authors go even further to suggest that 'the popularity of ... *The Namesake* in the United States is indeed due in part to its participation in the discourse of traditional versus cosmopolitan modernity' (Badruddoja 2008, 180). Gogol's identity conflicts are best represented by his two names, as the film title highlights, and the tribulations begin right at the moment of his birth, when the doctor at the hospital asks the Gangulis the baby's name (0:22:30): they tell him he has no name yet, as his grandmother is coming from India for the ceremony and that is the moment when he will be given a good name. They cannot understand the hurry—'some of my cousins were not named until they were six years old', Ashima says (0:22:45). This is the first occasion in the film in which the Gangulis are portrayed as traditionalists far removed from Western standards of civilization, and it is only at the insistence of the doctor —'in this country', he tells them with unconcerned bureaucratic diligence, 'a baby can't be released from the hospital without a birth certificate' (0:23:00)—that they agree to give their son a pet name, Gogol.

Gogol is how the main character will be addressed by his inner circle and his parents, portrayed as awkwardly traditional and enclosed in their all-Bengali values and relations. Nikhil, on the other hand (or its

Americanized version, Nick), is the one used by those outside his family. In what is probably the most meaningful sequence in this respect, we see Gogol telling his parents about his intention of adopting his real name: 'Gogol is okay on your high school diploma but can you imagine it on your résumé or on your credit card?' he tells his parents in the kitchen (0:50:39). He rejects his pet name, the one he is known by in that gendered space related to femininity and, at the same time, Gogol states he wants to adopt his real name, Nikhil, in order to enter the masculinized public space of labour and global capitalism, where your profession or your credit card (or lack therof) defines who you are. The radical contrast between Gogol and Nikhil is made visually explicit by the editing work: Nair takes us from Gogol sitting in the kitchen with his family to Nikhil signing a cheque at Tiffany's and stepping out into the phallic world of Manhattan skyscrapers. Once Gogol turns into Nikhil he will try to leave behind everything his parents represent to start anew with his white upper-class girlfriend, Maxine, and her family.

Nair's film seems to partake in the discourse of intolerance of interracial relationships in the USA. As several specialists have stated, diasporic individuals in general and artists in particular may either be resistant to (by challenging or questioning dominant understandings of both India and the United States) or complicit with the nation-state by adopting and reaffirming dominant values of their national communities. In this sense, the impossible love affair between Gogol and Maxine will please hegemonic understandings of the nation in both nation-states. There are in the film three sequences which highlight the alleged insurmountable distance between the dominant (white) community and racialized diasporas: the first one is at Maxine's party to celebrate her Masters in Fine Arts (0:52:28),[6] where a sophisticated, middle-aged white lady, unaware of the implicit racism, interrogates Gogol about his 'origins' ('how old were you when you moved to America?' she asks him) and he is obliged to explain he was born in the US, although his interlocutor seems to pay no attention at all.

The second sequence takes place at the Gangulis' (0:57:08), when Gogol introduces Maxine to his parents: despite the fact that he instructs his girlfriend about what she can and cannot do in front of Mr. and Mrs. Ganguli ('no kissing, no holding hands' he says), she ignores him

---

[6] A 'properly' gendered degree for a woman, in the same way that Gogol's job as an architect perfectly suits dominant gender roles.

and behaves 'naturally,' to Ashima's discomfort and Ashoke's surprise: she calls Gogol's parents by their first names, kisses both of them and holds hands with Gogol while having dinner, showing a disrespectful attitude, by the Gangulis' standards, to both her boyfriend and his parents.

The third sequence is the one at Ashoke's funeral: after sometime without having any news from Gogol,[7] she turns up at the Gangulis' where the family is mourning. Maxine is dressed up for the funeral, though only according to Western standards: she does not realize the inappropriateness of caressing Gogol's face; her bare arms; and, of course, the fact that she is wearing black and not white, the colour of mourning in India. All three sequences come to highlight (though in extremely kind terms, it is true) a discourse of miscegenation deeply rooted in hegemonic understandings of both the US and Indian nations.

As was the case with Ashoke, whose identity shifted between colonial and postcolonial discursive positions, Gogol's identity oscillates between two well-established Orientalist constructions. On the one hand, he plays a sexually appealing, attractively racialized young man, although confused about his identity; on the other hand, Gogol cannot escape his mother's influence and wishes to comply with her desires. Once again, the shadow of the effeminate Bengali hovers over the male characters in the film: 'Bengali men were alleged to be too close to their mothers and thus lacking virility because of overindulgence and protection' (Basu 2006, 484). Paradoxical as it may seem, this is a well-established stereotype in Orientalist representations of the male Other and it is this oscillation 'between emasculation and hypermasculinity which configures the ways in which ... South Asian men have come to be viewed, always deviant from the heteronormative white male' (Kalra 2009, 122).

In addition to this stereotypical construction of Gogol, following a popular Indian diasporic saying, he dates a white girl but ends up marrying a Bengali.[8] After having met the not-too-attractive young Moushumi when they were teenagers, they meet again years later following Ashima's insistent advice to date her (1:26:00), truly believing that what his son needs is a good Bengali woman to marry and to form a family. The first thing we see of her when Gogol dates her for

---

[7] Full of remorse as he was for having 'traded' his family for that of his white, upper-class girlfriend with whom he was spending most of his spare time.

[8] For a very similar case see, for instance, Deepa Mehta's *Bollywood/Hollywood*.

the first time is an extreme close-up of her fingers on her legs in fishnet stockings: the reverse shot shows us a mesmerized Gogol looking at the sophisticated, 'exoticized' beauty Moushimi has turned into. Nair alternates extreme close-ups of Moushimi—her lips while smoking, her eyes looking over her glasses, her neck—with Gogol's gaze:[9] while she is the one who leads the dialogue, Gogol is in control of the gaze and, thus, of what we see, and what we see is the embodiment of the femme fatale who will break Gogol's heart when she has an affair with one of her previous partners. Moushumi is portrayed as far more sophisticated than Gogol: she is doing her PhD in French, lived in Paris for some time, and her friends are all equally sophisticated (and white). Their relationship is marked by a reversal of roles: Desai poignantly states that 'nineteenth-century Indian nationalism was not a rejection of the West but rather a way to produce an Indian modernity by using selective understandings of European modernity ... The spiritual, home, and Indian were gendered feminine, and the material, public, and Western as (an unmarked) masculine' (Desai 2004, 133–4). In the case of Gogol and Moushumi, it is the young woman who is closer to modernity according to Eurocentric parameters, while Gogol is some sort of *desi* at her side.

Gogol's condition as an ABCD does not allow him to form a family with either Maxine or with his Bengali girlfriend Moushumi and, in this sense, he fails to meet the requirements of the non-resident Indian male because 'it is not enough to be heterosexual; this desire must lead to successful couplings and fulfil society's expectations' (Rajan 2006, 1109). By the end of the film, we find ourselves where it started, although this time it is Gogol who is on a train. He seems to follow his father's steps, but the trauma behind his need to travel is at his innermost level. He was born in the USA and has tried hard to assimilate and (dis)integrate into that society, becoming an architect and dating a white girl from an upper-class family that would give him the opportunity for upward mobility and (almost) total assimilation into US society. But after his father's death, and out of feelings of guilt, he goes back to his mother and embraces what she represents in terms of ethnic and

---

[9] Silverman has pointed out the difference between the male and female gaze and how classic cinema 'situates the female subject firmly on the side of spectacle, castration, and synchronization, while aligning her male counterpart with the gaze, the phallus, and what exceeds synchronization' (Silverman 1988, 50).

cultural background. I consider especially meaningful the fact that Nair includes a scene which is not in Lahiri's novel and comes to highlight Gogol's turning point: it is the scene in which Gogol shaves his head in mourning for his father's death, a melodramatic moment which will be enhanced, first, when he meets his mother at the airport and she realizes she has her son back by her side again; and later when, at the funeral, Maxine sees Gogol and both of them become aware that their relationship has come to an end.

The last sequence of the film is revealing in the way in which we are taken back to its opening, with Ashima 'back home' again,[10] singing Indian classical songs, closing the circle and evidencing her lack of adaptation to US life, despite having lived there for some thirty years and the fact that she has left her children behind. Some may state it is the natural consequence of the film being a family melodrama, in which according to the rules of the genre, 'woman, and everybody else rebellious, would seem to be restored to their appointed places' (MacKinnon 2004, 31). While some family melodramas depart from oppositional binary classifications (conservative/progressive, conventional/transgressive, affirmative/subversive), this is not the case in *The Namesake*. Far from challenging the hetero-normative patriarchal family model, by the end of the film both Gogol and Ashima yearn and long for one, a yearning neither of them can fulfil. This coincides with 'patriarchy's scopic regime' which, according to Rajan,

> is always already in operation in culture ... Contemporary viewers ... have certain expectations of how masculinities should or could operate in culture and derive pleasure from seeing such constructions either played out or aborted. ... Fantasies of modern masculinities are projected with a certain level of fluidity and patriarchal authority ... works from the base to keep these masculinities from straying so far from the norm as to become unrecognizable. (Rajan 2006, 1102–3)

In conclusion, we may affirm that the 'male Other' in *The Namesake* stands for (post)colonial constructions of South Asian masculinities, and gender relations are defined according to the normativities of both the

---

[10] It is worth considering that, as Desai points out about diasporic individuals in Gurinder Chadha's *Bhaji on the Beach*, 'home is a fiction', it is not home, but 'nostalgia for a home that [she has] not been to in twenty years' (Desai 2004, 139).

USA and India. As Kalra has stated, 'the idea of hegemonic masculinities means that racialized minorities are always produced in a dialogue with the dominant' (Kalra 2009, 119) and he wonders whether it will be 'possible ever to represent masculinity in a normative manner for a negatively racialized or religiously demonized group' (Kalra 2009, 119). In the case of Ashoke, he is portrayed as an almost ideal NRI, a successful professional with a loving wife and two children; at the same time, however, he reminds viewers of the colonial construction of the effeminate, bookish Bengali, and this 'lack' would set him apart from the traditional NRI patriarch. His could be an alternative masculinity model for both his host and home nation, but unfortunately, we are told, there seems to be no room for him in American society and he dies by the middle of the film.

Gogol, on the other hand, is an ABCD as well as an attractive racialized and successful professional, although too attached to his mother to fit white American masculinity canons. These are well-known (post)colonial constructions which still pervade public culture. In this sense, the film seems to have been made to appeal to portions of the audience from both West and East and to a certain extent it succeeds: some of the Western (white) public will reaffirm their (mis)conceptions about the insurmountable distance between themselves and the racialized Other; parts of the public in India may be satisfied when they witness how the protagonists look for shelter in the values and traditions inherited from their forebears. A part of the audience may even enjoy their rejection of American society:

> The deployment of Orientalist categories in contemporary American society by both normative Americans (the white gaze) and South Asian-Americans (the model minority myth) implies an unbridgeable cultural divide based on racial and ethnic structures. The binary categorization is not only between American/South Asian, but also includes masculine/feminine. ... The pressure to be American or South Asian ... is a general strand. (Baddruddoja 2008, 162)

This cultural divide is made even more explicit on the DVD cover (Nair 2007): we see Gogol walking and looking straight at us, addressing us, as if demanding an answer to his identity dilemmas, framed by the Taj Mahal and the Empire State building, highlighting his 'entrapment' between two cultures. Above him, as some sort of ghostly (even traumatic) presence, we see Ashoke and Ashima Ganguli looking serious and concerned, with Ashima's head leaning on Ashoke's shoulder. Significantly, in addition, Ashima is placed on top of the image of the Taj Mahal, while Ashoke's image is above the Empire State Building and, while Ashima's braided hair and earrings remit to her cultural and traditional Indian background, Ashoke is wearing a denim jacket, symbol of (Western) modernity. Finally, the leitmotiv on the front cover reads 'The greatest journeys are the ones that bring you home': if we apply the motto to the film, we find that Ashoke dies (there is no 'home' for his alternative masculinity in this world); Ashima goes back to Calcutta (her rooting in traditional Indian values and her inability to adapt to the 'multicultural' USA make her go and try to satisfy her longing and desires for what once was, but no longer is, 'home'); and last but not least in this heap of topics, Gogol is left on a train in an introspective journey which is where he and others like him are supposed to live forever.

Works Cited

Badruddoja, Roksana. 2008. Queer Spaces, Places, and Gender: The Tropologies of Rupa and Ronica. *Feminist Formations* 20 (2): 156–188.

Basu, Subho, and Sikata Banerjee. 2006. The Quest for Manhood: Masculine Hinduism and Nation in Bengal. *Comparative Studies of South Asia, Africa and the Middle East* 26 (3): 476–490.

Bose, Brinda. 2008. Modernity, Globality, Sexuality, and the City A Reading of Indian Cinema. *The Global South* 2 (1): 35–58.

Brod, Harry. 2002. Studying Masculinities as Superordinate Studies. In *Masculinity Studies and Feminist Theory. New Directions*, ed. Judith Gardiner, 160–175. New York: Columbia University Press.

Butler, Judith. 1990. *Gender Trouble. Feminsim and the Subversion of Identity*. New York: Routledge.

Chakravartty, Paula. 2000. The Emigration of High-Skilled Indian Workers to the United States: Flexible Citizenship and India's Information Economy. Working Paper 19: 1–37, San Diego: The Center for Comparative Immigration Studies CCIS University of California.

Desai, Jigna. 2004. *Beyond Bollywood. The Cultural Politics of South Asian Diasporic Film*. New York and London: Routledge.

Ebert, Roger. 2007. *The Namesake*. Film Review. http://www.rogerebert.com/reviews/the-namesake.

Gaonkar, Dilip Parameshwar. 2001. On Alternative Modernities. In *Alternative Modernities*, ed. Dilip Parameshwar Gaonkar, 1–23. Durham and London: Duke University Press.

Gilroy, Paul. 2004. *After Empire*. Oxford: Routledge.
Hall, Stuart. 1990. Cultural Identity and Diaspora. In *Identity: Community, Culture, Difference*, ed. Jonathan Rutherford, 222–237. London: Lawrence & Wishart.
Holden, Stephen. 2007. Film Review: Modernity and Tradition at a Cultural Crossroads. *The Namesake*. http://www.nytimes.com/2007/03/09/movies/09name.html.
Internet Movie Data Base. 2006. *The Namesake*. http://www.imdb.com/title/tt0433416/.
Kalra, Virinder S. 2009. Between Emasculation and Hypermasculinity: Theorizing British South Asian Masculinities. *South Asian Popular Culture* 7 (2): 113–125.
Kristeva, Julia. 1982. *Powers of Horror. An Essay on Abjection*, trans. Leon S. Roudiez. New York: Columbia University Press.
Lahiri, Jumpa. 2004. A Conversation with Jhumpa Lahiri. In *A Reader's Guide: The Namesake. Jumpa Lahiri*. Houghton Mifflin Company. http://www.houghtonmifflinbooks.com/readers_guides/pdfs/lahiri_namesake.pdf.
Lewis, Reina. 1996. *Gendering Orientalism: Race, Feminity and Representation*. London and New York: Routledge.
MacKinnon, Kenneth. 2004. The Family in Hollywood Melodrama: Actual or Ideal? *Journal of Gender Studies* 13 (1): 29–36.
Mani, Bakirathi, and Latha Varadarajan. 2005. 'The Largest Gathering of the Global Indian Family': Neoliberalism, Nationalism, and Diaspora at Pravasi Bharatiya Diva. *Diaspora: A Journal of Transnational Studies* 14 (1): 45–74.
McArthur, Colin. 1982. *Scotch Reels*. London: British Film Institute.
Mosse, George L. 1996. *The Image of Man: The Creation of Modern Masculinity*. Oxford: Oxford University Press.
Nair, Mira, dir. 2007. *The Namesake*. Twentieth Century Fox Home Entertainment.
Rajan, Gita. 2006. Constructing-Contesting Masculinities: Trends in South Asian Cinema. *Signs: Journal of Women in Culture and Society* 31 (4): 1099–1124.
Rotten Tomatoes. 2006. *The Namesake*. http://www.rottentomatoes.com/m/namesake/.
Shukla, Pankaj. 2006. Mira Nair's Name at Stake. http://www.smashits.com/mira-nair-s-name-at-stake/movie-review-6104.html.
Silverman, Kaja. 1988. *The Acoustic Mirror. The Female Voice in Psychoanalysis and Cinema. Theories of Representation and Difference*. Bloomington and Indianapolis: Indiana University Press.
Warnke, Georgia. 2008. *After Identity: Rethinking Race, Sex and Gender*. Cambridge and New York: Cambridge University Press.

(Un)Veiling Women's Bodies: Transnational Feminisms in Emer Martin's *Baby Zero*

Aida Rosende-Pérez

After the dramatic events of 11 September 2001, the controversial idea of the clash of civilizations developed by the American political scientist Samuel P. Huntington began to pervade and increasingly dominate mainstream Western imagination, and much of Western world politics.[1] Huntington's thesis apparently tries to delineate (and prophesy) the present and future of global politics in the post-Cold War world, predicting that this period will be characterized by a 'cultural conflict' (Huntington 1993, 22) occurring between what he calls 'civilizations' (Huntington 1993, 22)—taking culture and religion as their axes. Huntington theorizes the interactions between these civilizations as inevitably characterized by violence, something he finds 'particularly

---

[1] My use of the term 'Western' is a shortcut that is not meant to imply a particular set of countries located in the geographical West. Instead, I try to connote the cultural dominance of Eurocentric ideologies.

A. Rosende-Pérez (✉)
University of the Balearic Islands, Palma, Spain
e-mail: aida.rosende@uib.es

© The Author(s) 2017
B. Martín-Lucas and A. Ruthven (eds.), *Narratives of Difference in Globalized Cultures*, New Comparisons in World Literature,
DOI 10.1007/978-3-319-62133-3_12

true along the boundaries of the crescent-shaped Islamic bloc of nations' (Huntington 1993, 35), and he goes further to claim that 'Islam has bloody borders' (Huntington 1993, 35). What is made clear in Huntington's thesis is that, although he identifies a variety of civilizations and even sub-civilizations (Huntington 1993, 23), his focus is first and foremost the conflict between 'Islam' and 'the West'. Huntington's idea of the clash of civilizations has experienced an important revival in the European media since the terrorist attacks in Paris and Brussels in 2016, and also in relation to the revived conflict between 'the West'—particularly those countries belonging to the North Atlantic Treaty Organization (NATO)—and the Islamic State militant group (ISIS) in the Middle East.

In her novel *Baby Zero* (2007), Irish writer Emer Martin tackles this complex and vexed issue from a feminist point of view which focuses on the conviction that 'this clash of civilizations is really just a clash of like versus like' (Martin 2008). She has described her novel *Baby Zero* (2007) as a 'book about a family caught between the East and the West. A Western woman in an Eastern body' (Martin 2008, online). With these words, Martin refers to Marguerite, the youngest member of the Fatagagas family, born in a refugee camp in war-torn Orap, an imaginary (though sadly familiar) Middle Eastern state which combines features of the recent history of both Afghanistan and Iran. From there, the novel follows this family to their exile, first in Ireland as refugees, and later on as migrants in the United States.

When adult Marguerite returns to Orap at the beginning of the novel, which actually anticipates the end of the story, she finds herself in a country that, like Taliban Afghanistan, imposes full veiling for women and forbids their presence in the streets if not escorted by a male relative. Soon after arrival, Marguerite's aunt, a former dentist now in charge of the local women's hospital, pushes her to participate in a humanitarian protest against the mistreatment and abandonment of the women in the hospital. Marguerite's reaction to her aunt's call to help her 'countrywomen' (Martin 2007, 17) reveals her view not only of her own identity but of the overall gender politics which intermingle with the geopolitical relations between East and West: 'This [Orap] is not the country I grew up in. My countrywomen are not these black spectres, dying and mad in this filthy, shit-smelling place. I've been in America most of my life. My countrywomen are currently sipping cosmopolitans in bars and showing their belly buttons' (Martin 2007, 17). Marguerite's positioning of herself as part of a 'liberated' Western world as opposed to the 'oppressed'

Orapian women reflects both her dichotomous understanding of both cultures and also the realization that this dichotomy is played out in the covered or uncovered bodies of women. Her words depict a grim cartography of binary oppositions which is where I begin this examination of how transnational feminist politics can resist and redraw this map. To do this, I will concentrate on the symbolic functions of the veils in *Baby Zero* to analyze how the narrative questions hegemonic readings of Eastern veils and their most frequent metonymic association: the uncontested 'oppression of Muslim women' under the yoke of their own tradition.

Contrary to Huntington's focus on difference, Martin concentrates on commonality: '[b]oth cultures have something in common. Namely, the battleground fought over women's bodies' (Martin 2008, online). In this, Martin agrees with numerous feminist critics who have made similar claims in their diverse analyses of women's roles in the structural workings of globalization processes. Among them, and using a similar wording to that of Martin, Rosi Braidotti has argued that '[s]uch a clash of civilizations is postulated and fought out on women's bodies' (Braidotti 2005, 172). Braidotti chooses as a significant example George Bush's appropriation of the language and rhetoric of feminist discourses in his insidious invocation of women's rights with imperialist ends when invading Afghanistan for the sake of 'global justice'.[2] This cooptation and manipulation of feminist concerns is not only a core feature of neoliberalism widely described as a hijacking of feminism but, as Lila Abu-Lughod has pertinently noticed, it has 'haunting resonances' (Abu-Lughod 2013, 33) for anyone with a knowledge of colonial history. Abu-Lughod, as well as many other feminist authors, has resorted to Gayatri Spivak's well-known phrase: 'white men saving brown women from brown men' (Spivak 1988, 297; Abu-Lughod 2013, 33; Ahmed 2011, 222; Kahn 2008, 162; Puar and Rai 2002, 127) to emphasize the continuity of this strategy and to condense its underlying gendered and racist ideology. The period immediately following 9/11, involving the preparation for and then the actual US invasion of Afghanistan, was undoubtedly a key moment in the modelling of the stereotype

---

[2] One need only read/watch the news to see how this discourse prevails in the current confrontation with ISIS and women's participation in this global jihadist movement. These women are repeatedly portrayed as 'brainwashed' victims, 'seduced' and 'tricked' by 'their' men to act against 'their own interests' and consequently, in need of Western ('feminist') 'illumination' and 'rescue'.

of 'the oppressed Muslim woman', with Laura Bush and Cherie Blair contributing similar speeches on the righteousness of the war against terrorism as a battle 'for the rights and dignity of women' (Bush qtd. in Abu-Lughod 2013, 32), and a media invasion of images of burqa-clad Afghani women in need of 'rescuing'. The so-called 'war on terror' was thus predominantly portrayed as a war to liberate Muslim women from all the oppressions of their 'uncivilized civilization', that is, their patriarchal and repressive culture and religion that came almost to be represented by that one homogenized symbol: the burqa, which British reporter Polly Toynbee called the 'battle flag' of the war (qtd. in Ahmed 2011, 64).[3]

Leila Ahmed has analyzed the importance of visual media imagery in reinforcing and perpetuating the political rhetoric of the Bush administration and, hence, favouring the unstoppable advance of its war machinery—while also participating in the profitable marketing of the war. Ahmed also explores the way in which the oppression of Muslim women has progressively become over-exposed in cultural products that exploit the clash ideology, with, for instance, an avalanche of films and books that rapidly became blockbusters and best-sellers in the West (Ahmed 2011, 224). These narratives focus (mostly) on non-Western women as either helpless victims of an extreme patriarchal and religious system or heroines who are able to escape it, frequently finding refuge in a Western country where they become 'free'.[4] Marketing strategies also play an important role in the selling of the ideas sketched above, with film posters and DVD or book covers repeatedly featuring veiled women (Pazagardi 2010, 3).

In her article 'Do Muslim Women Really Need Saving?', Lila Abu-Lughod addresses the problematic insistence on a cultural approach that focalizes on the mistreatment of women in 'Other', non-Western parts of the world. She denounces this approach—and with it, Huntington's theory of a civilizational confrontation resulting from

---

[3] These are the roots of the current controversies over the image of women in ISIS who have chosen to dress this way, which constitutes a shock for Westerners.

[4] See Ahmad 2009; Mahmood 2008; Martín-Lucas 2014. Many of the chapters in this volume engage in discussions of the complex issue of representation which can be easily linked to the mis- and over-representation of Muslim women and, which enrich the reading of these problematic depictions. For a specific examination of the reception of narratives of difference, and especially the 'packaging' of the Third World for consumption in the markets of globalization, see Chap. 5 by James Procter.

cultural, religious and even 'ways of life' differences—as a dehistoricizing strategy that conceals the complex motivations and sets of relations that have led to the current state of affairs:

> [T]he question is why knowing about the 'culture' of the region, and particularly its religious beliefs and treatment of women, was more urgent than exploring the history of the development of repressive regimes in the region and the U.S. role in this history. Such cultural framing, it seemed to me, prevented the serious exploration of the roots and nature of human suffering in this part of the world. Instead of political and historical explanations, experts were being asked to give religio-cultural ones. Instead of questions that might lead to the exploration of global interconnections, we were offered ones that worked to artificially divide the world into separate spheres—recreating an imaginative geography of West versus East, us versus Muslims, cultures in which First Ladies give speeches versus others where women shuffle around silently in burqas. (Abu-Lughod 2002, 784)

Unlike most 'veil narratives', Emer Martin's novel *Baby Zero* distances itself from a civilizational clash reading, and endorses instead transnational feminist politics, thus offering an exemplary narrative for the purpose of this chapter.[5] First, Martin's novel historicizes the contextual meanings that can be derived from its reading, that is, it offers 'historical explanations' instead of religio-cultural ones, as Abu-Lughod demanded (Abu-Lughod 2002, 784). Second, this historicization of the different contexts addressed in the novel, not only the Middle East but also the West, focuses on the interdependent relations of both spaces in all their geopolitical (and violent) complexity. Third, it draws away from the Eastern–imprisonment–unfreedom versus Western–liberation–freedom dichotomic narrative to explore the ambiguities and instabilities that lie hidden under this narrative 'shroud': mainly the strategic resistances of

---

[5] My use of the term 'veil narratives' refers to any (visual or linguistic) type of text where (un)veiling features prominently as symbolic resource. It is worth clarifying that there is an obvious generalization and homogenization in the use of the English words 'veil' and 'veiling', Particularly in the West, 'veiling' is frequently employed to refer to a wide variety of women's Islamic dress codes, which obscures the differences between the indefinite number of practices this term is meant to convey while also erasing from view the reality of non-Muslim veiling practices such as those in Jewish, Christian or Hindu traditions (Pedwell 2007, 4).

non-Western women and the many unfreedoms wrapping hegemonic versions of Western femininities.[6]

Baby Zero plainly puts forward the implication of the Western world in the structuring of the conditions that lead to the fictionalized confrontational atmosphere of the novel without losing sight of the real histories that inspire it. In the novel, the intervention of the USA during the second revolution in Orap, which very much resembles that of the Taliban in Afghanistan, finds a direct rendering. Imprisoned after finally participating in her aunt's protest, Marguerite hopes her adopted country will intervene in her defence and asks her mother whether the American government is in fact planning to get involved:

> 'It's on the newspapers over there, Ishmael said. The American government knows about your case. They're using it as an excuse to come in and bomb and get the last oil reserves.' ...
>
> 'So the Americans know my case. They want to rescue me?'
>
> 'No. They want you as an excuse. They'd prefer to have you executed.' (Martin 2007, 299)

Marguerite has clearly bought into the discourse of the USA as 'the world's policeman', particularly in relation to its crusade against 'the oppression of Muslim women', oblivious to the fact that below its supposedly altruistic mission lie other much more selfish and powerful interests.[7]

A good many feminist thinkers (among them, Abu-Lughod 2002; Ahmed 2011; Braidotti 2005; Grewal and Kaplan 1994; Moallem 2012; Mohanty 2003) have openly criticized not only the neoliberal cooptation of feminist discourses but also the conscious or unconscious complicity of Western feminism. Braidotti, for instance, warns against Western feminist discourses and practices that—no matter how well

---

[6] I borrow the term 'unfreedom' from Moallem who explains that in spite of it not being a word in English, it expresses better than any other existing word 'the negation of the concept of freedom' (Moallem 2012, 199).

[7] Robin L. Riley, Chandra T. Mohanty and Minnie Bruce Pratt's edited collection *Feminism and War: Confronting U.S. Imperialism* (2008) contains a broad selection of articles that disclose the historical and geopolitical intricacies not only of the military intervention in Afghanistan but of the many US imperialist wars.

intentioned—participate in the further discrimination and oppression of non-Western women, reproducing the liberal idea that 'our women … are already liberated and thus do not need any more social incentives or emancipatory policies. "Their women", however, … are still backwards and need to be targeted for special emancipatory social actions or even more belligerent forms of enforced "liberation"' (Braidotti 2005, 4). Agreeing with this criticism of the Orientalist bias that has permeated Eurocentric feminism, Abu-Lughod points to a way for feminists to stop walking next to the anti-feminists that have become at times our travelling companions:

> [W]e need to look closely at what we are supporting (and what we are not) and to think carefully about why … I do not know how many feminists who felt good about saving Afghan women from the Taliban are also asking for a global redistribution of wealth or contemplating sacrificing their own consumption radically so that African or Afghan women could have some chance of having what I do believe should be a universal human right—the right to freedom from the structural violence of global inequality and from the ravages of war, the everyday rights of having enough to eat, having homes for their families in which to live and thrive, having ways to make decent livings so their children can grow, and having the strength and security to work out, within their communities and with whatever alliances they want, how to live a good life, which might very well include changing the ways those communities are organized. (Abu-Lughod 2002, 787)

Grewal and Kaplan, on their part, call for a 'struggle against all fundamentalisms' (Grewal and Kaplan 1994, 20) capable of generating a transnational feminist solidarity that in its theoretical and practical actions addresses 'the concerns of women around the world in the historicised particularity of their relationship to multiple patriarchies as well as to international economic hegemonies' (Grewal and Kaplan 1994, 17). In my view, *Baby Zero* interestingly responds to this call in its mapping out of an important set of ideological fundamentalisms lying ahead of us and, especially, lying ahead of women East and West. It is mainly in the misogynistic hostility of these milieus that Emer Martin claims the world as 'gripped by Western and Eastern fundamentalisms' (Martin 2008, online). This pluralization of the term in both Grewal and Kaplan's and Martin's words is key to understanding where the novel stands in this context of seemingly open conflict, working to deconstruct a false metonymic relation between 'fundamentalism' and 'Islamic fundamentalism' that may be wrongly deduced by the (ab)uses of this term on the part of Western mainstream political establishment and media, principally since 9/11.

In *Baby Zero*, Martin employs the veil as a complex, contested and multi-layered symbol of how cultures impact women's bodies and inscribe their patriarchal (but also imperialist, racist and classist) ideologies on them. There is not one veil in this novel but a multiplicity of (so-assumed) Eastern and Western veils, all of them moulding women's bodies and subjectivities in line with diverse (though not so disconnected) configurations of the male gaze in a multiplicity of patriarchies. The covering or uncovering, visibility or invisibility of female bodies in the novel is sustained throughout the narrative as a symbolic resource to reflect on issues concerning power relations and modes of representation, notions of agency and subordination, patriarchal oppressions as they intersect with other discriminatory paradigms of differentiation, such as racism and classism and, also, to both unearth and envision feminist resistance. The apparent opposition between the veiled and unveiled body, which appears to be almost always connected with the one caught between speech and silence, is dismantled in the novel to expose how both ends of the binary may be construed simultaneously as oppressive, protective or resistant depending on the discourse within which they are articulated and performed.

Related to these dichotomies, the question of 'free will' or 'choice', a rather controversial issue for feminism, is also recurrently invoked and questioned in the novel. In her exploration of discourses that set up the veil as a quintessential marker of Middle Eastern women's unfreedom, ignoring, for instance, violent impositions of 'unveiling' in countries such as Turkey (which has officially banned the veil since the 1980s) or Iran (1925–1941, under the dictatorship of Reza Sha),[8] or without exploring the logics of expressions such as 'the tyranny of fashion' (Abu-Lughod 2002, 786). In the West, Abu-Lughod has asked: 'What does freedom mean if we accept the fundamental premise that humans are social beings, always raised in certain social and historical contexts and belonging to particular communities that shape their desires and understandings of the world?' (Abu-Lughod 2002, 786). Inderpal

---

[8] A more recent example of this would be the so-called 'burkini ban' implemented in August 2016 by several cities and communes along the French coast.

Grewal has further convincingly argued that in spite of 'choice' being an essential concept in the language of feminisms to represent female agency, its use is also profoundly imbricated in neoliberal discourses that hold 'having choices' as proof of not being 'oppressed', and also in consumer culture: 'Consumer culture worked by producing desires and fantasies that could be linked to group as well as to individual identities and were also linked to a consumer citizenship through which liberal equality became possible' (Grewal 2005, 29). Therefore, Grewal concludes, '[t]he pervasiveness of liberal discourses of 'choice' within feminism, liberal democracy and consumer culture suggest that there are connections between these formations that deserve greater scrutiny, especially in the formation of what I have understood as the link between geopolitics and biopolitics' (Grewal 2005, 29). I will go back to this issue in my analysis of what I refer to as 'Western veils' to illustrate how this scrutiny materializes in specific moments in the novel.[9]

In Afghanistan-like Orap, Marguerite encounters a regime that literally expunges women from society and erases them from the public sphere. Secluded within the domestic space of the house which they cannot leave without the company of a male relative; abandoned to their luck in a women's hospital where they cannot be treated because '[m]ale doctors aren't allowed to see women patients, but there are no women surgeons' (Martin 2007, 14); imprisoned for having 'no understanding of tradition' (Martin 2007, 19); or covered by a full black veil, the women in this Orap seem to be vanishing from view. Forced by the socio-political circumstances to also wear the veil, Marguerite cannot but feel that in this clothing women become 'phantoms' (Martin 2007, 10), 'masks' (Martin 2007, 27), 'stripped of expression' (Martin 2007, 11) threatening presences whose bodies are made synonymous with danger: 'dark holes in the street. If you touched us, you would fall inside and disappear.' (Martin 2007, 11) The practices of *purdah*, which have mostly affected Hindu and Muslim women but also Christian ones with variations over time, seclusion conditions and regional demarcations, appear at this point in the novel in their most extreme form, one that recalls the Taliban's extremist positions regarding women's presence in the public arena. *Purdah*, a word coming from the Urdu and Persian term *parda* meaning 'veil' or 'curtain', cannot

---

[9] For a more extended examination of this complex topic, see Grewal 2005.

be reduced to the compulsory covering of women's hair, face and/or body with a distinctive type of veil although this is one of its most visible outcomes. What most of the different practices that come together under the generic term *purdah* have in common is, on the one hand, their policing of gender segregation in public space, where women are either forbidden to just 'be' or forced to cover and/or seek a male relative's 'protection'; and on the other, a justifying rhetoric based on principles of a moral propriety that configures women as guarantors and custodians of the family and the nation's honour. In the novel, wherever and whenever *purdah* is in place, it is mostly signified by a sense of women's confinement on three different levels: public institutions such as the hospital or the prison, private spaces such as the family house, and the burqa as 'portable seclusion' (Papanek qtd. in Abu-Lughod 2002, 785) and/or 'mobile homes' (Abu-Lughod 2002, 785) that negotiate the presence of the private (body) in the (body) public.

The novel's denunciation of *purdah* as a set of misogynist practices is more than evident. However, the narrative also foregrounds the difficulties and conflicts that emerge when addressing the question of how to resist these exclusions and discriminatory practices. Martin inserts the politics of the veil in the novel within this quandary. She offers a narrative that preoccupies itself with the visibilization of the often invisible resistant agency of non-Western women who are typically represented as victimized under local and global patriarchies, and with the imperative contextualization of these multiple oppressions.

Among Marguerite's initial remarks about women's non-presence in Orap we find a paradox that is closely entwined with the ambiguities of the shrouding versus overexposure of women and their bodies. Marguerite notices: 'there was the fact that we had disappeared but were everywhere' (Martin 2007, 11). In the non-fictional realm, covered Middle Eastern women are at the centre stage of national and foreign political strategies and their propagandistic campaigns; they saturate the narratives and covers of books which inundate the shelves and windows of bookshops in the West; they feature at the core of feminist debates; and, of course, they are everywhere in the media, as Martin satirizes in the novel through the voice of Marguerite: 'This covering does not diminish us according to plan. It mythologises us. Our story is larger. We are more photogenic, more iconic. I could see the press clamour to capture our images as one snake of draped femininity.' (Martin 2007, 247) Marguerite's words encapsulate the preponderance of this paternalistic version of Muslim femininity, suggesting how women's oppressions in the non-West become convenient and useful for the West, which can thus present itself as a saviour in the name of women's rights.

However, the novel makes clear that these women are also everywhere on their own terms because some resist their individual and collective oppressions. The protest Marguerite's aunt organizes against the terrible reality of the women's hospital is one such instance of local resistance through which *Baby Zero* points to the fact that 'women's rights are not a Western prerogative' (Martin 2008, online). This protest revolves once again around the notions of visibility and invisibility that run steadily below the development of the veiling trope in the novel. The plan involves driving the anguished women confined in the hospital to the government buildings and leaving them there for the entire city to see the kind of abandonment that they suffer. As such, even though all these women are fully covered in their burqas, their bodies' occupation of the public space in an act of rebellion defies the principle of extreme (social and political) invisibility that forcibly regulates women's existence in this society, and this transgression is violently punished. Marguerite's aunt is publicly stoned to death to prevent other women from daring to raise their voices against the regime and its denigrating treatment of women. Marguerite is taken to prison where she is raped and beaten by the guards in terrible episodes of violence that focus on the female difference of her body and her face as symbol of identity: 'This night … two men come into my cell. They pull my veil over my face, and they wrap all the material around my body tightly and face me to the wall. They spin me around and punch me in the face and on the breasts.' (Martin 2007, 23)

The body, and more significantly the face, feature prominently in the narration as symbols of women's identities and their embodied subjectivities, which can appear covered or uncovered depending on context and purpose and, also, on who decides ('freely' or not) over the covering or uncovering. Martin allows for some kind of ambiguity over the meaning of the Islamic veil to open the door for multiple readings of how this very symbolic but very material clothing operates in different contexts and situations. On the one hand, the novel documents how women may opt for taking up the veil in a conscious decision to confront other forces which also oppress them: for example, describing the poverty-ridden slums of an Orapian city before a previous revolution that had overthrown the ruling monarchy, it offers a picture where veiled women and rumours of revolution are entwined. This Orapian revolution, chronologically speaking the first one in the history of this fictional country, shows many parallels with the Iranian revolution of 1979. The variegated uses of the veil in the novel suggesting that women's decisions to take up or take off the veil are not as straightforward as Western hegemonic discourses on the barbaric patriarchal culture of the Muslim Other may wish to render them.[10] Under the dictatorship of Reza Shah (1925–1941), women were forced to unveil and men were required to wear Western-style clothes to offer to the world an image of a modern Iran: 'The signs of modernization were written on the body, as dress became the focal point of such identification' (Moallem 2012, 65). This forced unveiling was in many cases violent and traumatic for women, and for many of them meant, in practice, their total seclusion in a private sphere further reduced by the absence of the veil as a negotiating wall between their bodies and the men who were not related to them by family ties. Compulsory unveiling by force subsided slightly under the regime of Reza's son Mohammad Reza, and as a result of this relaxation some Iranian women began to veil themselves again. In the pre-revolution years, some women also started to veil for the first time 'in protest of Westernized models of femininity' (Moallem 2012, 4) or in solidarity with other women who had been persecuted and were now being stigmatized: veiled women were immediately ascribed an identity defined by traditionalism, religiousness, low-class status and limited education (Zahedi 2007, 84).

The acknowledgement of the heterogeneity of strategic functions and meanings under which the veil can be read does not amount in *Baby Zero* to a denial of the patriarchal implications that any conviction of the need to cover (or uncover) women's bodies entails, but a request to 'care about history' (Martin 2008, online). During this first revolution in Orap, for instance,

> [s]ome camp girls were becoming fundamentalists and joining the child soldiers, running off to join the enemy's ranks, claiming they would be respected for their fight and not looked at as objects for men's pleasure. But Farah thought that they got it wrong. The veils they were wearing were saying just that – that their whole existence was sexualised, while the

---

[10]For an exhaustive analysis of the contested uses of the veil in Iran, see Moallem 2012; Zahedi 2007.

men's was not. But it was a myth that the veils made women submissive, Farah noted. (Martin 2007, 140)

So the novel does not refute or soften the patriarchal connotations of the veil, but calls for a deeper awareness of the histories that surround its uses as the only way of generating truly effective resistance.

There are also examples in the novel where brutal violence against their bodies prompts women to cling to the veil as a kind of shelter. After days of being attacked and sexually abused in the now Taliban-like Orap, Marguerite is taken along with the other women in the prison to see their group lawyer. When asked to remove their veils, Marguerite is reluctant and observes a similar feeling in her companions: 'It can become a protection too. None of the women have faces. One has some, but her nose is cut off … Most faces have been melted by acid' (Martin 2007, 28). With their veils on, these women protect themselves from undesired gazes, those judging them as well as those exploiting their image and their suffering.

The redemptive act Marguerite's mother, Farah, performs at the end of the story, giving her life to save her daughter—pregnant as a result of being repeatedly raped while in prison—makes the different strands of the Islamic veil's symbolism in the novel converge. This is a strategic example of localized female resistance and unbounded love, even though it problematically implies the tragic death of the mother. After the birth of her child, Marguerite is set for execution and Farah is called upon to pick up the baby and take her away before the fatal moment. Farah arrives at the prison in her burqa and, after showing her ID to the guards in a final irony—how can an ID serve as identification for a woman whose body and face are fully covered and thus made invisible?—she is taken to Marguerite's cell. There, alone with her daughter, she instructs Marguerite to remove her burqa and exchange it for hers without saying a word. They have only a fleeting moment in which to see each other's face before the guard asks the woman with the non-ragged burqa to leave with the baby. In this final scene, invisibility and silence work together for these women to exchange their fates, the veil masking their identities to allow Farah to save her daughter while sacrificing her own life. The novel marks the veil as instrumental for Marguerite's survival at this point, though Farah's death works as contrapuntal reminder of the patriarchal ethos that imposes veiling for these women in the first place and ends up with the death of those that remain in Orap prison.[11]

The Islamic veil that, at different points in the novel, women wear or abandon seems to symbolically lie trapped in a complex spiral of contextual meanings that destabilize patriarchal dichotomies as they intersect with feminist notions of imprisonment and sheltering, oppression and resistance. Martin allows the Islamic veil this ambiguity of meaning and, especially, the potential strategic use that women may make of it—given the circumstances in which her characters find themselves—turning it from instrument of oppression to either protective tool or strategic weapon of resistance. This last meaning connects to the tricky terrain of feminist resistance in its problematic relationship both to the neoliberal devouring cooptation of its demands and achievements, and to the complex implication of Western feminism in it. *Baby Zero*'s engagement with this mine-filled issue appears to be in line with Braidotti's claim that there are 'great grey areas in between the pretentious claim that feminism has already succeeded in the West and the equally false statement that feminism is non-existent outside this region' (Braidotti 2005, 4). In light of the novel's politics, it can be claimed that for Martin, as for Braidotti, 'those in-between degrees of complexity are the ones that matter and they should be put at the centre of the agenda' (Braidotti 2005, 4).

I have outlined some of the complexities of meaning inscribed in the uses of the Islamic veil in the novel. As for the different veils more closely associated with Western culture, though not exclusive to it either, Martin allows for less, if any, ambiguity.[12] There does not seem to be much chance for feminist resistance in these. In California, we witness how Rita, the American girlfriend of Marguerite's cosmetic surgeon uncle Mo, is regularly injected with Botox—'A form of toxin

---

[11] Farah's martyrdom is highly problematic from a feminist point of view because it may seem to reinforce a rather conventional model of motherhood, the mother who sacrifices herself for her children, her family or her nation.

[12] In this sense, I agree with Carolyn Pedwell who argues that certain generalizations implied in dualisms such as 'Eastern' and 'Western' veils, for instance, are problematic. As well as obscuring other veiling practices, as made explicit before, Pedwell claims that 'labelling Muslim veiling "non-Western" obscures the wide practice of veiling in Western industrialised countries by women who may consider themselves both "Muslim" and "Western"' (Pedwell 2007, 5) and '[i]t is also clear that so called "Western" beauty procedures are practiced all over the world' (Pedwell 2007, 5).

that causes botulism. Technically ... a poison' (Martin 2007, 71)—and how she obsesses over clothes, make-up, beauty treatments and cosmetic operations that will stop or erase the signs of ageing and preserve her body as a young and sexually attractive one according to her society's beauty standards. The character of Rita acts in the novel as a reminder of the pervasive power, force and pressure of ageist discourses mostly but, again, not exclusively, in industrialized Western societies, with the USA being its apex and principal exporter through the globalized media. Rita's behaviour and remarks in the novel often illustrate how women and their bodies become early conceptualized as old when it comes to sexual attractiveness as related to physical appearance. However, Rita also functions as a powerful comment on what Diane Negra has termed 'the new aging' and 'its emphasis on marketing, consumerism, and personal responsibility for fending off the aging process' (Negra 2009, 72). Negra argues that in recent times, Western culture has witnessed a change in the meanings of ageing, particularly female ageing, by means of the creation of 'an idealized culture of "ageless" consumers and active populations' (Katz and Marshall qtd. in Negra 2009, 71). This idea is obviously connected to the capitalist investment in plastic surgery and other cosmetic technologies and belies at least two facts directly affecting women in a very negative way: the insistence on a liberal notion of citizenship based on individual achievement and consumer agency is used to justify the reduction of state care; and it also creates a space of further stigmatization of those women who do not respond to this 'ageless' norm as their bodies show the signs of ageing (Negra 2009, 71). These are bodies erased under the Western veil of anti-ageing ideology; real women are thoroughly absent in a Western public sphere saturated by the visual imagery of impossibly 'forever young' (and white, and affluent) female bodies. Cosmetic surgery is just one of the tentacles that trap women in their efforts to conform to this impossible ideal.

The female face emerges once more as potent symbol in the novel and, again, it disappears, covered by a mask, hidden. Discussing the latest hype in cosmetic treatments, Mo explains: 'AlloDerm is taken from corpses, and I can fold it, roll it and stack it so it fits into your face. It will even become you' (Martin 2007, 71). Mo's words describe this treatment almost as a cloth that instead of covering the skin is inserted under it. The way in which Botox is described adds to the symbolism of an annihilation of identity when Mo's recently arrived 10-year-old niece Leila 'thinks this woman was being killed' (Martin 2007, 71), and points to a paralysis that is muscular but may also be read as political: 'It paralyzes the facial muscles so you don't use your face, and as a result you don't get wrinkles' (Martin 2007, 71). In the same way that the veil robs women of expression, Botox cancels it. Women seem to be losing both their faces and their bodies, all trapped within the threads of patriarchy and its multiple manifestations.

The metaphorical paralysis of the Botox-injected face in the image above resembles the progressive depoliticization of feminism in invocations of a post-feminist fantasy more often than not linked to the concept of choice. Negra locates the changing face of (anti-)ageing discourses within this wider frame declaring that 'the overwhelming ideological impact that is made by an accumulation of post-feminist cultural material is the reinforcement of conservative norms as the ultimate "best choices" in women's lives' (Negra 2009, 4). In this context, Negra claims that

> [o]ne of the most distinctive features of the postfeminist era has been the spectacular emergence of the underfed, overexercised female body, and this ideal has drifted into middle age (and beyond). In sketching the preoccupations and interests attributed to the self-surveilling postfeminist subject, a key development with which I am concerned is the rising social expectation for American women to adhere to an intense regime of personal grooming (waxing, tanning, manicures, pedicures, facials, Botox treatments, etc.) and at younger and younger ages. (Negra 2009, 119)

Through the character of Rita, *Baby Zero* addresses the deceptive frivolousness of beauty regimes, exposing the dangerous manipulation and violence which women daily subject their bodies to in order to conform to an imposed ideal, normalized and hypervisibilized body— against which we are constantly measuring, disciplining and correcting ourselves (Bordo 1993, 25). And this discipline is insidiously imposed not only upon our bodies but also our minds. As Naomi Wolf has argued, the contemporary reification of the female body is the most pervasive and enduring strategy of patriarchal control in the Western world because '*[t]he beauty myth is always actually prescribing behaviour and not appearance*' (Wolf 1991, 14; italics in the original). In the US setting of the novel, the female body is visibly located within the context of a consumerist society that turns it into both sexualized object of consumption and essential target for the beauty industry. Patriarchy and capitalism working hand in hand to sustain their power. With this, the novel firmly departs from approaches that situate the beauty industry next to the concept of 'choice'.[13]

There is another character in the novel whose own manipulation of her body reflects the combined pressures of patriarchy and capitalism. Desiree, a US teenager who befriends the Fatagagases' son, is a 'proud bulimic' (Martin 2007, 105) who vomits after eating because 'Mother has promised me a whole wardrobe' (Martin 2007, 105). Although Desiree's eating disorders turn her into a thin young woman, she is pushed to endlessly continue to keep her body controlled into what for her is an unnatural and unhealthy slimness. Her body does not meet her family's (and society's) 'beauty' expectations and she is promised consumerist beauty goods if she is able to discipline her appetites. As a consequence, Desiree punishes her body for its hunger, not because she is particularly unhappy with it but to be able to 'dress' it in fashionable clothes. At the same time, Desiree's dysfunctional approach to her body is concurrently shown in her lack of sexual desire—'of all of my appetites, sex was never my thing' (Martin 2007, 282)—and most of all in her disgust at physical contact: 'Desiree did not like to be touched' (Martin 2007, 256). Desiree has become an object, a doll to be looked at.

Negra's words quoted above also signal the connection between the savage appetite of capitalism for women as consumers with the over-sexualization of girls' bodies. Girls are introduced to the beauty market at earlier and earlier ages, something that is also addressed in the novel in an almost grotesque scene where Rita takes Leila 'to do some shopping' (Martin 2007, 86):

> Leila arrived at Bubba Gumps with leopard-skin leggings and a pink halter-neck top that exposed her belly button. Her shoulder-length hair was bunched up in a sparkling scrunchie, and Rita had sprinkled glitter on

---

[13] The most notable example of this position is perhaps Kathy Davis's work on cosmetic surgery. Davis has defended the idea that cosmetic surgery is '*first and foremost* ... about taking one's life into one's own hands' (qtd. in Bordo 1993, 20; italics in the original) which was contested by Susan Bordo in her acclaimed book *Unbearable Weight*, initiating a debate that the two authors sustained for some years and one that feminist scholars continue to engage in.

her face. She wore pink lipstick and blue eye shadow and high white zebra shoes ...

'Doesn't she look amazing? They had the Extinct clothing line for kids too.' (Martin 2007, 86)

Hand in hand with this exposure of girls to an over-sexualized beauty and fashion market, there is, in consumer culture, an obvious 'girlification' of women; both issues are reflected in the novel as a powerful comment on the paedophiliac nature of society. This is the model Rita longs to achieve, entering a perverse rat race to look younger and younger, slimmer and slimmer, which keeps her permanently frustrated, and permanently consuming.

The juxtaposition of 'Eastern' and 'Western' veils in my analysis of the disciplining of women's bodies in *Baby Zero* is not meant to imply in any way that there are no differences between the everyday oppressions they are taken to symbolize. There are in fact many, cruel and violent ones, and they are indeed very relevant. However, what *Baby Zero* suggests is that true liberation must be sought and found in a different place or, in fact, in alternative spaces outside the false binaries defining concepts of freedom and unfreedom as they have been delineated above. As Martin puts it:

Is it more oppressive to cover the body entirely or to slice it open and put in implants, to inject botulism into women's heads? These are grim choice [sic] and we can only hope to steer away from such extremes. Neither furthers the cause of women, and women's equality is vital to changing the world, there is no freedom without it. (Martin 2008, online)

Both the female hair as symbol and cosmetic surgery as a very material intervention upon bodies feature in the novel as further related to other parameters of discrimination and oppression, such as racism or class prejudices. The sculpting of bodies to reflect dominant social standards does not apply only to the production of properly gendered bodies.

A variety of embodied disciplinary practices—hair bleaching and straightening, skin whitening, or surgical reconstruction of lips, eyelids or noses, to name but a few—participate prominently in the production of bodies which reflect the privileged position of some bodies over others (Lennon 2010). Farah, in the novel, dyes her hair blonde 'like all Orapian middle-class and upper-class women' (Martin 2007, 137) to improve her societal image; Marguerite spends hours dying and straightening hers in California where 'women are all blonde' (Martin 2007, 194). But the clearest instance of the normalization of bodies along racist and classist lines in the novel is the way in which the Fatagagas brothers earn their livelihood and acquire fame in Orap. The real Fatagagas, two brothers whose identity was usurped by Mo and Ishmael, 'performed cosmetic surgery, lopping the ends of the noses of the ruling class daughters' (Martin 2007, 34), and the identity-usurping brothers continued the business with notable success: '[a] visitor to Orap might have been forgiven for thinking that some genetic anomaly was taking place among the middle classes' (Martin 2007, 35). Marguerite herself has 'work done' (Martin 2007, 290):

> It is not really my nose but a nose Uncle Mo built for me after he plucked off the old, crooked Orapian nose. I was horrified when that ancient *ethnic nose* arrived on my face in early adolescence. I counted the days to when I could have it razed to the ground and have something *more modern*, more convenient, built instead. Really, I wanted *a more silent nose*. (Martin 2007, 243; my italics)

Nose modification was reserved for the upper sections of Orapian society, not only for economic reasons but also for ideological ones. Mo, Marguerite's uncle and later also professional mentor, selectively chooses his patients and decides who can or cannot be granted a pert nose: 'Get out of here … You are peasants and those are your noses' (Martin 2007, 35). And, although nose jobs are shown to be practised in the novel on both male and female bodies, there is a clear emphasis on the highest level of exigency for women: 'The young women and their mothers were invariably bleached blondes and he gave them new pert noses. Their men had long Semitic noses and jet-black hair' (Martin 2007, 35). Women are more, and differently, pressured to escape their racialized bodies and get into the prison of a rigidly maintained gendered model of a body that, apart from being as white(ned) as possible, is forced to satisfy several other conditions.

By focusing not only on the 'historical dynamism of veil' (Fanon qtd. in Moallem 2012, 211) and its changing contextual meanings, but also on those other veiled veils which hijack women's bodies and subjectivities in the West, *Baby Zero* offers an alternative approach to the (un)veiling trope as it has been articulated in post-9/11 gendered (political, media and cultural) narratives built on, and (re)producing, the rhetoric of the clash of civilizations. Critically exposing the female body as the main confrontational terrain upon which this clash is endlessly enacted, the novel provides an exploration of gendering as a disciplinary practice that operates transnationally, crossing paths with other categorizing and regulatory practices and, as a consequence, affecting women in different ways. Martin delineates in *Baby Zero* essential ideas that open the way to a better understanding of these 'multiple, overlapping and discrete oppressions' (Grewal and Kaplan 1994, 19) and thus, to a politics of resistance in line with transnational feminist claims—a feminist joining of forces which does not ignore women's unequal positions within global power relations and hierarchies, but which is able to articulate strategies of localized resistance to the different manifestations of patriarchal (hetero)sexism. As Grewal and Kaplan contend, analyzing 'how gender works in the dynamic of globalization and the countermeasures of new nationalisms, and ethnic and racial fundamentalisms ... [f]eminists can begin to map these scattered hegemonies and link diverse local practices to formulate a set of solidarities' (Grewal and Kaplan 1994, 19). It is in this way that the novel helps create new spaces where women's transnational affect, coalition and cooperation can emerge and flourish.

WORKS CITED

Abu-Lughod, Lila. 2013. *Do Muslim Women Need Saving?*. Cambridge, MA and London: Harvard University Press.
———. 2002. 'Do Muslim Women Really Need Saving? Anthropological Reflections on Cultural Relativism and its Others'. *American Anthropologist* 104 (3): 783–790.
Ahmad, Dora. 2009. Not Yet Beyond the Veil: Muslim Women in American Popular Literature. *Social Text 99* 27 (2): 105–131.
Ahmed, Leila. 2011. *A Quiet Revolution: The Veil's Resurgence from the Middle East to America*. New Haven and London: Yale University Press.
Bordo, Susan. 1993. *Unbearable Weight: Feminism, Western Culture and the Body*. Berkeley, Los Angeles and London: University of California Press.
Braidotti, Rosi. 2005. A Critical Cartography of Feminist Post-postmodernism. *Australian Feminist Studies* 20 (47): 169–180.
Grewal, Inderpal. 2005. *Transnational America: Feminisms, Diasporas, Neoliberalisms*. Durham NC and London: Duke University Press.
Grewal, Inderpal, and Caren Kaplan. 1994. Introduction: Transnational Feminist Practices and Questions of Postmodernity. In *Scattered Hegemonies:*

Postmodernity and Transnational Feminist Practices, eds. Inderpal Grewal, and Caren Kaplan, 1–33. Minneapolis: University of Minnesota Press.

Huntington, Samuel P. 1993. The Clash of Civilizations? *Foreign Affairs* 72 (3): 22–49.

Khan, Shahnaz. 2008. Afghan Women: The Limits of Colonial Rescue. In *Feminism and War: Confronting U.S. Imperialism*, eds. Robin L. Riley, Chandra Talpade Mohanty, and Minnie Bruce Pratt, 161–178. London and New York: Zed Books.

Lennon, Kathleen. 2010. Feminist Perspectives on the Body. In *Standford Encyclopedia of Philosophy*. http://plato.stanford.edu/entries/feminist-body/.

Mahmood, Saba. 2008. Feminism, Democracy, and Empire: Islam and the War on Terror. In *Women's Studies on the Edge*, ed. Joan Wallach Scott, 81–114. Durham NC and London: Duke University Press.

Martin, Emer. 2007. *Baby Zero*. Dingle and London: Brandon Books.

Martin, Emer. 2008. 'Interview by Niall McKay'. http://www.laurahird.com/newreview/emermartininterview.html.

Martín-Lucas, Belén. 2014. Of Saris and Spices: Marketing Paratexts of Indian Women's Fiction. In *Indian Writing in English and the Global Literary Market*, eds. Om Dwivedi, and Lisa Lau, 99–118. Houndmills: Palgrave Macmillan.

Moallem, Minoo. 2012. *Between Warrior Brother and Veiled Sister: Islamic Fundamentalism and the Politics of Patriarchy in Iran*. Berkeley, Los Angeles and London: University of California Press.

Mohanty, Chandra Talpade. 2003. *Feminism without Borders: Decolonizing Theory, Practicing Solidarity*. Durham, NC and London: Duke University Press.

Negra, Diane. 2009. *What a Girl Wants: Fantasizing the Reclamation of Self in Postfeminism*. London and New York: Routledge.

Pazargadi, Leila. 2010. Marketing "Honor Killing Memoirs": Confronting Western Depictions of Muslim Women. *Thinking Gender Papers*. University of California Los Angeles, Center for the Study of Women. http://escholarship.org/uc/item/57k2604f.

Pedwell, Carolyn. 2007. Tracing "the Anorexic" and "the Veiled Woman": Towards a Relational Approach. *New Working Papers Series* 20. London School of Economics, Gender Institute. http://www.lse.ac.uk/genderInstitute/pdf/C%20%20Pedwell.pdf.

Puar, Jasbir K., and Amit S. Rai. 2002. Monster, Terrorist, Fag: The War on Terrorism and the Production of Docile Patriots. *Social Text* 72 (20): 117–148.

Riley, Robin L., Chandra Talpade Mohanty, and Minnie Bruce Pratt (eds.). 2008. *Feminism and War: Confronting U.S. Imperialism*. London and New York: Zed Books.

Spivak, Gayatri. 1988. Can the Subaltern Speak? In *Marxism and the Interpretation of Culture*, eds. Cary Nelson, and Lawrence Grossberg, 271–313. Urbana and Chicago: University of Illinois Press.

Wolf, Naomi. (1991) [1990]. *The Beauty Myth: How Images of Beauty Are Used Against Women*. London: Vintage Books.

Zahedi, Ashraf. 2007. Contested Meaning of the Veil and Political Ideologies of Iranian Regimes. *Journal of Middle-East Women's Studies* 3 (3): 75–98.

Index

A
Abject, 40, 209
Ableism, 72
Aboriginal languages, 17
Abu-Lughod, Lila, 225–227, 229
Academia, 149, 157, 199
Academy, 16, 28, 98, 111
Activism, 191, 199
Aesthetics, 21, 24, 43, 82, 87, 136
Affect, 8, 23, 37, 54, 85, 120, 124, 154
Affective labour, 124
Afghanistan, 224, 225, 228
Africa, 43–46, 160, 169, 176, 178, 179
Agamben, Giorgio, 118
Ageism, 237
Agency, 7, 22, 47, 64, 117, 124, 129, 230, 237
Aging, 237, 238
AIDS, 190
Alienation, 204
Ali, Monica, 83, 88, 91, 98, 119
Alterity, 16, 18, 119
Ambiguity, 7, 46, 63, 66, 140, 149, 163, 209, 227, 232, 236
Americanisation, 172, 176
Anamorphosis, 59, 60
Androgyny, 61
Anglophone, 33, 82
Anonymity, 113, 123, 125
Answered by Fire, 49–51, 53
Anti-capitalist, 120
Anti-racist, 120
Anxiety, 18, 37, 63, 66, 75, 125, 169, 204
Apartheid, 7, 185, 191–193, 195, 196
Archetypal, 64, 165, 206, 212
Arranged marriage, 98, 104, 204, 213
Ashcroft, Bill, 42
Assimilation, 210, 218
Audience, 5, 81, 120–122, 133, 220
Australia, 3, 4, 8, 14, 16, 17, 19, 27, 31–33, 40, 41, 49, 51, 52
Australian literature, 32, 33
Authenticity, 2, 60, 71
Authority, 19, 54, 87, 88, 127, 148, 219

B

Baby Zero, 72, 224, 227, 229, 234, 241
Bhatt, Sujata, 4, 24
Bangladesh, 86, 106, 107, 204
Beauty
  as construct, 218, 237
  industry, 239
Bengali identity, 210, 212, 215, 217
Berlant, Lauren, 37, 53
Bewes, Timothy, 4, 40
Bhabha, Homi K., 159, 163, 169, 172, 173, 210
Biocapital, 123, 128
Biography, 29. *See also* Psychobiography
Biopolitics, 118, 124, 231
Biopower, 118, 125
Bisexuality, 193
Black Consciousness movement, 195
Bollywood, 205
Booysen, Anene, 187, 188, 191, 199
Border crossing, 26, 27, 29
Borderless, 5, 100, 119, 121, 123, 125–127, 129, 130
Boundaries, 100, 117, 124, 129, 159, 176, 224
Bourdieu, Pierre, 81, 87, 189, 190
Braidotti, Rosi, 225, 228, 236
Brand, Dionne, 120, 123
Brick Lane, 82–84, 86, 88, 90, 91, 102, 106, 111, 114
Bricolage, 86
Britain, 88, 91, 146, 164, 209
British colonialism, 163
British Council, 82
British Empire, 99, 144, 165, 207
Burqa, 7, 226, 232, 235
Butler, Judith, 119, 123, 126, 128

C

Cafre, 169
Calcutta, 204, 221
Caliban, 163, 167, 168
Camera, 48, 50, 121, 122, 170, 214
Canada, 3, 4, 16, 49, 51, 82, 84, 120, 121, 125, 127, 128, 134, 209
Capital, 2, 5, 82, 88, 98, 104, 113, 118, 124, 129, 208
Capitalism, 5, 71, 98, 99, 101, 102, 106, 111, 114, 123, 216, 239
Caribbean, 121, 129, 207, 209
Cartography, 172, 225
Casanova, Pascale, 81, 87, 89–91
Celebrity, 189, 196
Choice, 22, 48, 51, 62, 105, 106, 141, 230, 231, 239
Christianity, 125, 206
Cinema, 49, 218
Citizenship, 3
Clash of civilizations, 89, 223, 224, 242
Cliché, 50, 91
Colonial fantasies, 58, 63
Commerce, 103, 104
Commodification, 125, 158, 211
  of difference, 4
  of the Other, 3
  of the woman artist, 5
  of women's bodies, 7
Community, 76, 99, 105, 111, 113, 127, 128, 169, 204
Compassion fatigue, 53
Complicity, 38, 47, 62, 216
Consciousness, 6, 17, 18, 48, 49, 66, 99, 113, 138, 178, 197, 206
Consecration, 89
Consumer culture, 231, 240
Consumerism, 237

Cooptation, 225, 228, 236
Cosmetic surgery, 237
Cosmopolitan, 81, 88, 215
Costumbrista movement, 66
Counter-discourse, 4, 46, 136
Creative resistance, 158
Creative writing, 27, 109
Criticism, 58, 59, 83
Cultural capital, 87
Cultural commodity, 1
Cultural imperialism, 169

D

Debord, Guy, 142, 143
Decolonial, 15, 16
Dehumanisation, 65, 128, 129
Democracy, 7, 118, 130, 196, 231
Derrida, Jacques, 63
Deterritor, 81, 91, 170
Deterritorialization, 5
Diaspora, 82, 92, 179, 203, 204, 208, 212
Diasporic, 2, 3, 6, 7, 87, 203–205, 207–209, 211, 212, 214, 216, 217, 219
Dictatorship, 161, 230, 234
Dirty Pretty Things, 97, 123
Disability, 61, 66, 68–71, 125, 189
Disability Studies, 75
Disciplinary practices, 240, 242
Discriminatory practices, 232
Disenfranchised, 101, 106, 112
Dissent, 128, 130
Diversity, 5, 33, 90, 97, 127, 149, 207
Documentary, 5, 48, 49, 53, 128–130
Documentary film, 4
Docu-poem, 119–121, 124, 126
Domestic space, 188, 231

E

East is East, 205
Emancipation, 62, 99, 104, 110, 111
Emasculation, 206, 217
Embodiment, 119, 218, 233, 240
Empowerment, 99, 102, 105, 110, 148
English
   language, 14, 17, 18, 27, 29, 33, 84, 103, 104, 120, 140, 213
   nationality, 164, 173
Equality, 99, 106, 231, 240
Ethics, 1, 8, 24, 38, 44, 121, 124, 130, 136, 138
Europe, 3, 16, 43, 67, 158, 159, 161, 164, 167, 170, 174, 175, 177, 179, 200, 207
Exile, 158, 224

F

Fanon, Franz, 48, 210, 241
Fashion, 47, 127, 230, 240
Femininity, 63, 198, 210, 216, 232, 234
Feminism, 190, 225, 228–231, 236, 238
Feminist politics, 7, 225, 227
Fertility, 66, 169
A Fine Madness, 43, 44
First Nations, 149
Fluidity, 215, 219
Folklore, 67
Foreignness, 18, 20, 21, 26, 84, 85, 100, 163, 206, 214, 232
Foucault, Michel, 118
Four Inhabitants of Mexico, 66, 67
Frida Painting the Two Fridas, 73
Fulang Chang and I, 57, 61, 76
Fundamentalisms, 229, 242
Funding, 147, 148

G

Geopolitics, 7, 121, 176, 187, 224, 227, 228
Global city, 5, 98, 99, 102, 104, 107, 122
Globalization, 1, 2, 5, 8, 81, 82, 98, 100, 105, 119, 121, 129, 172, 176, 225, 226, 242
Global marketplace, 88, 170
Global North, 101
Global South, 101
Gomo, Mashingaidze, 4, 42, 43, 46
Gordimer, Nadine, 7, 191
Gramsci, Antonio, 141, 191
Grewal, Inderpal and Caren Kaplan, 229, 242
Grievable death, 126
Grotesque, 69, 239

H

Hardt, Michael and Antonio Negri, 8, 119, 124, 127–130
Hegemony, 4, 5, 15, 61, 125, 130, 147, 163, 165, 176, 209, 211, 220, 225, 234
Heteronormativity, 193, 199, 203, 205, 217, 219
Heterosexism, 242
Hilder, Jamie, 6, 136, 147
Hollywood, 190
Holocaust (narratives of), 38, 39
Homeland, 67, 170, 179, 204
House Gun, 7, 185, 191, 195, 199
Humanitarian fiction, 2, 3, 42, 54
Humanity, 197
Human rights, 40, 149, 191
Hybridity, 6, 29, 71, 90, 105, 158, 159, 163, 178, 204
Hyper-capitalist, 100, 102
Hypermasculinity, 206, 217
Hypervisibility, 3, 125

I

Iberian Peninsula, 159, 170, 177
Identity, 1, 64, 164, 169, 170, 177, 206, 209, 217, 241
Ideology, 62, 99, 107, 110, 111, 113, 206, 207, 213, 225, 226, 237
Impairment, 58, 61, 68, 69
Imperialism, 163, 165, 166, 211
Imperialist ideology, 8, 63, 164, 225, 228, 230
Indentured labour, 207, 209
Independence
  personal, 73, 104, 105, 113
  political, 44, 50, 207
India, 7, 26, 82, 123, 186, 187, 189, 206–209, 212, 213, 215, 217, 220
Indian diaspora. *See* Diaspora
Indigeneity, 65
Infertility, 72
Intelligibility, 62, 130, 210
International bestsellers, 82
Invisibility, 3, 33, 103, 122–124, 167, 209, 230, 233, 235
Iran, 224, 230, 234
Ireland, 224
Isolation, 66, 104, 105, 149, 170

K

Kahlo, Frida, 4, 57, 60, 76
Khan-Din, Ayub, 205
Khanna, Ranjanna, 62
Knowledge production, 16, 28, 123, 146

L

Lahiri, Jhumpa, 7, 203
Latin America, 160, 176
Levy, Andrea, 82, 84
Lexical empathy, 4, 8, 15, 23–25
Liminality, 22, 28, 117, 128, 210, 215

Lindauer, Margaret A., 58, 65, 66
  Devouring Frida, 58, 72
Lisbon, 175, 179
Literary awards, 32, 33, 91
Literary capital, 81, 87
London, 69, 70, 81–84, 86, 88, 91, 97–100, 103–107, 110
Love, 24, 31, 198, 216, 235

M

Marginalized communities, 2, 16, 19, 135
Marketing, 1, 2, 88, 178, 237
Martin, Emer, 224, 227, 229
Masculinities, 7, 203, 205, 219, 220
Mbembe, Achille, 8, 126
Me and My Doll, 72
Media, 2, 7, 8, 15, 33, 53, 58, 83, 102, 125, 170, 185, 187, 188, 191, 196, 200, 205, 209, 224, 226, 230, 232, 237, 242
Mestizo, 71, 74
Metropolis, 3, 4, 84, 98, 99, 113, 122, 159
Mexico, 5, 61, 63, 65, 68
Migrant, 2, 5, 17, 29, 98, 99, 102, 105, 110, 113, 120
Militarization, 118
Mimicry, 163
Modern, 29, 58, 91, 119, 142, 206, 207, 210, 213, 219, 234
Modernity, 90, 99, 188, 204, 211, 213, 215, 218, 221
Monolingual, 4, 8, 17, 21, 27, 31, 32
Mosse, George L., 207
Multiculturalism, 15, 33, 120

N

Nair, Mira, 7, 107, 203
Namesake, The, 7, 107, 203, 204, 210–212, 214, 215, 219

Nation, 2, 5, 6, 17, 64, 110, 124, 127, 130, 157–162, 165, 171, 176, 178, 179, 203, 206, 207, 216, 232
Necropolitics, 8, 126
Negra, Diane, 237, 239
Neocolonial discourse, 8, 51
Neoliberalism, 100, 101, 106, 107, 114, 118, 147, 225
Nigeria, 82, 85, 90
9/11, 6, 112, 118, 119, 126, 205, 225, 230, 241
Nomadism, 6, 168, 178

P

Passivity, 75, 85
Patriarchy, 7, 21, 23, 104, 111, 199, 205, 220, 226, 229, 230, 234, 236, 238, 239
  heteropatriarchy, 207, 214, 242
Performance, 2, 3, 29, 70, 75, 76, 109, 142, 145–148
Pistorius, Oscar, 185, 186, 189, 194
Poetry, 2, 3, 8, 19, 21, 22, 26, 29, 43, 143
Portrait of Lucha Maria, A Girl from Tehuacan, 70, 71
Post-apartheid, 186, 192
Postcolonial, 2–6, 40, 42, 46, 48, 58, 59, 61–66, 100, 101, 107, 160, 163, 208, 210, 211
  (post)colonial, 7, 219, 220
Postfeminism, 238
Precarity, 124, 128, 129
Privilege, 6, 20, 64, 106, 118, 125, 141, 188, 196–198
Psychoanalysis, 64
Psychobiography, 59, 62, 64
Public art, 134, 145, 147, 148
Public discourse, 32, 140, 147, 187, 210

Public gaze, 68
Public space, 26, 104, 123, 127, 148, 213, 214, 216, 232, 233
Public sphere, 2, 17, 105, 122, 123, 125, 128, 231, 237

R
Race, 7, 19, 186, 192, 193, 205
Racism, 85, 110, 164, 198, 205, 216, 230, 240
Rape, 3, 7, 186–188, 190, 191, 198
Reader, 8, 16, 17, 20, 23, 24, 27, 29, 59, 84–86, 88, 89, 91, 141, 171, 173, 175
Readership, 82
Reading public, 81, 83, 84
Realism, 38, 43, 47, 48, 51–53, 161
Resistance, 44, 48, 62, 105, 130, 163, 172, 206, 207, 230, 233, 235, 236, 242
Rojo, Tamara, 69

S
Sassen, Saskia, 122
Self Portrait for Marte R. Gómez, 74
Self Portrait on the Borderline between Mexico and the United States, 71
Semiperipheral, 159, 162, 172
Singh Pandey, Jyoti, 187, 199
Smith, Zadie, 82, 83
Soft diplomacy, 2
Sook Lee, Min, 119, 120
Sousa Santos, Bonaventura, 159, 162–164, 172, 175
South Africa, 7, 186, 188, 192
Sovereignty, 118, 126, 164, 165
Spivak, Gayatri, 62
Steenkamp, Reeva, 185, 188, 194, 196, 199
Stone Raft, The, 6, 158–160, 162, 163, 172, 175, 178

Strong woman, 61–63, 70
Subaltern, 159, 175, 179, 204, 211
Surrealism, 65
Surveillance, 118, 121, 125, 128
Susceptible bodies, 125

T
Teaching, 4, 16, 27, 28, 33, 121
Translation, 2, 16, 20, 24, 135
Transnational, 1, 2, 27, 82, 211
    affect, 242
    cultural markets, 203
    feminism, 7, 225, 227, 229, 242
    knowledge, 28
    migration, 101
    poetics, 26
Trauma, 38, 68, 69, 198, 215, 218
Trinidad, 82, 87, 88, 91

U
Undocumented workers, 119–121, 123, 124–126, 129
Unfreedom, 227, 228, 230, 240
United States, 26, 52, 63, 71, 101, 123, 164, 176, 177, 179, 200, 204, 206, 215, 216, 224
Urbanization, 98, 99, 101
Urban space, 6, 8, 97, 102, 105

V
Vancouver, 6, 133, 135, 142, 148
Veil, 230
    Eastern veils, 225
    Islamic veil, 233, 235, 236
    politics of, 232, 236
    veil narratives, 6, 227
    Western veils, 7, 231, 237
Victimization, 188, 197
Violence, 52, 62, 113, 186, 190, 195, 196, 233

colonial, 47
gender, 8, 24, 186–191, 199, 232
and intersectionality, 192
symbolic, 7, 89, 225

W
War on terror, 226
Whiteness, 19, 193
Winter Games
  Olympic and Paralympic, 134
Women
  labour, 122

and oppression, 7, 89, 110, 205, 224, 225, 228, 230, 231, 233, 236
women's bodies, 7, 225, 230, 234, 235, 240, 241
women's rights, 225, 233
The World Health Organisation, 189
World literature, 2, 8, 29
World reading, 82

Z
Zimbabwe, 44, 46, 47

CPSIA information can be obtained
at www.ICGtesting.com
Printed in the USA
LVHW081132090619
620619LV00027B/2072/P